BUSINESS SKILLS IMPROVEMENT EXERCISES

MW00675142

2D EDITION

LORETTA BARKER

Fontana High School
Fontana, California

H. MARK LOVERN

Atlanta, Georgia

Copyright © 1993
by South-Western Publishing Co.
Cincinnati, Ohio

ISBN: 0-538-60775-0

Library of Congress Catalog Card Number: 91-66754

Printed in the United States of America

2 3 4 5 6 7 8 DH 99 98 97 96 95 94 93

SOUTH-WESTERN PUBLISHING CO.

Senior Developmental Editor: Carol Lynne Ruhl
Acquisitions Editor: Janie F. Schwark
Production Editor: Nancy Shockey
Senior Designer: Jim DeSollar
Associate Photo Editor/Stylist: Kim Larson
Marketing Manager: Al S. Roane

ISBN 0-538-60775-0

Library of Congress Catalog Card Number: 91-66754

Printed in the United States of America

2 3 4 5 6 7 8 DH 99 98 97 96 95 94 93

CONTENTS

UNIT 2A

UNIT 2B

UNIT 2C

UNIT 2D

Contents

INTRODUCTION

Illus. I-1   You may fill this empty chair when you finish school.

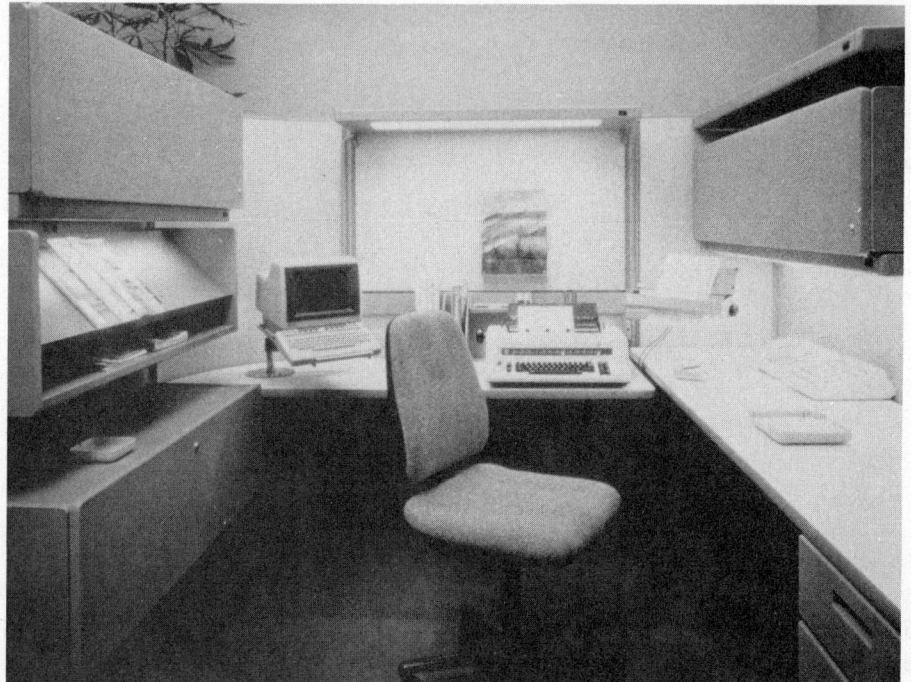

Photo Courtesy The Knoll Group

Notice that no one sits at the workstation in the above illustration. The work done in the whole office will slow down until a qualified person fills this empty chair. You may wish that an empty chair like this one will be waiting for you when you finish school. Many empty chairs will be filled by young persons like you who are well prepared for a job in business.

When you go for a job interview, you likely will be asked, "What skills do you have?" To have good skills, you must spend time in class and at home doing drills and practice exercises. As a result of your efforts, your skills will improve each day! So that you will be prepared for your future, you should begin *now* to think about practicing business skills that will help you get a job and succeed on that job.

BUSINESS SKILLS

This text-workbook contains exercises that will help you improve basic job skills. Each of these skills is described briefly in the following paragraphs. Read each description carefully. As you read, think of how improving these basic skills will help you when you apply for your first job in business.

SPELLING

Good spelling is needed in all jobs. Every time you add a word to your vocabulary, you should also learn to spell that word correctly. One way to improve your spelling is to spell a word slowly over and over in your mind. Writing the word several times is also helpful. To repeat new words or to drill upon them helps you to think about the sounds and the letters of the new words.

VOCABULARY

As you learn to pronounce and spell new words, you should also learn their meanings. You will add many new words to your vocabulary as you work the exercises in this text-workbook. You will also learn new words in other courses in high school. Many of the text-workbooks you will use in these courses will have word lists, glossaries, or vocabulary-building exercises.

CALCULATING

For a job in business, you may use a desk calculator, a hand-held calculator, or a computer for math calculations. Drills used in your business mathematics or business machines classes will prepare you for the kinds of calculations you will be expected to complete on a job.

FILING

There are two ways to file information. In *alphabetic* (or name) filing, you use the letters of the alphabet to guide you as you decide how to file. In *numeric* (or number) filing, you use only numbers and arrange them in a certain way. In some jobs you may use both letters of the alphabet and numbers, such as JBC496, for filing. Different businesses use different ways of filing. Filing rules are about the same in most businesses.

HAND PRINTING

Many business forms may be hand printed. Some forms must have ALL CAPITAL LETTERS printed in blocks or spaces. Always think of the person who will read what you print. Try to print the letters and numbers in the boxes or spaces neatly and clearly the way you would like them if you were reading the forms.

HANDWRITING

Your handwriting, like your printing, should be neat and easy to read. Some jobs may require you to write while you are under pressure. For example, a telephone call may require you to listen while you write on a form or note pad. Take your time and write all names and numbers clearly so someone else will not have a problem reading your message.

COMPARING

For some jobs you may have to *compare, match,* or *check* as one of your duties. You will see whether certain names and numbers are exactly the same as other names and numbers. Be sure to read slowly as you compare each letter in each word. When you compare two numbers, look for **transposed** numbers, which are two switched numbers. If the numbers *3498* are written *4398*, the 3 and 4 are switched or transposed.

REFERENCING

For your school assignments, you use the reference books in your school or home library. In a business you also have duties where you use reference books, charts, graphs, and other sources of information. Some common reference materials are:

- telephone directory
- telephone area code chart
- dictionary
- map of the United States
- ZIP Code directory
- price list
- airline guide
- databases

TELEPHONING

Answering the telephone is one of the most important duties in a business. You should be able to answer incoming calls, to place a caller on "hold," and to transfer calls to co-workers. You should learn how to handle these telephone situations in your high school business office and marketing classes. Some jobs also require beginning employees to place calls outside the business.

COMPLETING FORMS

Forms in a business may be filled in by handwriting, typewriting, or keyboarding for output from a computer. Each business has different kinds of forms and different ways of filling in the forms.

LEARNING GOALS

The activities in this text-workbook are divided into three units. You should try to finish the three units in 15 class periods. This means that you have four work days and one test day to finish each unit. You also may use time at home to complete the exercises.

Each exercise has a goal. Read the goal before you begin the exercise. Then work hard to meet the goal. Be sure to read and follow all instructions carefully. With practice, you will see how easy it is to reach the goals!

LEARNING OUTCOMES

After completing the exercises in this text-workbook, you should be able to:

- compare names and numbers to see if they are exactly alike
- write names and numbers with good handwriting
- print names and numbers in boxes or spaces
- put names and numbers in order for filing
- spell and define new words
- use references sources to find information
- tell time using analog and digital clocks
- solve math problems using addition, subtraction, and multiplication
- answer incoming telephone calls in the correct, businesslike manner
- use office files and databases to find information

UNIT 1A

EXERCISE 1
Goal: To see if the names of persons are exactly alike.

Look at the name in Column 1 and the name in Column 2. If the two names are exactly alike, circle the *A* in Column 3. If the two names are not exactly alike, circle the *N* in Column 3. An example is shown.

COLUMN 1	COLUMN 2	COLUMN 3	
0. Arnold V. Walthers	Arnold V. Walters	0. A	Ⓝ
1. Malcolm P. Howard	Malcom P. Howard	1. A	N
2. Ali Pirhalla	Ali Pirhalla	2. A	N
3. Millie G. Lohr	Millie C. Lohr	3. A	N
4. Philip J. Lawrence	Phillip J. Lawrence	4. A	N
5. Lawrence C. Holtzclaw	Lawrence G. Holtzclaw	5. A	N
6. Jayson Golberg	Jayson Golberg	6. A	N
7. Constansa Ruiz	Constanza Ruiz	7. A	N
8. Louise Manson	Louise Manson	8. A	N
9. Lori C. Conneaughey	Lori C. Conneaughey	9. A	N
10. Michelle Petersen	Michele Peterson	10. A	N
11. Rolf Stingo	Ralph Stingo	11. A	N
12. Wendolyn B. Gregory	Wendolyn P. Gregory	12. A	N
13. Linsay Thomas	Linsay Thomes	13. A	N
14. Vincent Fuschettio	Vincant Fuschettio	14. A	N
15. Kenneth L. Goings	Kenneth I. Goings	15. A	N

EXERCISE 2
Goal: To improve handwriting and spelling.

Look at the sample letters of the alphabet in Fig. 1-1. Look at the size and shape of each capital letter and each small letter. Look at how the letter fits on the line. As you do the handwriting exercises in this workbook, use the sample in Fig. 1-1 to improve the size and the shape of your letters.

Fig. 1-1 Sample of Writing the Alphabet

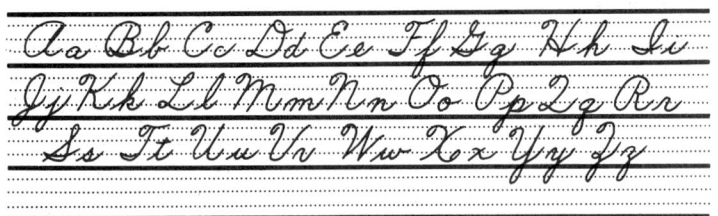

In this handwriting exercise, each word is divided into syllables (also called sounds). As you write each word, try to make each letter in the word easy to read. Also, spell the word to yourself as you write it.

The first word in the exercise, *annual*, is shown correctly divided into syllables. Then, *annual* is written one time in syllables and two times as a word. Do the exercise line by line. Pronounce the word in syllables. Write the word one time in syllables and two times as a word. *Do not write too fast.*

1. *An nu al   an nu al   annual   annual*

2. *ca reer*

3. *dif fer ence*

4. *frag ile*

5. *hun gry*

6. *in ter est*

7. *jour nal*

8. *le gal*

9. *man u al* _____

10. *nec es sar y* _____

11. *prac tice* _____

12. *re al ly* _____

13. *suc ceed* _____

14. *to ward* _____

15. *vis i tor* _____

EXERCISE 3
Goal: To index the names of persons for filing.

To file names in alphabetic order means to put names in the same order as the alphabet, or in ABC order. The first letter of each name tells the letter of the alphabet to use. Before you can put names in alphabetic order, you have to **index** them. *Indexing* the name of a person or business is putting the name in a certain order by the rules of filing. Each workday in this text-workbook, you will study rules of filing and finish exercises about the rules to help you when you work in a business.

RULE 1a   The name of a person is indexed in this way: (1) the last name (surname) is the key (or first) unit; (2) the first name (given) or initial is the second unit; and (3) the middle name or initial is the third unit. Unusual or foreign names are indexed in the same way. When indexing foreign names, if you cannot tell which name is the last name (surname), index the name as you see it. (See Sergio Zapata below.) A **cross-reference** system is used for unusual names or for papers that might be filed in more than one place. *Cross-referencing* means that a card or sheet is put in all the places in the file where a person might look for a paper. The card or sheet is usually of a color that makes it easy to see in a file folder. For example, Sergio Zapata would be indexed with Zapata as the last name. A cross-reference sheet would be placed in a file for Zapata Sergio (see below). On the sheet in the Zapata Sergio folder, a cross-reference note is written: *See Sergio Zapata.*

Look at the examples in Table 1-1 to learn how to index names of persons for filing. The letter with a line under it shows the change from one letter in the alphabet to another letter that comes later in the alphabet. This letter puts the names in alphabetic order. On the second line, the *H* has a line under it. The H in Harley comes after the C in Cassara. The last names in the Unit 1 column are in alphabetic order.

Table 1-1   Examples of Rule 1a

	INDEXING ORDER	
Name Before Indexing	**Unit 1**	**Unit 2**
	(Last Name)	(First Name)
Theodora Cassara	Cassara	Theodora
Marjean Harley	Harley	Marjean
Rodney Marlowe	Marlowe	Rodney
Sarah Suttles	Suttles	Sarah
Donald Upchurch	Upchurch	Donald
Margaret Yarbrough	Yarbrough	Margaret
*Sergio Zapata	Zapata	Sergio

*See Zapata Sergio. This name is on the cross-reference sheet in the Zapata folder.

If two or more *last* names are exactly the same, look at the *first* name of a person to see how it is different from the other first names. Look at Table 1-2. For the first three names, *Wilke* is the *last* name. Look at the three *first* names to see how they are indexed and put in alphabetic order. A line is placed under the first letter in the first name that is different than the one above it. You then use the underlined letter to place the name in alphabetic order.

For the last three names, *Wilkes* is the *last* name. *Wilkes* is indexed *after Wilke* because of the "s" in the last name. Each time you index last names that are identical, you will have to repeat the above procedure with the first names.

Table 1-2 Examples of Rule 1a

	INDEXING ORDER	
Name Before Indexing	**Unit 1**	**Unit 2**
	(Last Name)	(First Name)
Robert Wilke	Wilke	Robert
Roberta Wilke	Wilke	Rober<u>t</u>a
Robin Wilke	Wilke	Rob<u>i</u>n
Robateen Wilkes	Wilke<u>s</u>	Robateen
Robert Wilkes	Wilkes	Rob<u>e</u>rt
Robinette Wilkes	Wilkes	Rob<u>i</u>nette

EXERCISE 3a Read carefully each sentence in Column 1. If the sentence is *true*, circle the *T* in Column 2. If the sentence is *false*, circle the *F* in Column 2. An example is shown.

COLUMN 1	COLUMN 2
0. Marla Jeans comes before Marlo Jeanes.	0. T (F)
1. Kent Bryant Galina comes before Kent Bryan Galina.	1. T F
2. Regina Wells Nitka comes before Regis Walter Nitka.	2. T F
3. Felecia Bevis comes after Felesia Bevis.	3. T F
4. Erik Earl Plemmons comes before Eva Edwanda Plemmens.	4. T F
5. Helen Farris Hardy comes after Helena Ferris Hardy.	5. T F
6. Mathew Allen Knowlas comes after Matthew Allan Knowles.	6. T F
7. Rosalin Lee Waymon comes before Rosalyn Lee Wayman.	7. T F
8. Conrad Elvin Knopf comes after Conrad Elvane Knopf.	8. T F
9. Stephen Folle and Stanley Grimes come after Maria Hester.	9. T F
10. Paula Routh comes after Barbara Martz and Alton Thorpe.	10. T F
11. Michael Jorgenson and Jim Morrow come after Jennifer Klaas.	11. T F
12. Denny Jacobs comes after Mabel Bomar and Andrea Draper.	12. T F
13. Syble Hubbard and Cecile Jacoby come after Harry Lyndell.	13. T F

14. Willa Beatrice Leonard and William Beetrose Leonerd come 　14.　**T　F**
after Wylla Beatrise Leenard.

15. Ronald Odel Hervey comes before Ronalla Odelle Harvey 　15.　**T　F**
and Ronell Odella Hervay.

EXERCISE 3b　Look at the names listed below and study them carefully to see which names should be indexed first. After you have studied these names, write them in *alphabetic order* on the lines provided. Write the names in correct indexing order. Underline the letter in each name that determines the alphabetic order. The first two names (Coleman, Derek, and Collinge, Gail) are given as a guide.

Jamie Cusick	Derek Coleman	Franc Darnell
Nolan Davidson	Margaret Darling	Garth Collins
Hellena Davies	Maurice Davis	Kathy Colson
Gail Collinge	Noel Davidson	Midge Darwood

INDEXING ORDER

	Unit 1	Unit 2
	(Last Name)	(First Name)
0.	Coleman	Derek
0.	Collinge	Gail
1.		
2.		
3.		
4.		
5.		
6.		
7.		
8.		
9.		
10.		

EXERCISE 4
Goal: To improve writing numbers.

Use the sample in Fig. 1-2 to improve the size and shape of the numbers you write in the exercises of this text-workbook.

Fig. 1-2 Sample of Number Writing

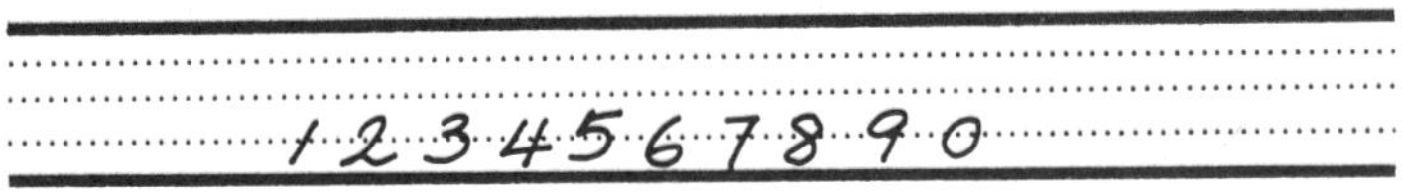

1 2 3 4 5 6 7 8 9 0

On the lines below, write the number 1 five times. Then, write the number 2 five times. Finish the line as you write 3, 4, 5, 6, 7, 8, 9, and 0 each five times. Try to keep the size and shape the same as you write each number. *Do not write too fast.*

_____

_____

_____

_____

_____

_____

_____

Use the lines below to write any numbers that need more practice.

_____

_____

_____

_____

_____

_____

Exercise 4

Look at Column 1. See how the amounts of money ($23.00 and $7.25) have been written in a column. Notice that the $ is not used. Instead of a decimal point, a line down the column divides the dollars and cents amounts. Look at the first two amounts in Column 1. Notice that the 7 in the second amount (7.25) is lined up beneath the 3 in the first amount (23.00). Lining up your figures carefully will make addition easier.

Not all lines in the column have amounts written on them. Use only the number of lines you need for an exercise. At the bottom of the column, add the amounts to find the total dollars and cents.

COLUMN 1

Total Expenses	
23	00
7	25
326	50
12	05
9	20
378	00

COLUMN 2

245.50
7. 00
25.25
106.00
37. 10

Total Expenses	
245	50

COLUMN 3

45.30
185.00
26.50
329.45
250.90

Total Expenses	

EXERCISE 5
Goal: To put numbers in order for filing.

In Exercise 3 you put names in order for filing by using filing rules and letters of the alphabet. In this exercise you will learn to put numbers in order for filing. You will not learn any rules for filing numbers.

In Fig. 1-3, the numbers are in order with the smallest number at the bottom of the group of file folder tabs. The largest number is at the top. See: 1035, 1036, 1037, 1038, and 1039. These numbers are in **consecutive order** from the front of the file to the back of the file. When you count 1, 2, 3, and so forth, you put numbers in consecutive order.

Fig. 1-3 A Number File

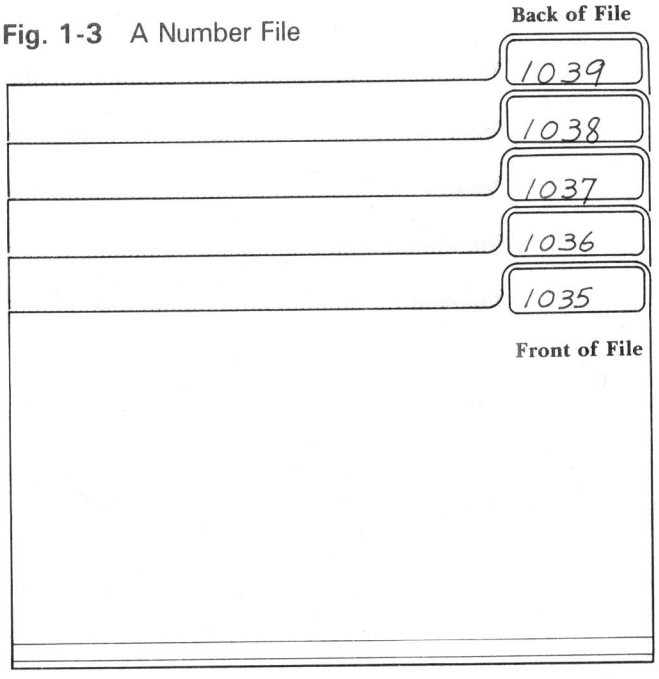

In Fig. 1-4, the numbers are in consecutive order from the bottom to the top: 1255, 1257, 1258, 1259, and 1260. You see that tab 1256 is not there. When this file folder is put back in order, the arrow shows the place where the tab will be put in correct numeric order.

Fig. 1-4 Number File with a Missing Folder

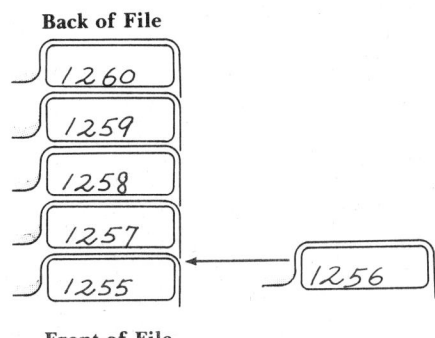

Exercise 5   **11**

In this exercise the numbers on the file folder tabs in Column 1 are in consecutive order. The number at the front of the file (1647) is the lowest number. The rest of the numbers are filed from smallest to largest behind this first number (this is consecutive order). The numbers in Column 3 should be written on the file folder tabs where they will be in consecutive order. On the file folder tabs in Column 2, write the numbers from Column 3 in the place where they will be in consecutive order. The first number (1658) is given as a guide. 1658 is larger than 1657 and is smaller than 1659, so it has been written on the file folder tab between these two numbers. As you read each number in Column 3, find the two numbers in Column 1 that it should fit between.

COLUMN 1	COLUMN 2	COLUMN 3
Back of File		
1665		
	1. _____	1658
1663		
	2. _____	1648
1661		
	3. _____	1662
1659		
	4. 1658	1652
1657		
	5. _____	1664
1655		
	6. _____	1646
1653		
	7. _____	1660
1651		
	8. _____	1650
1649		
	9. _____	1654
1647		
	10. _____	1656
Front of File		

EXERCISE 6
Goal: To use reference sources to find information.

If you were working in a business office, you would find answers to your questions by looking in many different books. Pages from common reference sources are found in the Reference Sources section of this text-workbook.

    To find the answers to the questions below, use the Reference Sources (pages 261–294). Write or print your answers in the space at the end of the line. Be sure to use your best handwriting or printing. To help you, the part of the Reference Sources you will need to use to find your answer is shown after the first question in each set.

ANSWERS

1a. In which area code are the telephone numbers in Arkansas? (Area Codes/Time Zones)   **1a.** _____

1b. In which time zone is Arkansas?   **1b.** _____

2a. What is the U.S. Postal Service abbreviation for the state of Maine? (USPS Abbreviations)   **2a.** _____

2b. How would you abbreviate the word *Heights*?   **2b.** _____

3a. How many hours difference is there between mountain time and eastern time? (Area Codes/Time Zones)   **3a.** _____

3b. The state of Wisconsin has how many area codes?   **3b.** _____

4a. For a $3.00 sale, what is the 4½ percent sales tax? (Sales Tax)   **4a.** _____

4b. For a $46.70 sale, what is the 5 percent sales tax?   **4b.** _____

5a. What is the price of one Auto Part 00145572? (Price Lists)   **5a.** _____

5b. What is the price of one Business Form UZ23?   **5b.** _____

6a. If you caught the Airport Express Bus at the Rugby Manor at 0730A, at what time would you arrive at the airport? (Bus/Airport Express Schedule)   **6a.** _____

6b. If you were staying at the St. Anne on the River Hotel and needed to be at the airport at 1215P, what time would you have to catch the bus?   **6b.** _____

EXERCISE 7
Goal: To add words to your vocabulary.

The words in Column 1 are the same words you used in Exercise 2 when you improved your handwriting and spelling skills. The words are divided into syllables in Column 2. The meanings in Column 3 will help you add the words to your vocabulary. These meanings are also called **definitions** and **synonyms.**

These words are very important parts of your study. They are among those words most frequently mispronounced and misspelled. Spend time in study and in drill before you finish the exercise. In your home study, pronounce the words as they are divided in Column 2. Learn the correct spelling and meanings. You will find these words and meanings on the unit test.

	COLUMN 1	COLUMN 2	COLUMN 3
1.	annual	an-nu-al	yearly, every year, yearlong, a yearly publication
2.	career	ca-reer	work, job, vocation, occupation, profession
3.	difference	dif-fer-ence	unlikeness, variation, contrast, distinction, dispute
4.	fragile	frag-ile	breakable, frail, flimsy, delicate, weak
5.	hungry	hun-gry	lacking food, starving, empty, longing for, craving
6.	interest	in-ter-est	drawing power, attention, attraction, arouse, entertain
7.	journal	jour-nal	diary, notebook, record, register, publication
8.	legal	le-gal	lawful, rightful, permissible, legitimate, judiciary
9.	manual	man-u-al	handbook, guide, physical, laborious, by hand
10.	necessary	nec-es-sar-y	needed, essential, required, principal, unavoidable
11.	practice	prac-tice	perform, do, act, drill, exercise
12.	really	re-al-ly	very, truly, genuinely, certainly, positively
13.	succeed	suc-ceed	follow, come after, win, gain, achieve
14.	toward	to-ward	to, near, in the direction of, not long before
15.	visitor	vis-i-tor	guest, caller, traveler, sightseer

Look at the meanings in Column 2. Find the word in Column 1 that correctly matches the meanings. In Column 3, write the *letter* of the matching word from Column 1. The first meanings are correctly matched for you.

COLUMN 1	COLUMN 2	COLUMN 3
A. annual	1. needed, essential, required	1. _J_
B. career	2. breakable, frail, weak	2. _____
C. difference	3. come after, win, achieve	3. _____
D. fragile	4. handbook, physical, by hand	4. _____
E. hungry	5. perform, drill, exercise	5. _____
F. interest	6. lawful, rightful, legitimate	6. _____
G. journal	7. attention, attraction, arouse	7. _____
H. legal	8. work, job, occupation	8. _____
I. manual	9. every year, yearlong, a publication	9. _____
J. necessary	10. to, near, in the direction of	10. _____
K. practice	11. lacking food, starving, empty	11. _____
L. really	12. guest, caller, traveler	12. _____
M. succeed	13. very, truly, certainly	13. _____
N. toward	14. unlikeness, variation, dispute	14. _____
O. visitor	15. diary, notebook, register	15. _____

EXERCISE 8
Goal: To write amounts of money on business forms.

You find many different ways to write amounts of money on business forms, such as receipts or checks. In a law office, business forms and papers may have amounts of money written in a special way. Your parents and friends may use a different way. Other textbooks may show another way. For the exercises in this text-workbook, use the examples in Fig. 1-5 as the way to write amounts of money.

Fig. 1-5 How to Write Amounts of Money on Business Forms

Amount of Money		
$75.00	*Seventy-five and no/100* ——————	DOLLARS
$25.75	*Twenty-five and 75/100* ——————	DOLLARS
$143.87	*One hundred forty-three and 87/100* —	DOLLARS
$2,504.50	*Two thousand five hundred four and 50/100*	DOLLARS
59¢	*Only fifty-nine cents* ——————	~~DOLLARS~~

Use the receipt shown in Fig. 1-6 as a guide as you fill in the receipt forms for this exercise. The numbers shown with the form are the numbers to follow as you read the instructions.

Fig. 1-6 Stub and Receipt Form

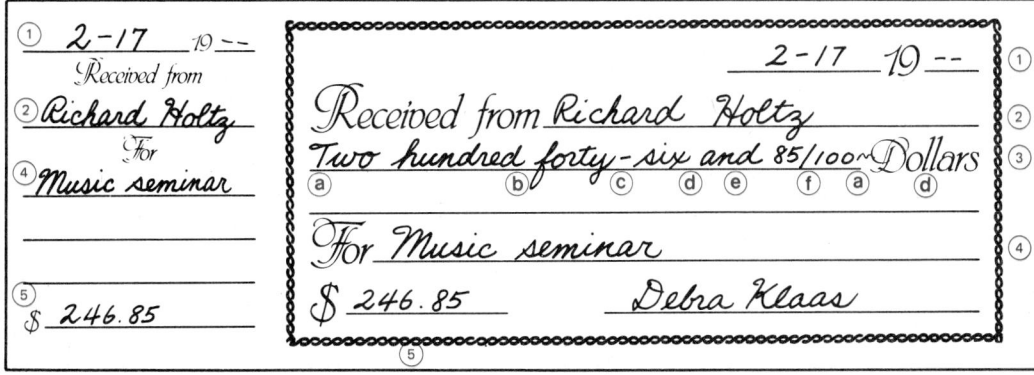

1. The date has only numbers in it. You may also write February 17, instead of 2-17. After the *19,* use the year when you write the receipt.
2. The name after *Received from* is the person who paid the money. The name at the bottom of the receipt is the person who received the money.
3. The amount of money has both words and numbers. Follow these guidelines when you write amounts of money:

a. Use a capital letter *only* for the first word in an amount. Begin the first word as close to the edge of the form as you can. After the last number in the amount, use a wavy line to fill in the space before the word *Dollars* at the end of the line. The words, *hundred, forty,* and *six,* do *not* have capital letters.

b. Do *not* use a comma or the word *and* after the word *hundred* for an amount of money more than $100.

c. Use a hyphen to divide numbers after twenty. You may have learned this grammar rule: Divide compound words or numbers with a hyphen.

d. Since the word *Dollars* is at the end of the line, do *not* use the word *Dollars* anywhere else on the line.

e. The word *and* comes between the number of dollars and the number of cents. You may also use an ampersand (&) instead of the word *and.*

f. The number of cents is written as a part of 100 (or $1). The number of dollars is written in words. Use a diagonal (/) to divide the number of cents and the 100.

4. After *For,* write the reason the money was paid.
5. After the $, write in numbers the amount you wrote in words in Step 3.

EXERCISE 8a Write the amount of money as you would on a receipt. Write neatly and small. The entire sum must fit on this line. You have very limited space on a receipt.

1. $48.95   _____ DOLLARS

2. $114.02   _____ DOLLARS

3. $219.00   _____ DOLLARS

4. $94.50   _____ DOLLARS

5. 19¢   _____ DOLLARS

6. $2,413.90   _____ DOLLARS

EXERCISE 8b Fill in the receipt forms below using this information:

Form 1: Use today's date. Write a receipt to Florence Needham for a contribution in the amount of $375.00. Sign the receipt with your own name.

_____ 19 ___
Received from
_____
For
_____
_____
_____
$ _____

_____ 19 ___
Received from _____
_____ *Dollars*
_____
For _____
$ _____ _____

Form 2: Use today's date. Write a receipt to John Ortig for a monthly payment in the amount of $248.50. Sign the receipt with your own name.

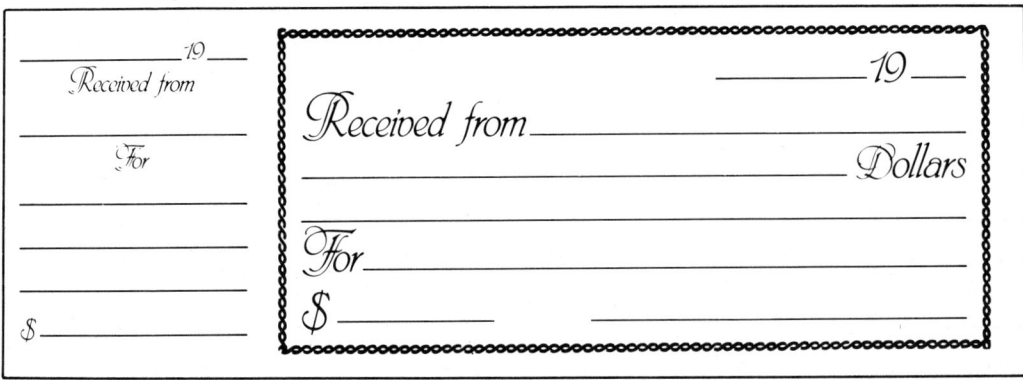

UNIT 1B

EXERCISE 9
Goal: To print information on business forms.

Some business forms used with a computer must have information printed in special boxes or spaces. Use the sample in Fig. 1-7 as you learn to print in ALL CAPITAL LETTERS the exercises with special boxes or spaces. Leave a blank box between words to indicate a space.

Fig. 1-7   Sample of All Capital Letters

A B C D E F G H I J K L M N O P Q R S T U V W X Y Z

Finish Exercise 9a. Print the information in Column 1 on the shipping labels in Column 2. Use ALL CAPITAL LETTERS. The first form is shown as a guide. If you need to abbreviate a word look at the USPS Abbreviations pages in the Reference Sources.

EXERCISE 9a

COLUMN 1   ### COLUMN 2

1.

Wingo School Supplies
Hugh Wingo
268 Palmetto Hwy Rm 200
Idaho Falls, ID 83401-2191

SHIP TO: (Fill in only if different from billing address.)

W I N G O   S C H O O L   S U P P L I E S
Firm Name

H U G H   W I N G O
ATTENTION

2 6 8   P A L M E T T O   H W Y   R M 2 0 0
Street Address   Floor, Room or Suite No.

I D A H O   F A L L S   I D 8 3 4 0 1 - 2 1 9 1
City   State   Zip

2.

Old Towne Pizza
Antonio Rossi
486 Telephone Rd
New Haven, CT 06511-2847

SHIP TO: (Fill in only if different from billing address.)

Firm Name

ATTENTION

Street Address   Floor, Room or Suite No.

City   State   Zip

Abacus Interiors
Wilfredo Henriquez
492 Front Street
    Suite 750
Albuquerque, NM
    87101 - 6029

3.

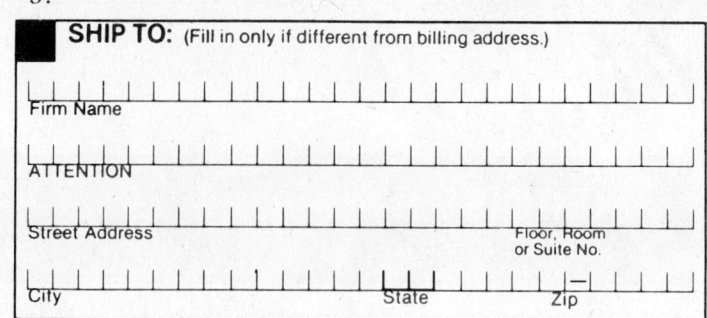

Some business forms must have information printed with proper names begin-ning with a capital letter followed by small letters. Use the sample in Fig. 1-8 as you print exercises in this text-workbook with forms where ALL CAPITAL LETTERS are not used.

Fig. 1-8 Sample of Capital and Small Letters

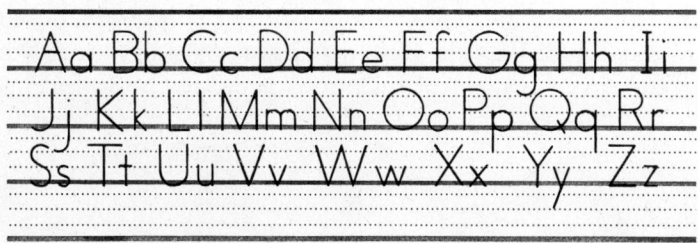

Finish Exercise 9b. *Print* the information in Column 1 on the airline baggage forms in Column 2. Use a capital letter followed by small letters. The first form is shown as a guide.

EXERCISE 9b

COLUMN 1

COLUMN 2

1.

J. Waldo Blum
596 Dover Ave.
Johnstown, Pa. 15901-1762

Herri Smith
726 Marigold Ct.
Myrtle Beach, SC
                29577-2263

James Simmons
4956 Orchid Lane
Hopkins, MN
                55343-6029

2.

Bend Tab To Release	**AIR TRANSPORT ASSOCIATION** BAGGAGE IDENTIFICATION LABEL
	NAME
	ADDRESS
	CITY STATE ZIP

3.

Bend Tab To Release	**AIR TRANSPORT ASSOCIATION** BAGGAGE IDENTIFICATION LABEL
	NAME
	ADDRESS
	CITY STATE ZIP

EXERCISE 10
Goal: To make change using the count-back method.

When you work in a store or fast-food restaurant, you will accept money from customers for items they purchase. It is important for you to be able to return the proper amount of change to your customers. Many electronic cash registers today will tell you what amount of money needs to be returned. Some businesses though still use the simple "cash drawer." Also, if the electronic cash register ever fails to work, you must be able to "count" the proper change.

When counting change it is important to begin with the smallest coins and work up to the larger bills as follows:

.01	pennies
.05	nickels
.10	dimes
.25	quarters
.50	half-dollars
	(these are used occasionally)

$	1.00	dollar bills
	5.00	five dollar bills
	10.00	ten dollar bills
	20.00	twenty dollar bills
	50.00	fifty dollar bills
	100.00	one hundred dollar bills
		(you will probably see very few $50 and $100 bills)

Example: You work at a fast-food restaurant. A customer orders a hamburger, salad, and large soft drink, which comes to $4.63. The customer hands you a $5 bill.

To use the "count-back" method, begin with the amount of the purchase—$4.63, and beginning with the smallest coin, "count" the change to add up to $5.00 as follows:

Counting money from cash drawer:

- take from the drawer .01 (1 penny) and say to yourself $4.64
- take from the drawer .01 (1 penny) and say to yourself $4.65
- take from the drawer .10 (1 dime) and say to yourself $4.75
- take from the drawer .25 (1 quarter) and say to yourself $5.00

Counting money to the customer:

Count the change to the customer just as you counted it when you took it from the drawer. The change you should give the customer will be two pennies, one dime, and one quarter.

In this exercise write in the *Take from cash drawer* column each coin or bill you would remove from your cash drawer to make the change for the sale. In the *Say to the customer* column, write what you would say to the customer. An example is shown.

	TOTAL OF SALE	CUSTOMER GIVES YOU	TAKE FROM CASH DRAWER	SAY TO CUSTOMER
0.	$4.82	$10.00	.01	4.83
			.01	4.84
			.01	4.85
			.05	4.90
			.10	5.00
			5.00	10.00
1.	$2.03	$3.00		
2.	$2.35	$5.00		
3.	$4.58	$5.00		
4.	$7.24	$10.00		
5.	$3.98	$20.00		

EXERCISE 11
Goal: To index the names of businesses for filing.

In Exercise 3 you learned to index the names of persons for filing. In this exercise you will learn the order to index the names of businesses for filing.

RULE 1b Business names are indexed and filed the same way they are written. Names of businesses or organizations may be banks, stores, shops, churches, schools, newspapers, and magazines. The name of a person may also be in the name of a business. Business names with personal names are indexed as written. For newspapers with the same names but not the city name, put the city name as the last indexing unit. You may put the state name after the city name.

Look at the examples in Table 1-3 to see how to index the names of businesses for filing. Look carefully at the letters that are underlined in Table 1-3. The letters with the lines under them show where the words differ from the ones directly above them. By matching the letters of words from left to right and by underlining the first change, you will be able to put lists of words/names/etc. in alphabetic order.

Table 1-3 Examples of Rule 1b

Name Before Indexing	INDEXING ORDER			
	Unit 1	Unit 2	Unit 3	Unit 4
Harris Wholesale Grocers	Harris	Wholesale	Grocers	
Harrisburg National Bank	Harrisburg	National	Bank	
Hawthorne Christian Church	Hawthorne	Christian	Church	
Health Hints Magazine	Health	Hints	Magazine	
Helen Hull Landscaping Service	Helen	Hull	Landscaping	Service
Helena Advertising Agency	Helena	Advertising	Agency	
Hilltop Dancing Academy	Hilltop	Dancing	Academy	
Hilton Head Gift Shop	Hilton	Head	Gift	Shop
Hometown News (Selma)	Hometown	News	Selma	
Hometown News (Tupelo)	Hometown	News	Tupelo	
Horton Harley Furniture Store	Horton	Harley	Furniture	Store
Houston Electronics Company	Houston	Electronics	Company	

EXERCISE 11a   In this exercise *A, B, C,* or *D* comes before each of the four names in each group. In the space shown, write the *A, B, C,* or *D* in the order that would put the four names in the correct alphabetic order. An example is shown.

0.   **A.** Wood Office Supply Company   0.   ___A, C, D, B___

    B. Woody Citrus Shippers

    C. Woodlawn National Bank

    D. Woodroe Woods Kennel

1.   **A.** *Weekly Neighbor News* (Roanoke, IL)   1. _____

    B. *Weekly Neighbor News* (Roggen, CO)

    C. *Weekly Neighbor News* (Roans Prairie, TX)

    D. *Weekly Neighbor News* (Robertson, WY)

2.   **A.** Davis Auto Parts   2. _____

    B. Davidson Plumbing Supplies

    C. Davison House of Fashion

    D. Davies Day Care Center

3.   **A.** Gracely Automatic Washers   3. _____

    B. Graceland Music Museum

    C. Grace Christian Church

    D. Gracalene Beauty Shop

4.   **A.** Howard Animal Motel   4. _____

    B. Howard Counseling Clinic

    C. Howard Hynes Transmission Repairs

    D. Howard National Life Insurance Company

5.   **A.** James River Travel Agency   5. _____

    B. James Rivers Cattle Breeders

    C. James Rivera Roofing Company

    D. James Rives Furniture Finishers

EXERCISE 11b In this exercise look carefully at the names in Column 1 to determine which name should come first alphabetically. Write that name on the first line in Column 2. Decide which name comes next alphabetically. Write that name on the second line. **BE SURE TO UNDERLINE THE LETTER THAT DETERMINES THE ALPHABETIC ORDER.** An example is shown.

COLUMN 1	COLUMN 2
0. Pauley Pilzin Printing Company Paulette Art Supplies Paul Porcet Dance Studio Paul Chamberlain Garden Shop	**0.** Paul Chamberlain Garden Shop Paula Porcet Dance Studio Paulette Art Supplies Pauley Pilzin Printing Company
1. Murata Paint Contractors Minute Markets of Madison Morrisey Optical Company Metro Industrial Clinic	**1.**
2. Torrida Stamp Trading Center Tutschek Outdoor Advertising Topware Home Parties Treadway Pawn Shop	**2.**
3. Eastridge Tree Trimmers Eskridge Upholstery Center Eldredge Marketing Research, Inc. Etheridge Animal Hospital	**3.**
4. Larette Marlin Art Studio Laramore Marlon Enterprises, Inc. Larry Marlon Chemical Co. Larrue Marlen Fashion Nook	**4.**
5. Universe Tennis Center Unique Hair Styles United Camper Sales Unlimited Auto Parts	**5.**
6. Davis Employment Agency Daves Distributors, Inc. Davies Computer Supplies Davis Alterations	**6.**

7. Andreas Blair Carpet Repairs

    Andrew Blane Exterminators, Inc.

    Andrews Blarr Upholstery Shop

    Andrea Blain Import Center

8. Geoffroy Factory Outlet

    Geffen Properties, Inc.

    Geffga Financial Group

    Geiger Aluminum Products

7. _____

   _____

   _____

   _____

8. _____

   _____

   _____

   _____

EXERCISE 12
Goal: To see if amounts of money are exactly alike.

Look at the amount of money in Column 1 and the amount of money in Column 2. If the two amounts are exactly alike, circle the *A* in Column 3. If the two amounts are not alike, circle the *N* in Column 3. An example is shown.

COLUMN 1	COLUMN 2	COLUMN 3
0. $556.55	$565.55	0. A (N)
1. $289.58	$289.53	1. A N
2. $821.70	$827.10	2. A N
3. $339.85	$339.35	3. A N
4. $650.51	$650.57	4. A N
5. $928.93	$928.98	5. A N
6. $6,539.00	$6,539.90	6. A N
7. $2,280.82	$2,280.82	7. A N
8. $1,777.75	$1,717.75	8. A N
9. $7,471.15	$7,471.15	9. A N
10. $5,545.55	$5,545.65	10. A N
11. $23,850.90	$23,850.90	11. A N
12. $78,359.80	$78,859.80	12. A N
13. $41,758.90	$41,758.90	13. A N
14. $84,587.00	$84,587.00	14. A N
15. $16,863.55	$16,868.55	15. A N

EXERCISE 13

Goal: To learn about push-button telephones and to use office files/databases to find answers to questions.

When you talk to someone on the telephone, you should think of talking to that person face to face. People often get their first impression about you and the company for which you work from a telephone conversation. These exercises about telephoning will teach you the correct ways to handle telephone calls. You will also learn about several kinds of telephone equipment and services. In each of the telephone conversations, you are the person who answers the call. As you read the telephone conversation in each exercise, be aware of the way you answer each call, the way you answer the questions of the person who called, and the way you end each call.

USING THE OFFICE FILES/DATABASES   With each telephone call, you will use the Office Files/Databases on pages 295–312. The Office Files/Databases section is different from the Reference Sources section. The pages in the Reference Sources come from many different places such as books, pamphlets, timetables, or lists. The information in the Office Files/Databases would be found in different files (paper files and files in computer memory) in your office. When you look for an answer to a question from a telephone caller, you will only need to look in the Office Files/Databases for the answer. In a real office you may look in many places to find answers to callers' questions.

You will use several kinds of telephone equipment as you complete the exercises. You will also learn about different kinds of filing equipment. In each exercise you will work for a different business. You will answer two calls in each exercise.

Illus. 1-1   Push-Button Telephone

USING A PUSH-BUTTON TELEPHONE   A push-button telephone is the kind of telephone used by most businesses. Push-button telephones can be connected to a computer, word processor, or other service center. Ten buttons have letters and numbers that are used for dialing a number. The other two buttons (∗ and #) are used for special purposes such as transferring calls to another number or sending information to certain computers. As you press each button when you dial a number, you hear a different tone. Now you can see why this telephone is sometimes called a touch (press) tone (sound) telephone. The buttons on this telephone may also be called keys.

In this exercise you will be using a push-button telephone with 12 buttons. You are the only person who handles calls for the small office of the Greenwood Realty Company. Four sales representatives who are also employed there call you from outside the office and ask for your help with sales or service. JoAngela Tibbs and Armando Martinez are two of these people. When you are responsible for answering a telephone in an office, always try to answer all calls on the *first* ring.

Read the two conversations carefully. *Fill in the blanks as you answer the calls.* To find the answers to questions asked, use the Office Files/Databases (pages 295–312).

Note: You call someone by his or her first name only with permission. In the following conversations, assume the sales representatives have told you to call them by their first names.

Call 1   *The telephone rings.*

YOU   Good morning, Greenwood Realty, _____
                                            YOUR FIRST AND LAST NAME

speaking. May I help you?

CALLER   Good morning, _____ This is JoAngela Tibbs. Please
                              YOUR FIRST NAME

look at the lease for Michael Farmer. I need to know the *term* of the

lease and the monthly *rental.*

(PAUSE)   (A **term** of a lease is the number of years the lease lasts. The **monthly**

rental is the amount of money paid each month for rent on the build-

ing. Turn to the Office Files/Databases. Find the files of Greenwood

Realty. Find the answers to the questions. Write the answers in the

space below.)

YOU   Thank you for waiting, JoAngela. The term of the Michael Farmer

lease is _____ years. The monthly rental is _____

CALLER	Thank you, _____. Have a nice day! Good-bye.
	<small>YOUR FIRST NAME</small>
YOU	You are welcome. You have a nice day, too. Good-bye.

Call 2   📞   *The telephone rings.*

YOU	Good morning, Greenwood Realty Company, _____ <small>YOUR FIRST AND</small> _____ speaking. May I help you? <small>LAST NAME</small>
CALLER	Yes, _____. You can. This is Armando Martinez. <small>YOUR FIRST NAME</small>
(PAUSE)	(You have a special telephone service called **call waiting.** When you are talking on the phone and another call comes through, you hear a special tone.)
YOU	Excuse me, _____. Will you hold, please? <small>CALLER'S FIRST NAME</small>
(PAUSE)	(You press the receiver hook once to put the first call on hold. Not all push-button telephones will let you hold a call. You must have this special service added. You may now speak to the second caller.)
	Good morning, Greenwood Realty Company. Will you hold, please? Thank you.
(PAUSE)	(You press the receiver hook to put the second call on hold. You may now talk to the first caller.)
	Thank you for waiting, _____. What may I do for <small>CALLER'S FIRST NAME</small> you?
CALLER	I need the home cities for the two new employees. Do you have their W-4 forms on file?
YOU	Yes, I do. Will you hold, please?
(PAUSE)	(Look in the Office Files/Databases for the answers. Write them in the spaces.)

Thank you for holding, _____. Cheryl Nix lives in
                          CALLER'S FIRST NAME

_____ and Ivan Wells lives in
       CITY

_____.
       CITY

CALLER   Thank you, _____. Good-bye.
                    YOUR FIRST NAME

EXERCISE 14
Goal: To improve spelling and handwriting of proper names of states, capitals, and territories.

As you write and spell the proper names in this exercise, follow the same steps that you used in the other handwriting and spelling exercises. The capital city is shown with the state or territory. Spend time in study and in drill. Pronounce the capital and state or territory in syllables. Spell and write the cities and states or territories one time in syllables and two times as words. Boise, Idaho, is shown as a sample of the correct way to finish this exercise. *Do not write too fast.* You will have these same proper names on the unit test. Spend time during your home study to drill on which city is the capital of which state or territory.

Use the sample in Fig. 1-9 to help you with the size and shape of letters.

Fig. 1-9 Sample of Writing the Alphabet

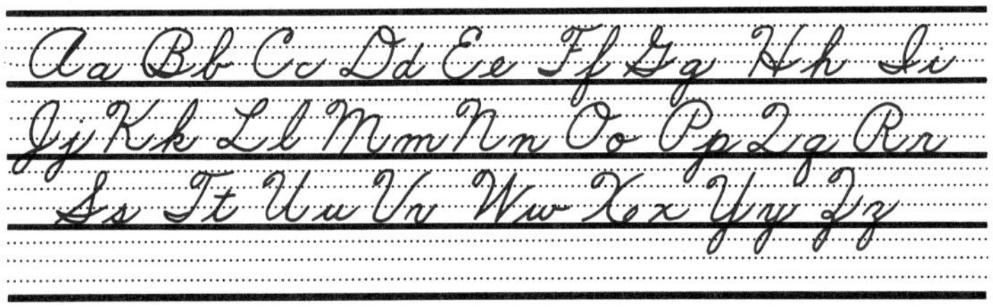

Aa Bb Cc Dd Ee Ff Gg Hh Ii
Jj Kk Ll Mm Nn Oo Pp Qq Rr
Ss Tt Uu Vv Ww Xx Yy Zz

Boi se, Id a ho   At lan ta, Geor gia
Boi se, Id a ho   _____
Boise, Idaho   _____
Boise, Idaho   _____

Aus tin, Tex as   Den ver, Col o ra do
_____   _____
_____   _____
_____   _____

Sa lem, Or e gon

Do ver, Del a ware

Au gus ta, Maine

A gan a, Guam

Co lum bus, O hi o

EXERCISE 15

Goal: To use telephone message forms with good handwriting or printing.

Use the telephone call form in Fig. 1-10 as a guide as you fill in the forms in this exercise.

Fig. 1-10   Telephone Message Form

PHONE CALL		

① FOR *Frank Biggs*   DATE *10/03*   TIME *9:45* (A.M.) P.M.

② M *iss Clare Lear*

③ OF *Camilla Public Library* ✓ TELEPHONED

④ PHONE *912   555-2335   104* | | RETURNED YOUR CALL
   AREA CODE   NUMBER   EXTENSION

⑤ MESSAGE *Call before 5 P.M.* ✓ PLEASE CALL

today eastern standard | | WILL CALL AGAIN

time | | CAME TO SEE YOU

⑥   *J.E.* | | WANTS TO SEE YOU
SIGNED

1. After *For,* write the name of the person to whom the call was made. The *Date* is shown in numbers, 10/03 (October 3). You may use the abbreviation *Oct. 3.* The time is 9:45 in the morning. Circle *A.M.*
2. The *M* has *iss* written after it to let Frank Biggs know Miss Lear's title. Miss is the title used for an unmarried woman. *Mrs.* is the title for a married woman. Some women prefer *Ms.* as a title. Ms. can be used for a married or unmarried woman. For a man, write *Mr.* Use abbreviations for a doctor (Dr.), minister (Rev.), or other title.
3. After *Of,* write the name of the place where the caller works. If the caller does not tell you the place, leave the line blank. A call from a home telephone would be an example of when to leave a blank line.
4. Always ask a caller to repeat the area code, telephone number, and the extension. You may say, "Did you say 9-1-2, 5-5-5, 2-3-3-5, Extension 1-0-4?"
5. The *Message* line may or may not be filled. In this sample, a time is written. Also, the time zone is given. For long-distance calls, be sure to ask for the caller's time zone.
6. Only the initials, *J.E.,* were used for the space above *Signed.* You may write your name.
7. The last part of the form has check marks for Mr. Biggs to learn more about the call. He sees that someone *Telephoned* and has left the message to *Please Call.* He can read the message to find out more about the call. Use the blank telephone message forms that follow. Write or print the information given in the example calls as you complete the call forms.

Call 1:   Use today's date and 10:30 in the morning. Randy Foxwood received a call from Dr. Martha Johnson of Auburn University. She wants Randy to call her before noon today, central standard time. Her telephone number is area code 205-555-2300, Extension 338.

```
┌─────────────────────────────────────────────────────────────────────┐
│                                               ╭─────────────────────╮ │
│                                               │    PHONE CALL        │ │
│                                               ╰─────────────────────╯ │
│                                                                  A.M.  │
│   FOR _____ DATE _____ TIME _____ P.M.      │
│                                                                        │
│   M _____                          │
│                                              │    │ TELEPHONED         │
│   OF_____        │    ├────────────────────┤
│                                              │    │ RETURNED           │
│   PHONE _____       │    │ YOUR CALL          │
│          AREA CODE   NUMBER     EXTENSION    │    ├────────────────────┤
│   MESSAGE _____       │    │ PLEASE CALL        │
│                                              │    ├────────────────────┤
│   _____      │    │ WILL CALL AGAIN    │
│                                              │    ├────────────────────┤
│   _____      │    │ CAME               │
│                                              │    │ TO SEE YOU         │
│   _____      │    ├────────────────────┤
│                                              │    │ WANTS              │
│                                              │    │ TO SEE YOU         │
│   SIGNED                                                               │
└─────────────────────────────────────────────────────────────────────┘
```

Call 2:   Use today's date and 11:40 in the morning. Mandy Southworth had a call from Alex Westwood. He wants Mandy to call him at 555-2410, Extension 670. (No area code is needed for a local call.) He wants her to speak at the annual meeting of the Diabetes Support Group.

```
┌─────────────────────────────────────────────────────────────────────┐
│                                               ╭─────────────────────╮ │
│                                               │    PHONE CALL        │ │
│                                               ╰─────────────────────╯ │
│                                                                  A.M.  │
│   FOR _____ DATE _____ TIME _____ P.M.      │
│                                                                        │
│   M _____                          │
│                                              │    │ TELEPHONED         │
│   OF_____        │    ├────────────────────┤
│                                              │    │ RETURNED           │
│   PHONE _____       │    │ YOUR CALL          │
│          AREA CODE   NUMBER     EXTENSION    │    ├────────────────────┤
│   MESSAGE _____       │    │ PLEASE CALL        │
│                                              │    ├────────────────────┤
│   _____      │    │ WILL CALL AGAIN    │
│                                              │    ├────────────────────┤
│   _____      │    │ CAME               │
│                                              │    │ TO SEE YOU         │
│   _____      │    ├────────────────────┤
│                                              │    │ WANTS              │
│                                              │    │ TO SEE YOU         │
│   SIGNED                                                               │
└─────────────────────────────────────────────────────────────────────┘
```

EXERCISE 16
Goal: To add words to your vocabulary.

The words in Column 1 are among those words most frequently mispronounced and misspelled. Spend time in study and in drill before you finish the exercise. In your home study, pronounce the words as they are divided in Column 2. Drill on the correct spelling and meanings. You will find these words and meanings on the unit test.

COLUMN 1	COLUMN 2	COLUMN 3
1. assume	as-sume	suppose, believe, acquire, take up, take over
2. business	busi-ness	job, work, occupation, firm, concern
3. dynamic	dy-nam-ic	active, energetic, forceful, vigorous, magnetic
4. equipment	e-quip-ment	supplies, appliances, utensils, furnishings, gear
5. fascinate	fas-ci-nate	charm, attract, lure, enthrall, captivate
6. identical	i-den-ti-cal	same, equal, alike, duplicate, equivalent
7. mutual	mu-tu-al	common, similar, shared, joint, reciprocal
8. neglect	ne-glect	ignore, forget, omit, overlook, pass up
9. opinion	o-pin-ion	belief, view, idea, feeling, estimate
10. problem	prob-lem	puzzle, question, mystery, riddle, dilemma
11. strictly	strict-ly	exactly, sternly, firmly, rigidly, particularly
12. truly	tru-ly	really, actually, indeed, honestly, in fact
13. usually	u-su-al-ly	regularly, habitually, ordinarily, customarily, normally
14. visible	vis-i-ble	noticeable, obvious, clear, prominent, evident
15. withhold	with-hold	hold back, deduct, hinder, retain, hide

Look at the meanings in Column 1. Write or print in the blank space in Column 2 the word in today's lesson that correctly matches the meanings in Column 1.

COLUMN 1	COLUMN 2
1. active, energetic, vigorous	1. _____
2. ignore, forget, omit	2. _____
3. hold back, deduct, retain	3. _____
4. same, equal, alike	4. _____
5. supplies, appliances, utensils	5. _____
6. really, actually, honestly	6. _____
7. suppose, believe, take over	7. _____
8. regularly, habitually, normally	8. _____
9. exactly, sternly, firmly	9. _____
10. puzzle, dilemma, question	10. _____
11. obvious, clear, evident	11. _____
12. job, work, occupation	12. _____
13. belief, view, idea	13. _____
14. charm, attract, lure	14. _____
15. common, similar, shared	15. _____

UNIT 1C

Write the social security numbers in Column 1 in the boxes in Column 2. The first number has been written as a guide.

COLUMN 1	COLUMN 2
288-40-9337	0. $\boxed{2}\boxed{8}\boxed{8}$-$\boxed{4}\boxed{0}$-$\boxed{9}\boxed{3}\boxed{3}\boxed{7}$
752-01-6652	1. □□□-□□-□□□□
363-29-4417	2. □□□-□□-□□□□
518-90-0674	3. □□□-□□-□□□□
256-88-1953	4. □□□-□□-□□□□
890-33-7674	5. □□□-□□-□□□□
161-64-8065	6. □□□-□□-□□□□

EXERCISE 18
Goal: To see if the names of persons are exactly the same.

Look at the handwritten name in Column 1 and the typewritten name in Column 2. If the two names are exactly the same, circle the *S* in Column 3. If the two names are different, circle the *D* in Column 3. An example is shown.

COLUMN 1	COLUMN 2	COLUMN 3
0. *Juan Ramirez*	Juan Ramirez	0. Ⓢ D
1. *Davison Tuggle*	Davison Tuggle	1. S D
2. *Catherine C. Lacy*	Catherine C. Lacy	2. S D
3. *Luyin Chiang*	Luin Chiang	3. S D
4. *Erlene Champaign*	Erlene Champaign	4. S D
5. *Rex L. Deardof*	Rex L. Deardorff	5. S D
6. *Chandra Lanham*	Chandra Lanham	6. S D
7. *Roderick C. Owensby*	Roderick C. Owenby	7. S D
8. *Forsythia C. Batcha*	Forsythia O. Batcha	8. S D
9. *Simon R. Sprayberry*	Simeon R. Sprayberry	9. S D
10. *Andrea Pinnenger*	Andreas Pinnenger	10. S D
11. *Marsha L. Ortkiese*	Marsha L. Ortkeise	11. S D
12. *Levi G. Sheperd*	Levi G. Shepard	12. S D
13. *Micaela O. Salas*	Miceela D. Salas	13. S D
14. *Woody C. Terbeck*	Woody C. Terbeek	14. S D
15. *Emanuel Eeraerts*	Emanuel Eeraerts	15. S D

EXERCISE 19
Goal: To index business names with symbols and certain parts of speech for filing.

RULE 2   Prepositions, conjunctions, symbols, and articles are parts of some business names. Index them in the same order as they come in the name. Use the word that stands for the following symbols: (&) and; (¢) cent or cents; ($) dollar or dollars; (#) number; and (%) percent. Index prepositions (in, at, with, on, for, of, out); conjunctions (and, or); and articles (a, an) as they are used in the name. **If the is the first word in a business name, put the as the last indexing unit.**

Look at the examples in Table 1-4 to see how to index business names with symbols and certain parts of speech. The letter with a line under it shows the change from one letter in the alphabet to another letter that comes later in the alphabet. This letter puts the names in alphabetic order.

Table 1-4   Examples of Rule 2

	INDEXING ORDER				
Name Before Indexing	Unit 1	Unit 2	Unit 3	Unit 4	Unit 5
On Guard Alarm Systems	On	Guard	Alarm	Systems	
The On Time Delivery Service	On	Time	Delivery	Service	The
Out of This World Bakery	Out	of	This	World	Bakery
Out of Town Newspaper Center	Out	of	Town	Newspaper	Center
The Outer Banks Garage	Outer	Banks	Garage	The	
Outside & Inside Decorators	Outside	and	Inside	Decorators	
Outside and Inside Home Repairs	Outside	and	Inside	Home	Repairs
Outside the City Motel	Outside	the	City	Motel	
The Pay Less $'s Store	Pay	Less	Dollars	Store	The
Pedro Ruiz Office Supplies Company	Pedro	Ruiz	Office	Supplies	Company
Pedros and Ruiz Building	Pedros	and	Ruiz	Building	
Place in the Sun Resort	Place	in	the	Sun	Resort
Place on the Bay Villas	Place	on	the	Bay	Villas

Note: Hyphens were omitted from some names to show the indexing order of some parts of speech.

In Column 1 the number (first, second, third, fourth, or fifth) is the *indexing unit* you should find in the name in Column 2. Write or print the name in the space in Column 3. An example is shown.

COLUMN 1	COLUMN 2	COLUMN 3
0. second	0. Early Bird Wakeup Callers	0. ___Bird___
1. second	1. Over the Rainbow Nursery School	1. _____
2. first	2. Around Town Delivery Service	2. _____
3. fourth	3. Between Two Cities Animal Hospital	3. _____
4. third	4. End of the Pier Cafe	4. _____
5. second	5. More $'s Savings Bargain Barn	5. _____
6. fifth	6. The Prado Mall Secretarial Center	6. _____
7. fourth	7. Away from the Crowd Boutique	7. _____
8. third	8. Tomas the Chef Cooking School	8. _____
9. first	9. By the Sea Party Supplies	9. _____
10. fifth	10. The Ramarez Family Sports Center	10. _____
11. second	11. Drummond & Lasky Marketing Group	11. _____
12. third	12. Citadel School of Broadcasting	12. _____
13. second	13. Off the Beaten Path Antiques	13. _____
14. fifth	14. A View from the Top Motel	14. _____
15. first	15. The University of Selma	15. _____

EXERCISE 20
Goal: To check for errors in putting employee numbers in order.

In Exercise 5 you put numbers in order for filing. When using a numeric filing system, some file folders may be put in the wrong place if the worker is not careful. Always read the names and numbers very carefully before you put a folder in a file drawer.

Check for errors in the sequential order of the employee numbers shown in Column 1 as you read from left to right across the line. In the example *(0)*, the number 7143 is out of sequence. It should fall between 7140 and 7144. If the numbers are in correct order, write "yes" in the space at the end of the line in Column 2. If the numbers are *not* in correct order, circle the misfiled number in Column 1. Then write that number in the space at the end of the line in Column 2. **Reminder: Always read the numbers across the line from left to right to check the correct order.**

	COLUMN 1						COLUMN 2
0.	7135	7140	7144	7146	7147	(7143)	0. _7143_
1.	1225	1226	1227	1224	1228	1229	1. _____
2.	4283	4284	4235	4286	4287	4288	2. _____
3.	8530	8533	8538	8549	8552	8585	3. _____
4.	3858	3855	3859	3860	3863	3865	4. _____
5.	6230	6231	6234	6235	6237	6240	5. _____
6.	2281	2282	2284	2285	2286	2237	6. _____
7.	5583	5584	5585	5588	5593	5598	7. _____
8.	9171	9178	9181	9179	9189	9180	8. _____
9.	7717	7718	7771	7719	7721	7727	9. _____
10.	4663	4664	4668	4673	4788	4879	10. _____
11.	1338	1339	1343	1345	1348	1350	11. _____
12.	6641	6647	6648	6663	6668	6669	12. _____
13.	8171	8177	8191	8197	8771	8777	13. _____
14.	5024	5184	5374	5237	5388	5491	14. _____
15.	2211	2217	2231	2373	2238	2384	15. _____

EXERCISE 21
Goal: To improve handwriting and spelling.

Use the sample in Fig. 1-11 as you try to improve the size and shape of your letters.

Fig. 1-11 Sample of Writing the Alphabet

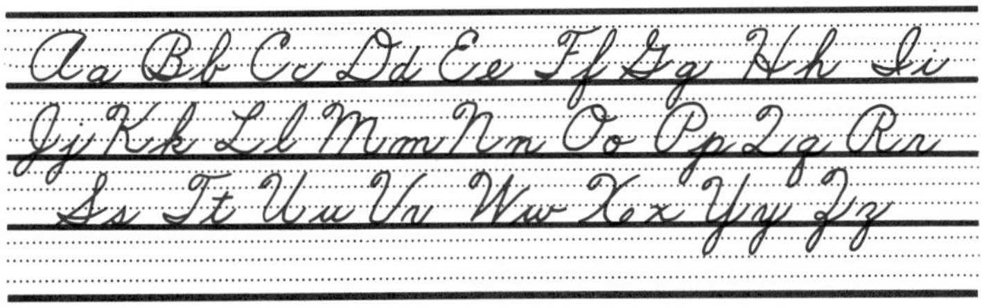

Follow the same steps that you used in Exercise 14. Handwriting is a very important skill in a business office. This exercise will help you to improve the handwriting skills you learned in your first years of school. Like keyboarding, handwriting requires practice. Your goal is to improve with each practice. You will improve your spelling skills, too, if you spell as you write.

1. _a ban don_ _____

2. _bank rupt cy_ _____

3. _com mit tee_ _____

4. _def i nite ly_ _____

5. _ex ag ger ate_ _____

6. _gov ern ment_ _____

7. _haz ard_ _____

8. _i tin er ar y_ _____

9. _length en_ _____

10. _mea ger_ _____

11. *nui sance* _____

12. *phy si cian* _____

13. *to geth er* _____

14. *u nan i mous* _____

15. *with draw al* _____

EXERCISE 22
Goal: To use reference sources to find information.

To find the answers to the questions below, use the Reference Sources of this text-workbook (pages 261–294). Write or print your answers in the space at the end of the line. To help you, the part of the Reference Sources you will need to use to find your answer is shown after the first question in each set.

ANSWERS

1a. In which zone is ZIP Code 63550? (Freight, UPS—Zone Chart)

1a. _____

1b. What is the fee to mail a 6-pound parcel by ground service? The package is to be mailed to a place of business in Zone 3.

1b. _____

2a. What kind of aircraft is used for Flight 625? (Airlines)

2a. _____

2b. What is the flying time of Flight 435?

2b. _____

3a. What is the mark *to delete*? (Proofreader's Marks)

3a. _____

3b. What is the mark to *insert an apostrophe*?

3b. _____

4a. At the Postal Service, what is the telephone number for passport information? (Telephone Directory)

4a. _____

4b. If you wish to file a claim with the Postal Service, what telephone number should you dial?

4b. _____

5a. What is the distance between Atlanta and Chicago? (Travel Chart)

5a. _____

5b. What is the distance between Dallas and Washington, DC?

5b. _____

6a. Which ocean is along the west coast of the United States? (Map—United States)

6a. _____

6b. Look at the map of the South. Find Florida. Which city is farther south, Miami or St. Petersburg? (Map—Pacific Coast States and the South)

6b. _____

EXERCISE 23
Goal: To deposit checks into a personal checking account at a bank.

When you open a personal checking account at a bank, you will fill in a signature card. On this card you will sign your name the way you plan to sign your name on the front of your checks. The way you sign your name on the front of your checks is also the way you will sign your name when you endorse checks for deposit in your checking account.

When you open a checking account, you must put money in the account. This is known as making a **deposit.** Before you make a deposit, **endorse** (sign) all checks you will deposit. In Fig. 1-12 Rachel used a **blank endorsement** on the back of the one check she deposited.

Fig. 1-12 Blank Endorsement

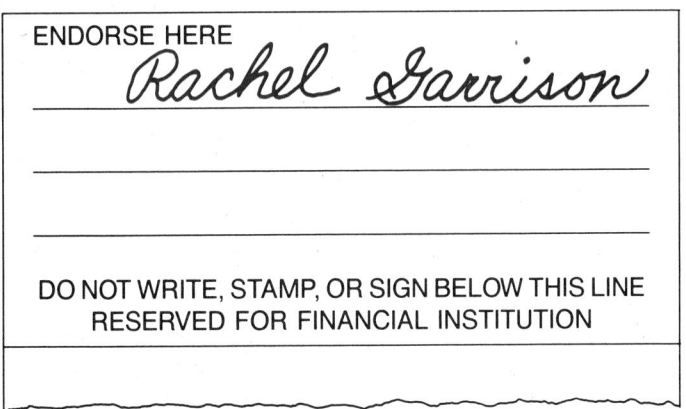

ENDORSE HERE

Rachel Garrison

DO NOT WRITE, STAMP, OR SIGN BELOW THIS LINE
RESERVED FOR FINANCIAL INSTITUTION

You may deposit as often as you have money to deposit, but a **deposit slip** (or deposit ticket) must be used each time you make a deposit. Look at Fig. 1-13 to see how Rachel filled in her first deposit slip.

Fig. 1-13 Completed Deposit Slip Showing a $500 Deposit

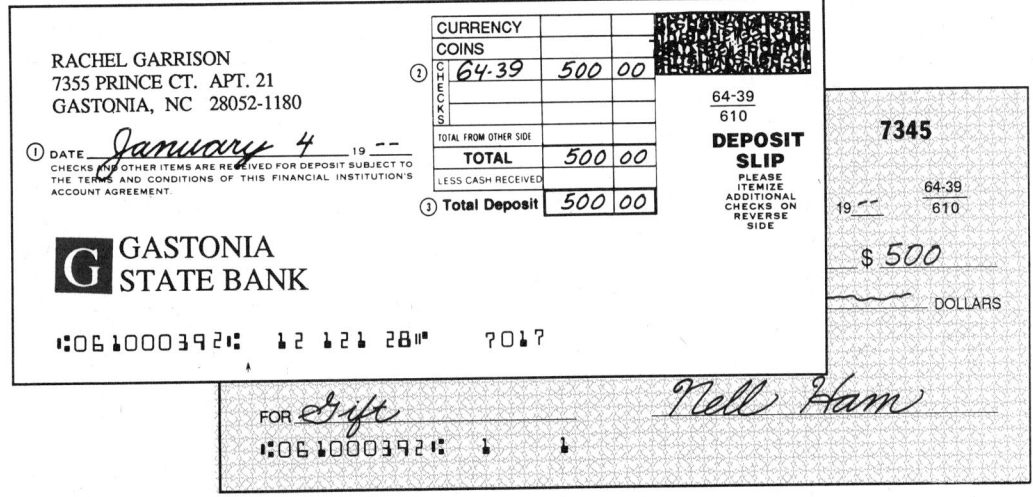

1. The date is written with words and numbers. You may also use abbreviations (such as Jan.) or numbers (such as 1-4).
2. Three parts of the deposit slip are: *Currency* (one dollar, five dollar, ten dollar, etc.), *Coins* (pennies, nickels, dimes, etc.), and *Checks.* In Fig. 1-13 the currency (bills) and coins have no amounts written because only one check is in the deposit. On the first line for checks, the dollars and cents ($500.00) are divided by a line down the column. On the same line, to the left of the deposit amount is the number 64-39. This number is found on the check to be deposited. Look under the check number 7345 and you will see 64-39 written over 610. At some banks, you may find that this number does not always have to be written on the deposit ticket. If you do use the number, always use the *top* number given that bank by the American Bankers Association. Do not use the bottom number from the Federal Reserve System.
3. Near the bottom of the slip, across from *Total,* the $500.00 is written in the proper blank. Since no cash was received by the depositor, the next line is skipped. The $500.00 is also written after *Total Deposit.* You will learn in later units about using other parts of the deposit slip that were not used in this exercise.

You must keep a record of your bank account in a **check register.** You may also hear it called a **checkbook** or a **bankbook.** You must write in this register every time you make a deposit or write a check.

Look at Fig. 1-14 to see how Rachel's $500 deposit is shown in her check register.

Fig. 1-14   Check Register

① CHECK NO.	② DATE	③ CHECK ISSUED TO	④ BAL. BR'T. F'R'D'.	✓	⑤		
	1/4	TO	AMOUNT OF CHECK OR (DEPOSIT)		500	00	⑥
		FOR	BALANCE		500	00	
		TO	AMOUNT OF CHECK OR DEPOSIT				
		FOR	BALANCE				

1. Nothing is written in the *Check No.* column because a check was not written.
2. The date of the deposit is written in the *Date* column.
3. Nothing is written in the *To* and *For* spaces under the *Check Issued To* column because a check was not written.
4. The word *Deposit* has a circle around it to show a deposit was made and a check was not written.
5. The amount of the deposit is written with the dollars and cents shown with a line between them.
6. The balance is the same as the amount of the deposit because you are opening an account. You will learn more about the balance when you learn to write checks.

Use the forms shown on page 57 to open a checking account in YOUR NAME.
1. Use your name for the blank endorsement on the back of the check you are depositing. Look at Fig. 1-12 on page 55 as you write the endorsement.

2. Fill in the deposit slip. Use today's date. Look at Fig. 1-13 on page 55 and read the instructions at the top of page 56 as you fill in the deposit slip.

3. Fill in the check register. Use today's date. Look at Fig. 1-14 on page 56 and read the instructions at the bottom of page 56 as you fill in the check register.

ENDORSE HERE

_____

_____

_____

DO NOT WRITE, STAMP, OR SIGN BELOW THIS LINE
RESERVED FOR FINANCIAL INSTITUTION

Back of Check

Student's Name
4289 Center Avenue Apt. G-9
Garwood, NJ 07027-1389

DATE_____ 19_____
CHECKS AND OTHER ITEMS ARE RECEIVED FOR DEPOSIT SUBJECT TO
THE TERMS AND CONDITIONS OF THIS FINANCIAL INSTITUTION'S
ACCOUNT AGREEMENT.

CURRENCY	
COINS	
CHECKS	
TOTAL FROM OTHER SIDE	
TOTAL	
LESS CASH RECEIVED	
Total Deposit	

48-93
610

DEPOSIT
SLIP
PLEASE
ITEMIZE
ADDITIONAL
CHECKS ON
REVERSE
SIDE

G GARWOOD
CITY BANK

⑆061000937⑆ ⑇2 ⑈2⑈ 28⑈

3772

19 _ _   48-93
              610

$ *900.00*

_____ DOLLARS

FOR *college tuition*   *Catherine Jackson*

⑆061000937⑆ ⑇3 ⑈⑈⑈ 49⑈

Deposit Slip

CHECK NO.	DATE	CHECK ISSUED TO	BAL. BR'T. F'R'D'.	✓		
		TO	AMOUNT OF CHECK OR DEPOSIT			
		FOR	BALANCE			
		TO	AMOUNT OF CHECK OR DEPOSIT			
		FOR	BALANCE			

Check Register

EXERCISE 24
Goal: To add words to your vocabulary.

The words in Column 1 are among those words most frequently mispronounced and misspelled. Spend time in study and in drill before you finish the exercise. In your home study, pronounce the words as they are divided in Column 2. Drill on the correct spelling and meanings. You will find these words and meanings on the unit test.

COLUMN 1	COLUMN 2	COLUMN 3
1. abandon	a-ban-don	leave, quit, forsake, desert, evacuate
2. bankruptcy	bank-rupt-cy	failure, broken, in the red, insolvency, poverty-stricken
3. committee	com-mit-tee	board, bureau, council, commission, advisory body
4. definitely	def-i-nite-ly	exactly, precisely, certainly, surely, positively
5. exaggerate	ex-ag-ger-ate	overstate, boast, magnify, overrate, inflate
6. government	gov-ern-ment	rule, command, management, control, administration
7. hazard	haz-ard	threat, risk, danger, chance, accident
8. itinerary	i-tin-er-ar-y	route, path, trip, journey, schedule
9. lengthen	length-en	extend, stretch, elongate, increase, prolong
10. meager	mea-ger	inadequate, scanty, deficient, skimpy, slight
11. nuisance	nui-sance	annoyance, pest, bother, irritation, inconvenience
12. physician	phy-si-cian	doctor, medic, M.D., healer, practitioner
13. together	to-geth-er	as a whole, in common, hand in hand, side by side, as one
14. unanimous	u-nan-i-mous	of one mind, solid, undivided, unified, agreeing
15. withdrawal	with-draw-al	retreat, departure, leave, exit, separation

Read each sentence carefully. Look at the meaning under the space with the number. In the *Answers* space, write or print the word from the word list that matches the meaning.

Small children _____(1)_____ what they see at the
overstate

circus.

1. _____

Though the pep rally crowd was _____(2)_____ ,
scanty

the cheering seemed louder than usual.

2. _____

Driving on an icy street is a _____(3)_____ to the
danger

driver and other motorists.

3. _____

If your headache continues, see a _____(4)_____ .
doctor

4. _____

Chicago, St. Louis, and Kansas City were the only

three cities shown on the _____(5)_____ .
journey

5. _____

The general called for a _____(6)_____ of the
departure

troops from the front lines.

6. _____

In the summertime, daylight hours will

_____(7)_____ .
increase

7. _____

Did someone _____(8)_____ the stolen car on the
desert

beach?

8. _____

To which _____(9)_____department does the
administration

Customs Service belong?

9. _____

Noise in the hallway was a _____(10)_____ during
annoyance

the testing session.

10. _____

The company had to file for _____(11)_____
insolvency

because of excessive losses.

11. _____

To honor outstanding student leaders was the

_____(12)_____ decision of the school board.
undivided

12. _____

The warehouse fire was _____(13)_____ a case of
surely

arson.

13. _____

The nominating _____(14)_____ reported its choice

advisory body

of a new slate of officers.   14. _____

The student body and the faculty worked

_____(15)_____ to raise the gift of money for the needy

as one

family.   15. _____

UNIT 1D

EXERCISE 25
Goal: To see if dates are exactly the same.

Look at the date in Column 1 and the date in Column 2. If the two dates are exactly the same, circle the *S* in Column 3. If the two dates are different, circle the *D* in Column 3. An example is shown.

COLUMN 1	COLUMN 2	COLUMN 3
0. 04-17-71	04-11-71	0. S ⒟
1. 10-04-75	10-04-75	1. S D
2. 12-01-72	12-07-72	2. S D
3. 07-22-73	07-22-73	3. S D
4. 09-15-82	09-15-82	4. S D
5. 11-11-77	11-17-77	5. S D
6. 01-22-63	01-22-68	6. S D
7. 06-26-66	06-20-66	7. S D
8. 05-09-68	05-09-63	8. S D
9. 10-20-66	10-20-66	9. S D
10. 03-08-68	08-03-68	10. S D
11. 04-07-71	04-01-71	11. S D
12. 12-10-81	12-10-81	12. S D
13. 08-31-85	08-31-85	13. S D
14. 11-12-78	11-12-87	14. S D
15. 09-07-79	09-07-79	15. S D

EXERCISE 26

Goal: To use a multi-line push-button telephone and to use office files/databases to find answers to questions.

In Exercise 13 you learned about a basic telephone with 12 buttons (1, 2, 3, 4, 5, 6, 7, 8, 9, *, 0, and #). Another kind of push-button telephone is called the **six-button desk telephone.** This telephone has the same 12 buttons as other touch-tone equipment, but *six large buttons* are at the bottom of the telephone under the 12 buttons. The hold button is the first one on the left side of the telephone. The "pick-up" buttons (2, 3, 4, and 5) are used to make and receive calls on separate outside lines. This telephone actually has four separate lines that it uses. The sixth button may be a COM or intercom button.

Illus. 1-2   A Six-Button Push-Button Telephone

The HOLD button allows you to place an incoming call on "hold" while you let another person in your office know he or she has a call. An intercom button lets you use the telephone to talk to someone in the same building with you.

When the telephone rings, a light flashes on one of the pick-up lines to tell you a call is coming in. To answer the call where the light is flashing, press the flashing button and then pick up the receiver. The light will stay on while the line is being used. If the call is for another person, you can place this call on "hold" by pressing the HOLD button. You would then press the COM button and dial a number to reach the desired person. When the person answers the telephone, you will tell that person he or she has a call. You will also tell that person which pick-up line to use.

To make a call outside the office, press a pick-up button with no light flashing and then make the call.

You are working for Bradford Office Supplies. Since the name of the company is so long, you answer telephone calls with only the first name, Bradford's.

Call 1   *The telephone rings.*

YOU   Good morning, Bradford's. _____ speaking. May
                     YOUR FIRST NAME
                     I help you?

OPERATOR   I have a collect call for anyone from Nicole Prenz. Will you accept?

                     (A *collect call* will be charged to Bradford Office Supplies. You can

                     accept the call because Nicole Prenz is a buyer who calls you each

                     day when she is out of town.)

YOU   Yes, Operator, I will accept the charges.

OPERATOR   Go ahead.

CALLER   Hello, _____. Please check your price quotations
                     YOUR FIRST NAME
                     database. What is the least amount we pay for jiffy mailers and

                     which supplier offers us the lowest price?

YOU   One minute, please, Nicole.

(PAUSE)   (Look in the Office Files/Databases for Bradford Office Sup-

                     plies.)

                     Thank you for waiting. The lowest price is _____ from
                                               AMOUNT

                     _____ in _____.
                     COMPANY NAME   CITY AND STATE

CALLER   Do you have any file folder prices less than $55 per 500?

YOU   Yes. _____ in _____, _____
                     COMPANY NAME   CITY   STATE

                     charges _____ per 500.
                          AMOUNT

CALLER   Thank you very much. I will return to the office tomorrow to han-

                     dle this order. Good-bye.

YOU   You are welcome. Good-bye.

Call 2 🖅   *The telephone rings.*

The blinking light on the COM button tells you the call is from inside the building. You may answer this call with your first name since you know most of the employees by their first names.

YOU   _____ speaking. May I help you?

                     YOUR FIRST NAME

CALLER   Yes, _____. This is Ricky Wolfe in the shipping de-

                     YOUR FIRST NAME

partment. Can you tell me the number at the post office I would

call to learn about sending parcels to the military?

YOU   Yes, _____. Will you please hold?

                  HIS FIRST NAME

(PAUSE)   (Look in the Office Files/Databases for Bradford Office

Supplies).

Thank you for holding, _____. Be sure to use a push-

                            HIS FIRST NAME

button telephone when you dial 555-7689. The recorded

instructions will tell you when to press the buttons for message

number _____.

CALLER   Thank you. That was 555 what?

YOU   Dial 555-7689 and wait for the recorded instructions. Then press

_____ for the message about parcels to the military.

CALLER   Do you have a message number for how to file a claim for items lost

in the mail?

YOU   Yes, I do. You do not have to dial 555-7689 again if you make this

call immediately after the first one. You wait for the tone and then

dial message number _____ to learn how to file a claim for

a lost item. Also, if you want a message repeated, wait for the tone

and dial the message number again.

Note: Ricky asked you to repeat the number. For callers who do not ask, always offer to repeat numbers. You want to be sure the caller heard the correct number.

Exercise 26   **67**

EXERCISE 27
Goal: To print information on business forms.

In Exercise 9 you printed information on shipping labels in ALL CAPITAL LET-
TERS. You also printed information on airline baggage forms and used a capital
letter followed by small letters. Look at the samples in Exercise 9 to help you with the
size and shape of letters as you finish this exercise.

   Use the information below as you print in ALL CAPITAL LETTERS the information on the business forms. The only punctuation you will use on these forms is the
hyphen in the ZIP Code. Abbreviate as many words as you can. Use the USPS Abbreviations pages in the Reference Sources to see which words can be abbreviated.

Ms. Kerin Marie Preston
169 Morepark Drive
Apartment 47
Island Heights, New Jersey 08732-2008

Form 1

Mr. Mrs. Ms.	First Name	Middle Initial	Last Name

Address			Apt. No.

City		State	ZIP

Mr. Mark William Milne
4473 South Beach Boulevard
Apartment D-621
Newport Beach, California 92663-4441

Form 2

Mr. Mrs. Ms.	First Name	Middle Initial	Last Name

Address			Apt. No.

City		State	ZIP

Look at the sample in Exercise 9 to help you with the size and shape of the capital and small letters as you finish this exercise. Use the information shown below to fill in the membership cards. Print with a capital letter followed by small letters. Use as many abbreviations as you can. *Do not print too fast.*

19562935
Phone: (703) 555-2000
Janet M. Lund
Assistant Staff Manager
National Fine Arts Bureau
Winslow Plaza West, Building C-45, Suite 120
Arlington, Virginia 22202-6120

Form 1

MEMBER #		PHONE ( )	
NAME			
TITLE			
COMPANY			
ADDRESS			
CITY	STATE		ZIP CODE

02117538
Phone: (915) 555-7350
Marc B. Eddlemann
Director, Information Processing Center
Sage Electric Corporation
Southwest Utilities Plaza
El Paso, Texas 79921-6563

Form 2

MEMBER #		PHONE ( )	
NAME			
TITLE			
COMPANY			
ADDRESS			
CITY	STATE		ZIP CODE

EXERCISE 28
Goal: To use reference sources to find information.

To find the answers to the questions below, use the Reference Sources of this text-workbook (pages 261–294). Write or print your answers in the space at the end of the line. To help you, the part of the Reference Sources you will need to use to find your answer is shown after the first question in each set.

ANSWERS

1a. Who is the author of *Good Grief, Good Grammar*? (Reference Books)

1a. _____

1b. What is the name of the publisher of *How to Find and Apply for a Job*?

1b. _____

2a. What is the Postal Service abbreviation for *Terrace*? (USPS Abbreviations)

2a. _____

2b. What is the abbreviation for *Mountain*?

2b. _____

3a. What is the income tax withheld for a single person on a monthly payroll if wages are $985 with one allowance? (Payroll—Monthly)

3a. _____

3b. What is the income tax withheld for a married person on a monthly payroll if wages are $1,625 with four allowances?

3b. _____

4a. What is the capital of Illinois? (Map—United States)

4a. _____

4b. The state of Michigan touches how many of the Great Lakes?

4b. _____

5a. Who was the caller to St. Louis, MO, on 7/5? (Calls Register)

5a. _____

5b. Who placed the incoming collect call on 7/29?

5b. _____

6a. What was the balance at the beginning of check stub 1314? (Checkbook)

6a. _____

6b. What was the balance at the end of the day on March 31?

6b. _____

EXERCISE 29
Goal: To use a forms register to write a receipt.

In some stores and offices, the business forms are found in a machine called a **forms register.** This register has blank forms with numbers on them. The top copy, or original copy, has other copies underneath with carbonless paper. As the top copy is filled in, the other copies are being made at the same time. When a form is finished, all the copies slide out of the register. You may have from two to six copies. A tray or drawer usually is a part of the register. One copy of a form is put in this tray or drawer. One copy goes to the customer. The other copies are filed or mailed to different places.

A forms register is shown in Illus. 1-3.

Illus. 1-3 Forms Register

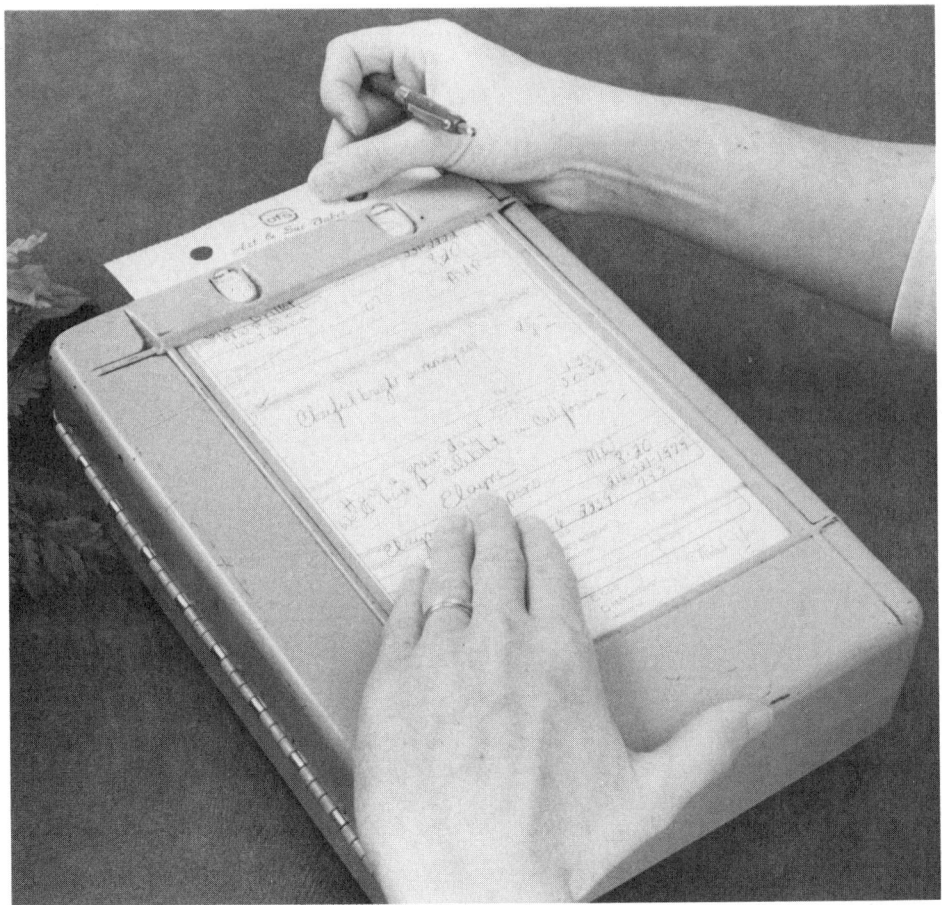

In Exercise 8 you learned to write a receipt with a stub. The sample receipt in Fig. 1-15 is the kind you find in a forms register. Use the receipt in Fig. 1-15 as a guide as you fill in the receipt forms for this exercise.

Fig. 1-15 A Sample Receipt Form

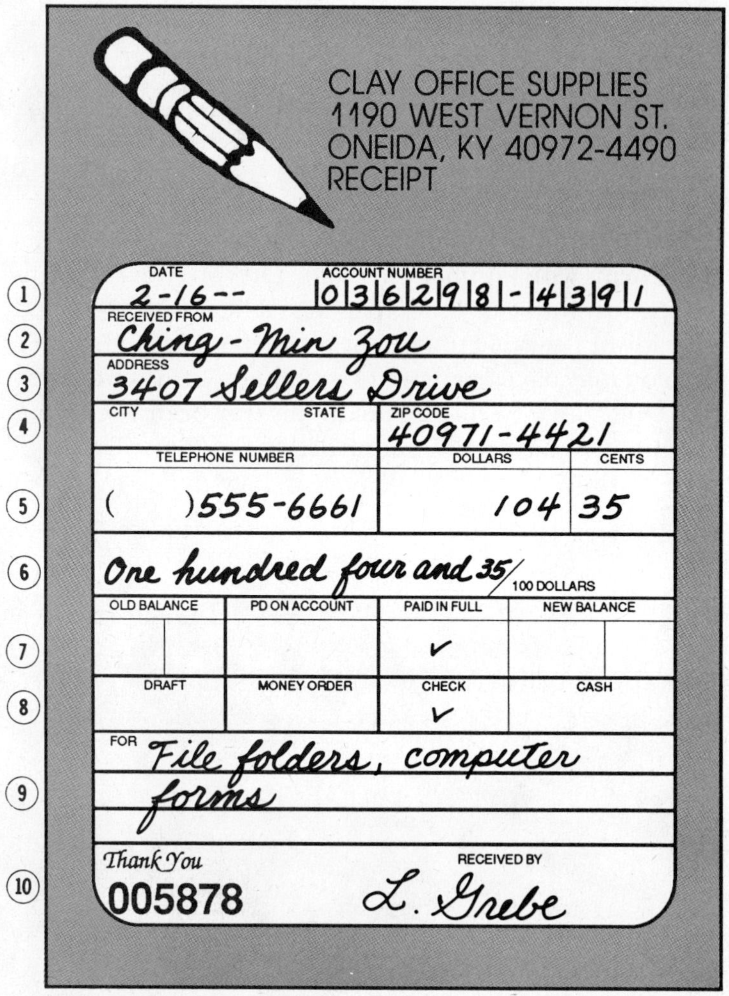
CLAY OFFICE SUPPLIES
1190 WEST VERNON ST.
ONEIDA, KY 40972-4490
RECEIPT

1. DATE 2-16-- ACCOUNT NUMBER 0362981-4391
2. RECEIVED FROM Ching-Min Zou
3. ADDRESS 3407 Sellers Drive
4. CITY STATE ZIP CODE 40971-4421
5. TELEPHONE NUMBER ( )555-6661 DOLLARS 104 CENTS 35
6. One hundred four and 35/100 DOLLARS
7. OLD BALANCE PD ON ACCOUNT PAID IN FULL ✓ NEW BALANCE
8. DRAFT MONEY ORDER CHECK ✓ CASH
9. FOR File folders, computer forms
10. Thank You 005878 RECEIVED BY L. Grebe

1. The date is written in numbers or the month may be written as a word. The account number is the way the person who paid the money is listed in the computer. A charge card number may be used here. A list of customer account numbers may be in a file or a list close by.
2. The name after *Received From* is the person who paid the money.
3. The address should have the house number, the street name, and the apartment number, if the person has one. Also, a post office box or a rural route number could be written here.
4. The city may be omitted IF it is in the same city as the store. *Always* include the full ZIP Code. If the city is not the same, then write the city, state, and ZIP Code. With such a small space, be careful to write clearly so it is easy to read. Be sure the numbers are written very plainly.
5. The telephone number is written without the area code IF it is the same area code as the store's. For the *Dollars and Cents,* use the line in the middle of the column as the decimal point. Use only numbers for the dollars and cents.
6. Write the amount of dollars in words. Before the */100 Dollars,* write the number of cents.
7. For the amount of *Old Balance,* you would look up the person's bill or use the computer keyboard to call up the amount. *PD on Account* is checked if the person

is paying on the old account balance. If the amount paid is the same as the old balance, then check *Paid in Full*. If the amount paid is not the amount of the old balance, subtract the amount paid from the old balance amount. Write the difference in the *New Balance* box.

8. Check one of the following ways to pay on account: draft, money order, check, or cash.
9. If there is a message, write it after *For*.
10. Sign your name or initials after *Received by* to show that you did take the money from the person who paid it.

Use the following forms to finish this exercise. Use as many abbreviations as you can for the addresses.

Form 1: Write or print a receipt to Heidi Barker who resides at 7480 Appleton Road, Oakland, California 94603. Use today's date. Her account number is 003629439. Her telephone number is 555-9326. Her old balance is $152.50. She paid you $70.50 cash on account. You will need to figure her new balance.

Form 1

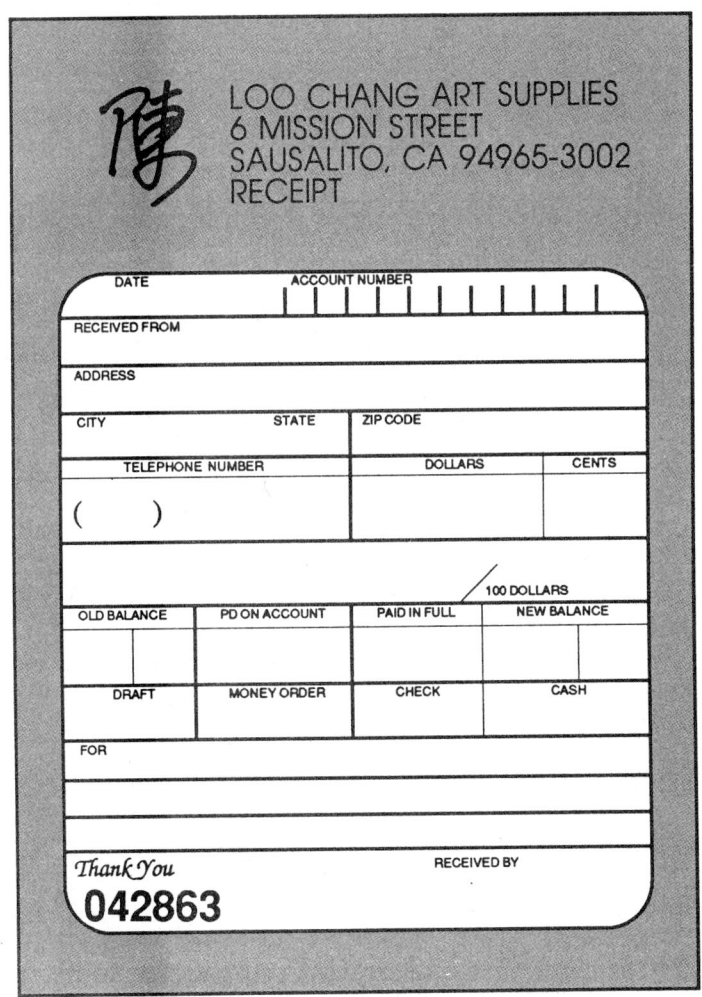

Form 2: Write or print a receipt to Timothy Taylor who lives at 720 Velva Court, Tomales, California 94971-3280. Use today's date. His account number is 003633691. His telephone number is 555-3141. His old balance is $250.85. He paid $150.85 on account by check. What is his new balance?

Form 2

陳 LOO CHANG ART SUPPLIES
6 MISSION STREET
SAUSALITO, CA 94965-3002
(415) 555-0450
RECEIPT

DATE	ACCOUNT NUMBER

RECEIVED FROM

ADDRESS

CITY	STATE	ZIP CODE

TELEPHONE NUMBER	DOLLARS	CENTS
( )		

100 DOLLARS

OLD BALANCE	PD ON ACCOUNT	PAID IN FULL	NEW BALANCE

DRAFT	MONEY ORDER	CHECK	CASH

FOR

Thank You
042864

RECEIVED BY

EXERCISE 30
Goal: To index names with certain punctuation marks for filing.

RULE 3 Commas, periods, hyphens, apostrophes, and parentheses are *not* used in indexing the names of a person or a business.

Look at the examples in Table 1-5 to see how to index names where punctuation marks are written, but not indexed. The letter with a line under it shows the change from one letter in the alphabet to another letter that comes later in the alphabet. This letter puts the names in alphabetic order.

Table 1-5 Examples of Rule 3

	INDEXING UNIT				
Name Before Indexing	**Unit 1**	**Unit 2**	**Unit 3**	**Unit 4**	**Unit 5**
Ari, Blau, & Chay Imports	Ari	Blau	and	Chay	Imports
Carol M. Bank	Bank	Carol	M		
Bank of Augusta	Bank	of	Augusta		
Banks & Hewitt, Roofers	Banks	and	Hewitt	Roofers	
Anniesue L. Banks	Banks	Anniesue	L		
Bank's Cut Rate Drugs	Banks	Cut	Rate	Drugs	
Banks' Dry Cleaners	Banks	Dry	Cleaners		
Bank-View Art Supplies	BankView	Art	Supplies		
Bankville Auto Repairs	Bankville	Auto	Repairs		
Beale's $ Stretcher Stores	Beales	Dollar	Stretcher	Stores	
China-Tone Music Shop	ChinaTone	Music	Shop		
Chinatown Gift Scene	Chinatown	Gift	Scene		
Barney J. Cholton	Cholton	Barney	J		
Chow-Time Restaurants	ChowTime	Restaurants			
The Clear-Vue Mirror Company	ClearVue	Mirror	Company	The	

EXERCISE 30a Put the four names in each group in correct alphabetic order. In the space shown write 1, 2, 3, or 4 to show the order where the name with the line under it would come in this correct alphabetic order. An example is shown.

0. Charles and Cowan Freight Lines   **0.** _____3_____

    Charlestown Shopping Mall

    Charlesy Coffee Vendors

    Charleston Commercial Bank

1. Belle of the Ball Studios   1. _____
   <u>Bell's Baby Products</u>
   Baal Motorcycle Sales & Service
   Bells' Supermarkets

2. Offen, Scott, and Lane Department Stores   2. _____
   Off the Square Flower Mart
   <u>Office Mates Employment Agency</u>
   Leola R. Offi

3. Fair Hills Convalescent Center   3. _____
   Fairies & Clowns Day Care Circus
   Michelle G. Fair
   <u>Fairfax Mobile Home Park</u>

4. <u>Middleburg Historical Society</u>   4. _____
   Mid-Town Garden Apartments
   Middy & Mike Chimney Sweepers
   Middleton Automobile Club

5. Mills & Kane Land Developers   5. _____
   Milne Paint and Body Shop
   <u>Millie Myrick Antiques</u>
   Milano, Dewey, and Ogle Associates

6. <u>Horsell's Discount Pharmacy</u>   6. _____
   Horsley Formal Rental Shop
   Horse Town Trading Post
   Horseshoe Bend Camera Cove

EXERCISE 30b   In this exercise look at each set of names to decide the correct alphabetic order. After you study each set of names, write these names in the correct alphabetic order on the lines to the right. An example is shown.

0. The Travellers' Choice Inn   0. <u>Travel Club of Austin</u>
   Travel Treads Footwear   <u>Travel Treads Footwear</u>
   Travel with Us Tours   <u>Travel with Us Tours</u>
   Travel Club of Austin   <u>Travellers' Choice Inn The</u>

1. Pearson's Car Rental Agency   1. _____
   Parson Paper Company   _____
   Parreson Produce Market   _____
   Perslon Sandwich Company   _____

2. Glen-Dale Broadcasting Systems
   Eudella C. Glenn
   Glenoaks Cabinet Works
   Glenridge Office Park

   2. _____
   _____
   _____
   _____

3. Lillian Lea Fabric Centers
   Lil's & Lee's Fantastic Photography
   Lilly Linn's Animal Shelter
   Lil Lee Chocolatiers

   3. _____
   _____
   _____
   _____

4. Top of the World Inn
   Top $ Food Marts
   Top-Notch Cleaners
   Top-Flight Chimney Sweep

   4. _____
   _____
   _____
   _____

5. Jay and Faye General Store
   Jason, Massey, and Scott Gem Labs
   Jack and Jill Playskool
   The J & L Marketing Service

   5. _____
   _____
   _____
   _____

6. Cross Points Clothing Company
   Cross-Rhodes Wrecker Service
   Crossroads Flooring, Inc.
   Cross Creek Sign Co.

   6. _____
   _____
   _____
   _____

7. The Summit Recreation Center
   Summit Hills Stables
   Harold Summers Dental Lab
   Summertime Outdoor Theatre

   7. _____
   _____
   _____
   _____

8. Tore's Technical Institute
   Torras Auto Paints
   Toras' Printing Co.
   The Toras' Italian Restaurant

   8. _____
   _____
   _____
   _____

EXERCISE 31
Goal: To tell time using an analog clock.

There are two basic types of clocks. An *analog* clock has a "face" that usually shows the numbers 1 to 12, which represent the hours of the day. Analog clocks have two hands which move and show the hours and minutes of the day. There are 24 hours in each day. The hour hand on the clock will go around twice for each 24-hour period. Each hour has 60 minutes. The clock has two hands: an hour hand and a minute hand. The hour hand is the short hand. The minute hand is the long hand. Both hands move in the same direction, which is called *clockwise*.

Fig. 1-16   Clock Face with Hour and Minute Hands

Fig. 1-17   Clockwise Direction

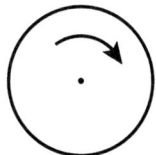

The long minute hand moves around the face of the clock once every hour. Look at Fig. 1-18. Do you see the *thin* black lines? Each of these lines represents one minute. Each group of five minutes is represented by a *thick* black line on the clock face.

Fig. 1-18   Clock Face Showing Minute Groupings

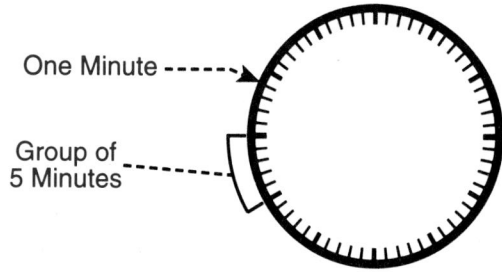

The short hand on the clock face indicates the hour. This short hand will move clockwise around the face of the clock also. This hour hand moves more slowly than the minute hand. It will move from one number to the next once each hour.

Fig. 1-19   Clock Face with Hour and Minute Hands

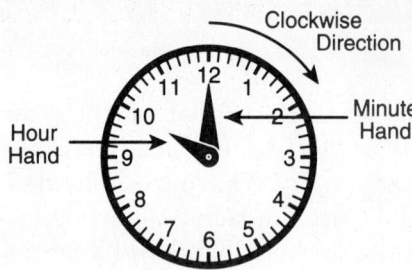

TELLING TIME   When the hour hand is pointed directly at a number and the minute hand is on 12, this is the beginning of an hour. The clock shown on the right reads 2:00.

Look at the clock on the right. The minute hand is on 6 and the hour hand is between the 2 and the 3. When the minute hand is on 6 it means that 30 minutes have passed. Count the thick five-minute marks. You will count 6 five-minute marks ($6 \times 5 = 30$). This clock reads 2:30 (or 30 minutes past 2).

As the minute hand moves around the clock, you will count the minutes that the minute hand has passed. Use the five-minute markings by counting by five. When you have counted all the five-minute marks, you will have to count individual minutes. Look at the clock on the right. This clock reads 2:51 (or 51 minutes past 2). You should say the hour first, followed by the minutes.

Look at the clocks shown below. Look at the hour hands and the minute hands. Count the minutes using the five-minute markings when you can. Write the time below each clock. An example is shown.

0. 7:00 _____   1. _____   2. _____   3. _____

EXERCISE 32
Goal: To add words to your vocabulary.

The words in Column 1 are among those words most frequently mispronounced and misspelled. Spend time in study and in drill before you finish the exercise. In your home study, pronounce the words as they are divided in Column 2. Drill on the correct spelling and meanings. You will find these words and meanings on the unit test.

COLUMN 1	COLUMN 2	COLUMN 3
1. **author**	au-thor	writer, novelist, essayist, founder, creator
2. **balance**	bal-ance	evenness, level, fairness, estimate, amount owed or owned
3. **cautious**	cau-tious	careful, watchful, on the safe side, guarded, wary
4. **develop**	de-vel-op	grow up, age, mature, progress, unfold
5. **embarrass**	em-bar-rass	shame, confuse, upset, bother, fluster
6. **fatigue**	fa-tigue	weariness, exhaustion, boredom, tired, exhausted
7. **gradual**	grad-u-al	slow, little by little, progressive, moderate, measured
8. **hectic**	hec-tic	disorderly, turbulent, flurrying, chaotic, feverish
9. **initial**	in-i-tial	first, beginning, opening, original, introductory
10. **label**	la-bel	tag, seal, name, slip, stamp
11. **manager**	man-ag-er	boss, supervisor, director, controller, organizer
12. **promptly**	prompt-ly	quickly, rapidly, swiftly, speedily, without delay
13. **specific**	spe-cif-ic	exact, definite, clear-cut, plain, clear
14. **territory**	ter-ri-to-ry	region, area, locale, land, district
15. **usable**	us-a-ble	can be used, available for use, utilizable, employable

Look at the meanings in Column 1. Circle the *correctly spelled* word in Column 2 that matches the meanings in Column 1.

COLUMN 1

1. disorderly, chaotic
2. shame, confuse
3. can be used, employable
4. evenness, amount owed
5. region, area
6. weariness, exhaustion
7. tag, slip
8. careful, watchful
9. first, beginning
10. writer, novelist
11. exact, definite
12. slow, little by little
13. quickly, rapidly
14. grow up, age
15. boss, supervisor

COLUMN 2

1. hecktic hectic heckict hecktict
2. embaris embarras embarrass embarrus
3. usable useable useble usible
4. balance ballance balence ballence
5. teritory terretory teritory territory
6. fatigue fatig fitigue fatige
7. labul lable label labbel
8. cauchious cautious caushous cautous
9. initial inishal inichul initual
10. arthur aurther arther author
11. pacific specific pacifick specifict
12. grajul gradjul grajel gradual
13. promply promptly prommly promptally
14. developp devellop develup develop
15. maneger manejer manager manger

Congratulations! You have now finished the exercises for Unit 3. Before you ask your teacher for the unit test, study the vocabulary, spelling, and filing exercises in this unit. You will also need to know the states and capitals. Ask your teacher for instructions for turning in your work. Do not begin work on the exercises in Unit 4 until your teacher tells you to do so.

UNIT 2A

EXERCISE 33
Goal: To improve writing numbers in columns.

In Exercise 4 you learned to write numbers in a column. In that exercise the column was divided with a line between the dollars and cents amounts. In this exercise the column has a line to divide each number. Look at the sample in Column 1.

    Use these steps to finish the exercise:

1. Write the numbers to the left of Column 2 down the lines of Column 2.
2. Find the total. Write the total at the bottom of Column 2.
3. Fill in Column 3 using the same steps you used for Column 2.

COLUMN 1	COLUMN 2	COLUMN 3

COLUMN 1 — AMOUNT

AMOUNT	
11 671 90	1
84 35	2
6 10	3
3 004 65	4
12 125 00	5
867 00	6
	7
	8
	9
27 759 00	10

COLUMN 2

486.30
1,822.00
5.50
18,006.20
95.00
677.00

AMOUNT	
	1
	2
	3
	4
	5
	6
	7
	8
	9
	10

COLUMN 3

5,396.00
741.70
12.50
21,684.30
985.00
5.50

AMOUNT	
	1
	2
	3
	4
	5
	6
	7
	8
	9
	10

EXERCISE 34
Goal: To index single letters and abbreviations in personal and business names for filing.

RULE 4a   An initial in a *personal* name (W. C. Yates, D. Marie Cully, Gena K. Law) is indexed as a separate unit. Abbreviations of personal names (Wm., Geo., Thos.) and brief personal names (Liz, Theo, Bob) are indexed as they are written.

RULE 4b   Single letters in *business* names are indexed as written. If there is a space between single letters, index *each letter* as a separate unit.
   An acronym is a word made of the initials of other words. WHO (World Health Organization) and VISTA (Volunteers in Service to America) are examples of acronyms. Index an acronym as *one* unit.
   Abbreviations (AA, YMCA, Y.W.C.A.) are indexed as *one* unit—with or without spaces and periods. Radio and television station call letters (WLW, WQXI, WGST) are indexed as one unit.

Table 2-1   Examples of Rule 4

| | INDEXING ORDER | | | |
Name Before Indexing	Key Unit	Unit 2	Unit 3	Unit 4
T. A. Specht	Specht	T	A	
T. A. Specht Bakery	T	A	Specht	Bakery
T & A Grocers	T	and	A	Grocers
TAN Motel	TAN	Motel		
Jas. Tanero	Tanero	Jas		
Teach-Toddlers Day School	TeachToddlers	Day	School	
TeachTots Toys	TeachTots	Toys		
U.A.L. Sporting Goods	UAL	Sporting	Goods	
United Athletic League	United	Athletic	League	
USA Travel Service	USA	Travel	Service	
WABE Radio Station	WABE	Radio	Station	
Wear-Ever Work Shoes	WearEver	Work	Shoes	
Wears Marine Supplies	Wears	Marine	Supplies	
Wear's Pharmacy	Wears	Pharmacy		

On the front of each group of cards on pages 89 and 90 is a group number (1, 2, 3, etc.). Before the name shown on each card is a letter (A, B, C, D, or E).

Use these steps to finish this exercise:

1. Look at the cards in Group 1. Put the five cards in correct alphabetic order by the name on each card.
2. Write the letters found in the corner of the card (A, B, C, D, or E) in the order in which the names come in alphabetic order.
3. Write the letters in the *Answers* column.
4. Follow the same procedure for the other nine groups.

An example is shown below. Notice that the letters (A, B, C, D, E) have been written in the *Answers* column in the correct alphabetic order. Card C (O & L Drywall & Roofing Co.) would be the first card in correct alphabetic order. Card D (Oberlin Mountain Inn) would be next. Card A (Old Tyme Card & Gift Shop) is third. Cards B and E would be the last two cards. In the *Answers* column are the letters for the cards in correct alphabetic order: *C, D, A, B, E*.

EXAMPLE

ANSWERS

Example 0. <u>C, D, A, B, E</u>

Group 1. _____

Group 2. _____

Group 3. _____

Group 4. _____

Group 5. _____

Group 6. _____

Group 7. _____

Group 8. _____

Group 9. _____

Group 10. _____

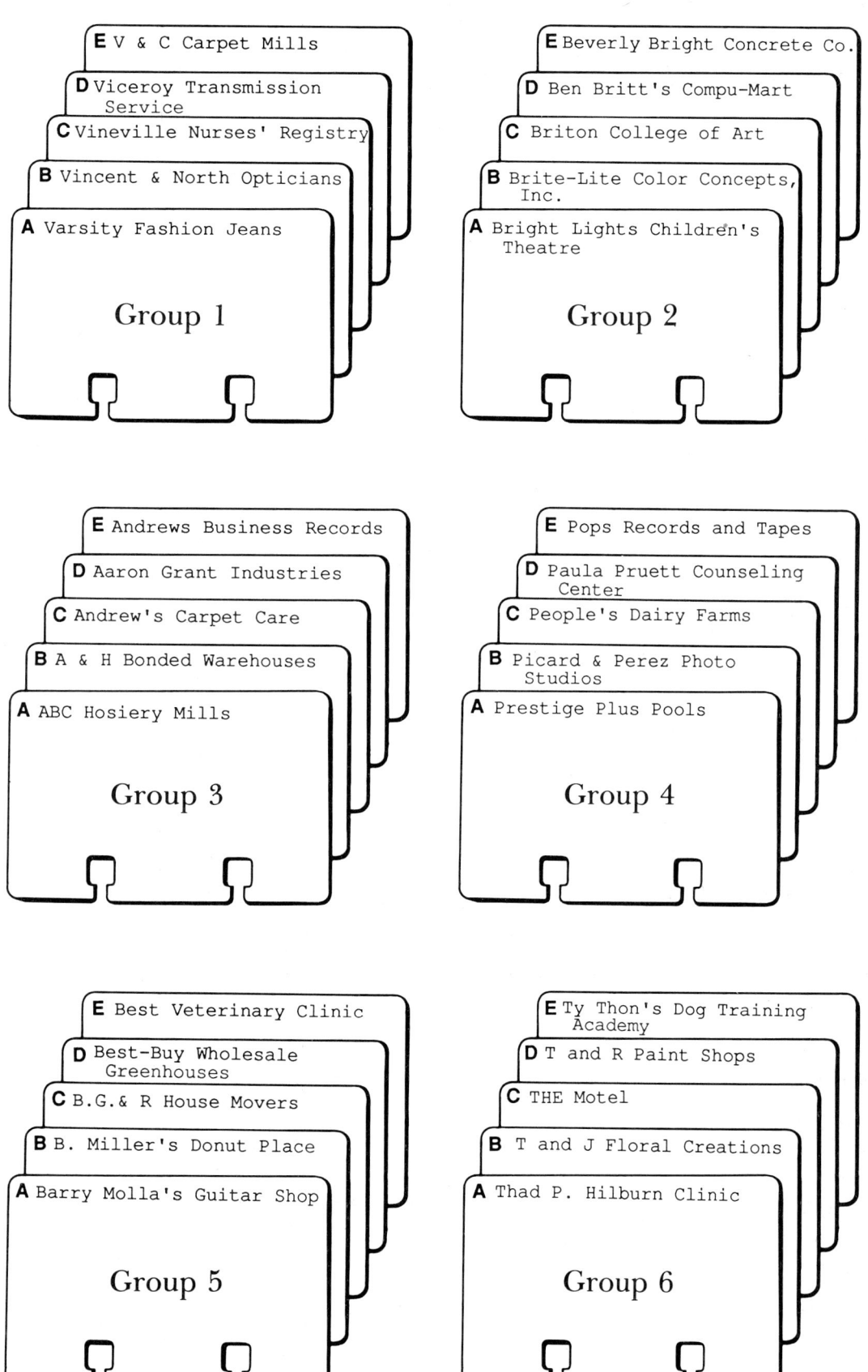

Group 1

- **E** V & C Carpet Mills
- **D** Viceroy Transmission Service
- **C** Vineville Nurses' Registry
- **B** Vincent & North Opticians
- **A** Varsity Fashion Jeans

Group 2

- **E** Beverly Bright Concrete Co.
- **D** Ben Britt's Compu-Mart
- **C** Briton College of Art
- **B** Brite-Lite Color Concepts, Inc.
- **A** Bright Lights Children's Theatre

Group 3

- **E** Andrews Business Records
- **D** Aaron Grant Industries
- **C** Andrew's Carpet Care
- **B** A & H Bonded Warehouses
- **A** ABC Hosiery Mills

Group 4

- **E** Pops Records and Tapes
- **D** Paula Pruett Counseling Center
- **C** People's Dairy Farms
- **B** Picard & Perez Photo Studios
- **A** Prestige Plus Pools

Group 5

- **E** Best Veterinary Clinic
- **D** Best-Buy Wholesale Greenhouses
- **C** B.G.& R House Movers
- **B** B. Miller's Donut Place
- **A** Barry Molla's Guitar Shop

Group 6

- **E** Ty Thon's Dog Training Academy
- **D** T and R Paint Shops
- **C** THE Motel
- **B** T and J Floral Creations
- **A** Thad P. Hilburn Clinic

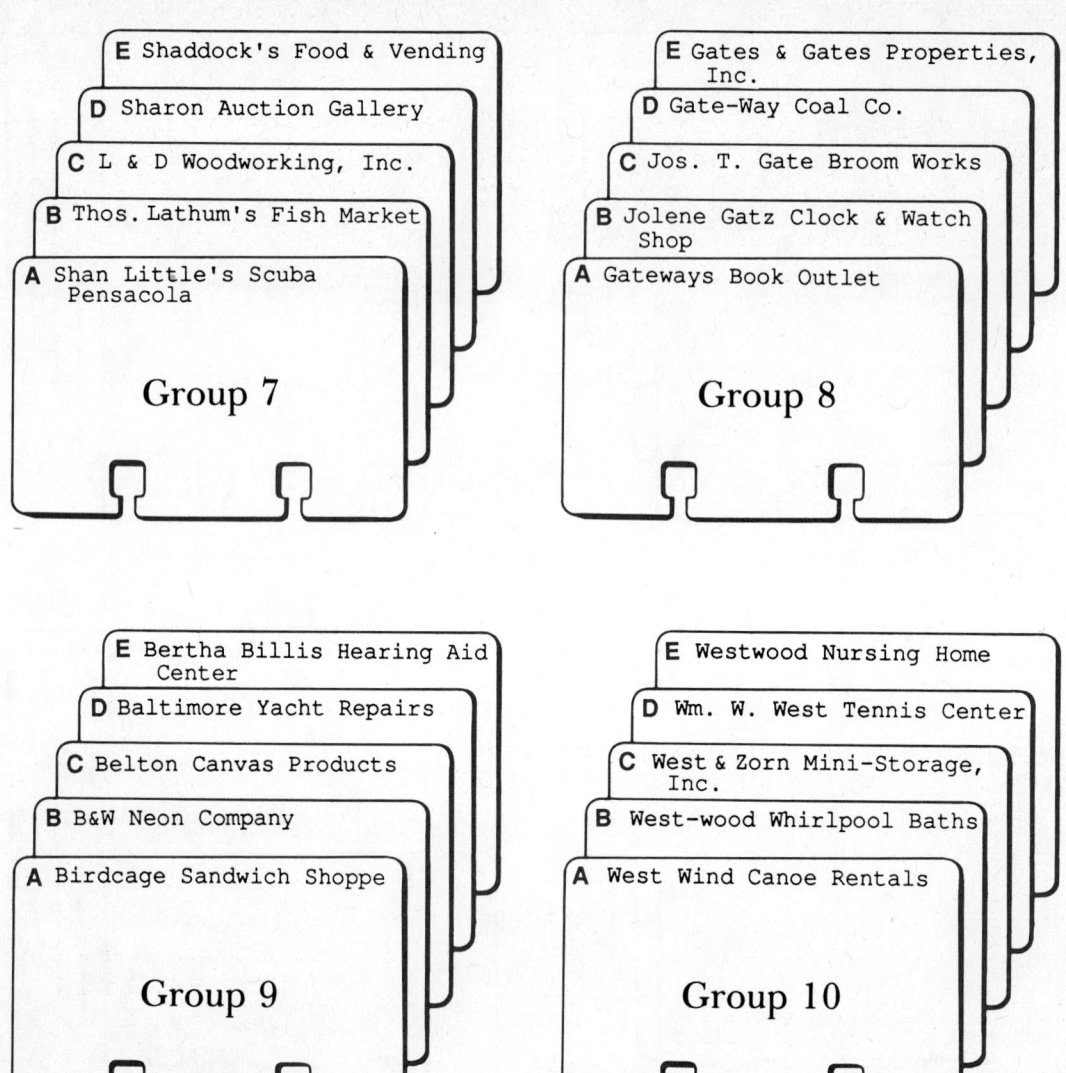

Group 7

E Shaddock's Food & Vending
D Sharon Auction Gallery
C L & D Woodworking, Inc.
B Thos. Lathum's Fish Market
A Shan Little's Scuba Pensacola

Group 8

E Gates & Gates Properties, Inc.
D Gate-Way Coal Co.
C Jos. T. Gate Broom Works
B Jolene Gatz Clock & Watch Shop
A Gateways Book Outlet

Group 9

E Bertha Billis Hearing Aid Center
D Baltimore Yacht Repairs
C Belton Canvas Products
B B&W Neon Company
A Birdcage Sandwich Shoppe

Group 10

E Westwood Nursing Home
D Wm. W. West Tennis Center
C West & Zorn Mini-Storage, Inc.
B West-wood Whirlpool Baths
A West Wind Canoe Rentals

EXERCISE 35
Goal: To write personal checks and to keep a check register.

In Exercise 23 you learned to open a personal checking account at a bank. After you completed a signature card, endorsed the check, and filled in the bank deposit ticket, you made a deposit. You also made the first entry in the check register.

You are now ready to write checks. Use Figs. 2-1 and 2-2 as a guide to finish the exercises about check writing in this text-workbook.

Always write in the check register before you write a check. You will add all deposits and subtract all checks in the register.

Use Fig. 2-1 as a guide for writing in the check register.

Fig. 2-1 Check Register

①	②	③	④		⑤	
CHECK NO.	DATE	CHECK ISSUED TO	BAL. BR.'T. F'R'D.	√		
	1/4	TO	AMOUNT OF CHECK OR (DEPOSIT)		500 00	
		FOR	BALANCE		500 00	
101	1/5	TO *Carolina Electric Authority*	AMOUNT OF CHECK OR DEPOSIT		72 58	
		FOR *monthly service*	BALANCE		427 42	
		TO	AMOUNT OF CHECK OR DEPOSIT			
		FOR	BALANCE			
		TO	AMOUNT OF CHECK OR DEPOSIT			
		FOR	BALANCE			
		TO	AMOUNT OF CHECK OR DEPOSIT			
		FOR	BALANCE			
		TO	AMOUNT OF CHECK OR DEPOSIT			
		FOR	BALANCE			

1. The check number is the same number as the one on the check in the checkbook. This number is printed on the check when you buy the checks from the bank. Checks are numbered in *consecutive* order. Check 102 comes after Check 101.
2. The date is 1/5 and the current year, the same date as shown on the check. You can also write January 5, if you do not want to use numbers.
3. The column for *Check Issued To* has two lines under it. After *To,* write the name of the person or company that is shown on the check after *Pay to the Order Of.* After *For,* write the same reason that is shown on the check after *For.*
4. In the next column you find *Amount of Check or Deposit.* In Exercise 23 when the deposit amount was written in the register, a circle was made around the word *Deposit.* When you write a check, do not circle anything. Since so many checks are written, the check register would be filled with circles. You would find the column hard to read. Circle only the word *Deposit* in this column when a deposit amount is written.

5. The last column always shows the *balance,* which is the amount in the bank account after a check is written or a deposit is made. Since a check is a way to take money from the bank account, *subtract* the amount of the check from the balance. Write the difference as the new balance. **Note: Always** *subtract* **the amount of a check and** *add* **the amount of a deposit to the amount shown as the balance.**

After you write all the information in the check register, then write the check. Be sure the amounts, names, and check number in the check register are the same information you write on the check.

Use Fig. 2-2 to help you when you write checks in the exercises in this text-workbook.

Fig. 2-2 Sample Check

1. The check number is the same number you wrote in the check register under the *Check No.* column.
2. The date may be written in numbers (1/5) or in words (January 5). Use the current year.
3. After *Pay to the Order Of,* write the name of a person or a company. Draw a wavy line after the name so that another name cannot be added. For long company names, abbreviate words such as Company (Co.), Incorporated (Inc.), Limited (Ltd.), International (Intl.), or Association (Assn.).
4. Use the same rules for writing numbers on checks as you used in writing receipts in Exercise 8.
5. Write the reason for writing the check after *For.*
6. The signature on a check must be the same signature that you wrote on the signature card when you opened the account.

Use this information to fill in the check register and the two checks on pages 93 and 94.

The check register should *always* be filled out before you write the checks. The reason for completing the check register first is so that you will not forget to do it. Sometimes when you are in a hurry it is easy to forget this task. Later when you try to remember to whom you wrote the check it may be hard to remember!

CHECK NO.	DATE	CHECK ISSUED TO		BAL. BR.'T. F'R'D.	V				
	1/4	TO		AMOUNT OF CHECK OR (DEPOSIT)		5 0 0	00		
		FOR		BALANCE		5 0 0	00		
101	1/5	TO *Carolina Electric Authority*		AMOUNT OF CHECK OR DEPOSIT		7 2	58		
		FOR *monthly service*		BALANCE		4 2 7	42		
		TO		AMOUNT OF CHECK OR DEPOSIT					
		FOR		BALANCE					
		TO		AMOUNT OF CHECK OR DEPOSIT					
		FOR		BALANCE					
		TO		AMOUNT OF CHECK OR DEPOSIT					
		FOR		BALANCE					
		TO		AMOUNT OF CHECK OR DEPOSIT					
		FOR		BALANCE					

Check 102: Write a check for $60.00 for a donation to the All-City School Fund. Sign Rachel Garrison's name on the check. The date is January 7. Use the current year.

RACHEL GARRISON   **102**
7355 PRINCE CT. APT. 21
GASTONIA, NC 28052-1180

_____ 19_____   64-39
                            610

PAY TO THE
ORDER OF _____ $ _____

_____ DOLLARS

G GASTONIA
   STATE BANK

FOR _____   _____

⑆061004421⑆ 12 121 128⑈

Exercise 35   **93**

Check 103: Write a check for $55.86 to the Madison Electric Company for the monthly electric bill. Sign Rachel Garrison's name on the check. The date is January 7. Use the current year.

RACHEL GARRISON   **103**
7355 PRINCE CT. APT. 21
GASTONIA, NC 28052-1180

_____ 19_____ 64-39
                                610

PAY TO THE
ORDER OF _____ $ _____

_____ DOLLARS

G GASTONIA
    STATE BANK

FOR _____   _____

⑆0610044⑈ 12 121 128⑆

EXERCISE 36
Goal: To see if the names of businesses are exactly alike.

Look at the name of the business in Column 1 and the name of the business in Column 2. If the two names are exactly alike, circle the *A* in Column 3. If the two names are not exactly alike, circle the *N* in Column 3.

COLUMN 1	COLUMN 2	COLUMN 3
1. Francis Chiropractic	Frances Chiropractic	1. A N
2. Auto Electric Specialists	Auto Electric Specialists	2. A N
3. Maywood Shops, Inc.	Maywood Shops, Inc.	3. A N
4. Dayne Mold Supplies	Dayne Mold Suppliers	4. A N
5. Checks For Cash	Checks for Cash	5. A N
6. Pacific Finance	Pacific Financial	6. A N
7. Veterans Memorial Hospital	Veterans' Memorial Hospital	7. A N
8. Food-for-Thought Institute	Food-For-Thought Institute	8. A N
9. Peach Tree Apartments	Peach Tree Apartments	9. A N
10. First National Bank of Tray	First National Bank of Troy	10. A N
11. Above Board Catering	Above Board Catering	11. A N
12. Ferro Electronics Group	Ferro Electronic Group	12. A N
13. Merlin Drive Upholstery	Merlin Drive Upholstery	13. A N
14. Golden Eagle Travel, Inc.	Golden Eagle Travel, Inc.	14. A N
15. China Motels	Chino Motels	15. A N

EXERCISE 37
Goal: To learn about PBX switchboards and to use office files/databases to find answers to questions.

Large businesses have many telephones throughout the business. Businesses with many telephones will often use a PBX (Private Branch Exchange) system like the one in Illus. 2-1. A PBX is able to handle a large number of calls. An attendant (operator) will answer incoming calls. By the touch of a button the attendant is able to send the call to the correct **extension.** An extension is a telephone away from the switchboard, such as the one on your desk, on your supervisor's desk, or on the wall in the shipping department.

Most PBX systems today are controlled by a computer. Switchboards are usually small, desk-top models. The attendant only answers incoming calls. Outgoing calls are made by other employees from the extensions. To make an outgoing call, you first must dial 9 or some other number. When a dial tone is heard, you may dial the outside number you wish to call. Calls may also be made within the company. In some businesses you will only need to dial the last four numbers to call within the company.

Other telephone systems will be discussed in the exercises in this text-workbook. These systems, which offer many time-saving features, are a result of today's rapidly changing telephone technology.

Illus. 2-1   PBX System

Courtesy of AT&T Archives

You are working for Travel America Magazine in the Advertising Department. A PBX switchboard accepts all the incoming calls.

Call 1   *The telephone rings.*

YOU   Advertising Department, _____
                                   YOUR TITLE (MS./MR./MISS), LAST NAME

           speaking. May I help you?

CALLER   Yes, I am Sally Englund at Englund Travel Agency. Could you please

           give me the place of our next National Travel Association meeting?

(PAUSE)   (Find the Travel America Magazine files in the Office Files/

           Databases. Look in the **tickler file** behind March 11.)

           Thank you for holding, Ms. Englund. The meeting is _____,
                                                                 DAY

           _____, at _____ in the _____ Room of
                 DATE   TIME   NAME

           the _____ Hotel.
                    NAME

CALLER   Who is the speaker?

YOU   _____.
              NAME OF SPEAKER

CALLER   Is he the national president?

YOU   Yes, he is, Ms. Englund.

CALLER   May I send my reservations to you?

YOU   No, I do not handle the dinner reservations. You may call _____
                                                                      TELEPHONE

           _____ and _____ will help you.
             NUMBER   NAME AFTER TELEPHONE NUMBER

CALLER   Thank you very much. I will call her. Good-bye.

YOU   You are welcome. Good-bye.

Note: You gave more information than the one answer she requested first. You made the call shorter by giving her the name of the person in charge of reservations.

Call 2  *The telephone rings.*

YOU   Advertising Department, _____.
                                      YOUR TITLE (MS./MR./MISS), LAST NAME

CALLER   Cindy Baden, please.

YOU   I'm sorry, Ms. Baden is not in this department.

CALLER   Is this the Legal Department?

YOU   No, this is Advertising. Please hold for a moment while I find Ms. Baden's extension.

(PAUSE)   (Look in the Office Files/Databases for Travel America Magazine. Find the display of the Human Resources Directory on your computer screen.)

                 Thank you for holding. Ms. Baden's extension is _____.

                 Would you like me to transfer you?

CALLER   Yes, please. Thank you very much.

YOU   You are welcome. One moment, please.

(PAUSE)   (You press a button on your telephone, then dial the extension for Ms. Baden, press the button again, and the call is transferred automatically.)

Note: A *transfer call* is a call that you will move from your extension to another extension in your company. You helped the caller when you found the correct extension. You also kept the caller from having to dial the switchboard again.

EXERCISE 38
Goal: To improve handwriting and spelling.

Follow the same steps that you used in other handwriting and spelling exercises. *Do not write too fast.* Pronounce the word in syllables and as a word. Your goal is to improve your handwriting and your spelling.

1. *an swer* _____

2. *cit i zen* _____

3. *dan ger ous* _____

4. *es ti mate* _____

5. *fa mil iar* _____

6. *gen u ine* _____

7. *im por tant* _____

8. *mar i tal* _____

9. *o rig i nal* _____

10. *pam phlet* _____

11. *rou tine* _____

12. *suc ceed* _____

13. *trag e dy* _____

14. *ver i fy* _____

15. *with stand* _____

EXERCISE 39
Goal: To file records using the numeric system.

Some businesses use numeric (number) filing rather than alphabetic filing. With a numeric filing system, records are indexed by number. For example, prescriptions from a doctor are usually filed numerically. When you have a prescription for medicine from your doctor, the pharmacist will put a number on the prescription form. This number is used each time you need more medicine for that prescription.

Fig. 2-3 Two File Cabinets Used for Numeric Filing

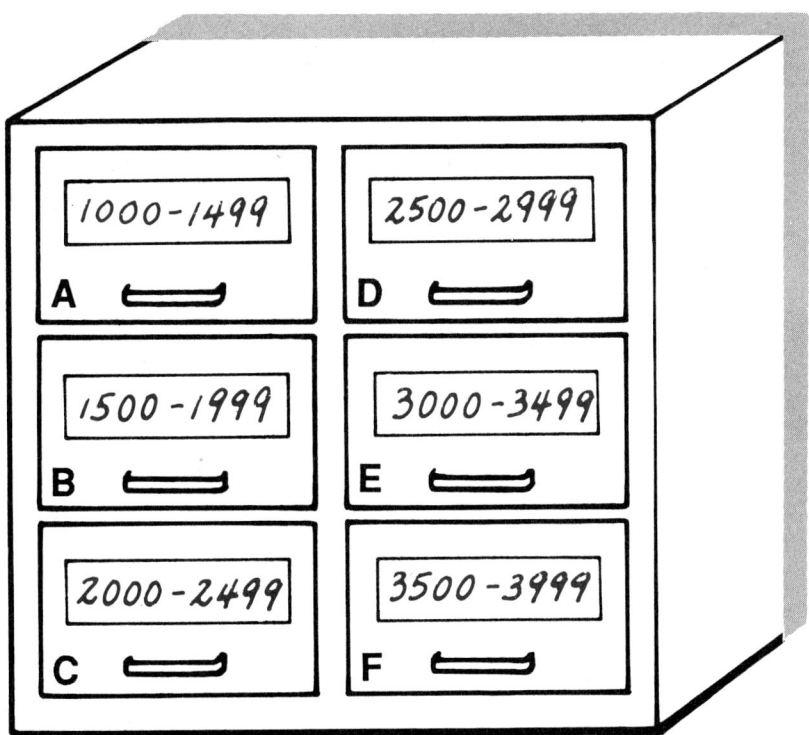

The two file cabinets in Fig. 2-3 each have three drawers. On the left of each drawer is a letter (A, B, C, D, E, or F). Each drawer has a label with numbers of the prescriptions filed in the drawer. For example, the label on Drawer A shows numbers 1000–1499 are filed in that drawer. Numbers 1500–1999 will be filed in Drawer B. Use the letter of the alphabet and the numbers on each drawer label as you finish this exercise.

Look at the number of the prescription file folder in Column 1. Find the drawer (*A, B, C, D, E,* or *F*) where you would file the folder. Write the letter of the file drawer in Column 2. An example is shown.

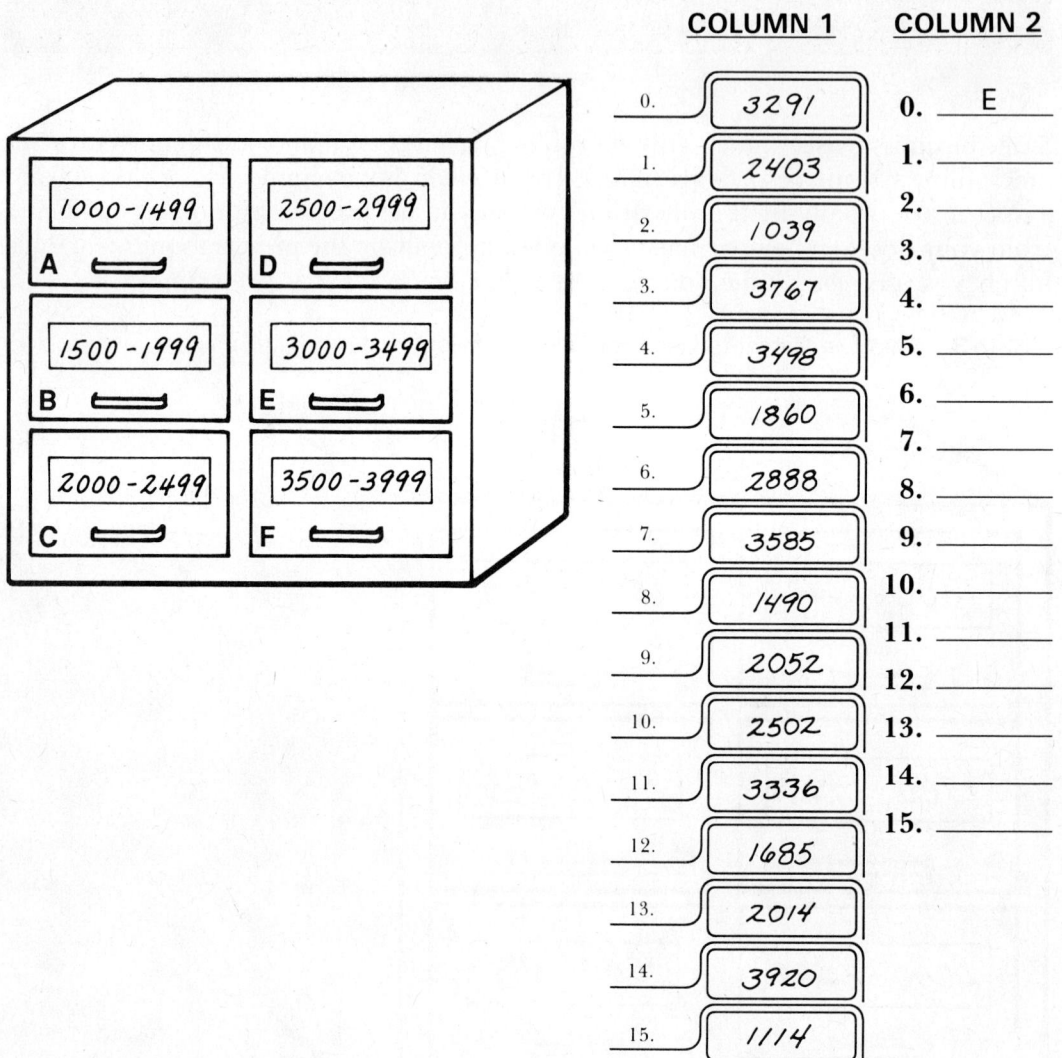

	COLUMN 1		COLUMN 2
0.	3291	0.	E
1.	2403	1.	
2.	1039	2.	
3.	3767	3.	
4.	3498	4.	
5.	1860	5.	
6.	2888	6.	
7.	3585	7.	
8.	1490	8.	
9.	2052	9.	
10.	2502	10.	
11.	3336	11.	
12.	1685	12.	
13.	2014	13.	
14.	3920	14.	
15.	1114	15.	

Drawers:
A 1000-1499
B 1500-1999
C 2000-2499
D 2500-2999
E 3000-3499
F 3500-3999

NAME _____ CLASS _____

EXERCISE 40
Goal: To add words to your vocabulary.

The words in Column 1 are among those words most frequently mispronounced and misspelled. Spend time in study and in drill before you finish the exercise. In your home study, pronounce the words as they are divided in Column 2. Drill on the correct spelling and meanings. You will find these words and meanings on the unit test.

COLUMN 1	COLUMN 2	COLUMN 3
1. answer	an-swer	reply, respond, response, reaction, acknowledgment
2. citizen	cit-i-zen	native, dweller, resident, inhabitant
3. dangerous	dan-ger-ous	harmful, unsafe, hazardous, injurious, risky
4. estimate	es-ti-mate	value, judge, compute, gauge, computation
5. familiar	fa-mil-iar	known, common, frequent, well known, closely acquainted
6. genuine	gen-u-ine	real, proven, actual, sincere, honest
7. important	im-por-tant	major, valuable, significant, serious, powerful
8. marital	mar-i-tal	wedded, matrimonial, married, wifely, husbandly
9. original	o-rig-i-nal	earliest, first, introductory, basic, model
10. pamphlet	pam-phlet	folder, leaflet, booklet, circular, brochure
11. routine	rou-tine	habit, custom, customary, everyday, normal
12. succeed	suc-ceed	follow, come after, win, gain, achieve
13. tragedy	trag-e-dy	misfortune, adversity, grief, disaster, calamity
14. verify	ver-i-fy	prove, evaluate, test, analyze, examine
15. withstand	with-stand	resist, endure, combat, oppose, face up to

Look at the meanings in Column 2. Find the word in Column 1 that correctly matches the meanings. In Column 3 write the *letter* of the matching word from Column 1.

COLUMN 1	COLUMN 2	COLUMN 3
A. answer	1. habit, custom, everyday	1. _____
B. citizen	2. earliest, first, introductory	2. _____
C. dangerous	3. real, proven, actual	3. _____
D. estimate	4. prove, evaluate, analyze	4. _____
E. familiar	5. native, dweller, resident	5. _____
F. genuine	6. folder, leaflet, booklet	6. _____
G. important	7. value, judge, compute	7. _____
H. marital	8. follow, come after, achieve	8. _____
I. original	9. wedded, matrimonial, married	9. _____
J. pamphlet	10. reply, respond, response	10. _____
K. routine	11. resist, endure, face up to	11. _____
L. succeed	12. major, valuable, significant	12. _____
M. tragedy	13. misfortune, disaster, calamity	13. _____
N. verify	14. harmful, unsafe, risky	14. _____
O. withstand	15. known, common, closely acquainted	15. _____

EXERCISE 41
Goal: To use reference sources to find information.

To find the answers to the questions below, use the Reference Sources of this text-workbook. Write or print your answers in the space at the end of the line.

Note: In Unit 1 you were told where in the Reference Sources you would look to find the information you needed. Now **YOU** must decide where to look for the information. You'll find it helpful to use the contents listing on page 262.

ANSWERS

1a. Find the map of the South. Use the directional indicator on this map. Which state's coastline is farthest east?

1a. _____

1b. Again looking at the map of the South, what is the capital of Mississippi?

1b. _____

1c. Find the map of the United States. Which state has the largest border in common with Mexico?

1c. _____

2a. Find the price of one Auto Part 43536655. If you bought five of these parts, what would the total cost be? (Do not add sales tax.)

2a. _____

2b. If you bought 12 Business Forms WA77, what would the total price be? (Do not add sales tax.)

2b. _____

2c. If you bought two boxes of 3.5" double sided, double density disks, what would the total cost be? (Do not add sales tax.)

2c. _____

3a. On the freight shipping record, to whom in Pontiac, MI, was the parcel shipped on 09/01?

3a. _____

3b. What was in the parcel?

3b. _____

3c. What was the fee for shipping the parcel?

3c. _____

4a. To reach the airport no later than 0225P, what time should you leave the St. Anne on the River Hotel?

4a. _____

4b. If you board the bus at Rugby Manor at 0900P, how many minutes will it take you to reach the airport?

4b. _____

4c. You must be at the bus pick-up station 20 minutes before it leaves for the airport. At what time should you be at the Union Plaza to get the bus that arrives at the airport at 0525P?

4c. _____

5a. What two cities are serviced by Flight 290? (Give names, not codes.)

5a. _____

5b. What is the flying time (hours, minutes) of Flight 185?

5b. _____

5c. For which city is LAX the three-letter code?

5c. _____

UNIT 2B

EXERCISE 42
Goal: To improve spelling and handwriting of proper names of states and capital cities.

As you write and spell the proper names in this exercise, follow the same steps that you used in the other handwriting and spelling exercises. The capital city is shown with the state. Spend time in study and in drill. Pronounce the capital and state in syllables. Spell and write them as cities and states one time in syllables and two times as words. *Do not write too fast.* You will have these same proper names on the unit test. Spend time during your home study to review these proper names. Use the sample in Fig. 2-4 to help you with the size and the shape of each letter.

Fig. 2-4 Sample of Writing the Alphabet

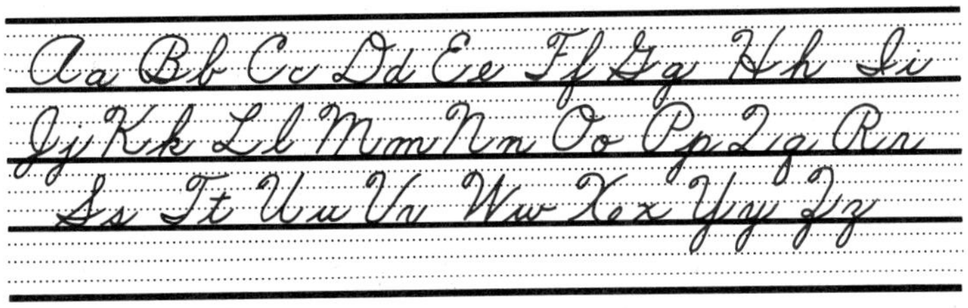

Ju neau, A las ka   *Chey enne, Wy o ming*

To pe ka, Kan sas   *Des Moines, I o wa*

Al ba ny, New York

Lan sing, Mich i gan

Phoe nix, Ar i zo na

Frank fort, Ken tuck y

Lin coln, Ne bras ka

EXERCISE 43
Goal: To learn about mobile (or cellular) telephones and to use office files/databases to find answers to questions.

Mobile (or cellular) telephones are very popular today. You see people using cellular telephones almost anywhere. You may see someone using a cellular telephone while at a sporting event or at a concert. While waiting at a traffic light, a salesperson may use a mobile telephone to call a customer or a doctor may call a hospital.

Mobile telephones are used for both local and long-distance calls. In many cities the number for a mobile telephone is found in the telephone directory under the name of the business. In other cities you must dial a telephone operator and ask for the mobile service operator to find the number. Today, many ships, airplanes, and trains have telephones on board for passengers to use while traveling.

Illus. 2-2 A Sales Representative Using a Cellular Car Phone to Keep in Touch with a Customer

You work as an office clerk in the sales department of the Christiansen Insurance Agency. All salespersons in this insurance agency have mobile telephones in their automobiles so they can keep in touch with the office. These salespersons often call to see if they have any messages. All incoming calls are answered by a receptionist who then transfers the calls to you.

> **Note:** In this company you are to answer the telephone by stating your department and your name. Use a courtesy title (Miss, Mr., Ms., Mrs.) and the person's last name when addressing a salesperson.

Call 1 🕿 *The telephone rings.*

YOU   _____ speaking. May I help you?
             <small>DEPARTMENT, TITLE, LAST NAME</small>

CALLER   Hello, _____. Ron Abbott speaking. Do I have any
                <small>YOUR FIRST NAME</small>
messages?

YOU   Yes, _____, you do. _____
              <small>HIS TITLE, LAST NAME</small>   <small>TITLE, LAST NAME</small>
_____ of the Minnesota Insurance Commission wants you to

call her as soon as possible about the _____

_____.

Her telephone number is _____.

CALLER   Thank you, _____. Also, would you please look at my
                  <small>YOUR FIRST NAME</small>
appointments for tomorrow. Whom do I see at 10 a.m.? at 2:30 p.m.?

YOU   At 10:00 a.m. you see _____ and at 2:30 p.m. you see

_____. Remember you have a full schedule in the of-

fice tomorrow, _____.
               <small>TITLE, LAST NAME</small>

CALLER   Thank you. Yes, I do remember my full schedule tomorrow. Have a

nice day! Good-bye.

YOU   You have a nice day, too _____. Good-bye.
                       <small>TITLE, LAST NAME</small>

Call 2 🕿 *The telephone rings.*

YOU   _____ speaking. May I help you?
             <small>DEPARTMENT, TITLE, LAST NAME</small>

CALLER   Good afternoon, _____. This is Yoko Umeki. Do you
                   <small>YOUR FIRST NAME</small>
have any messages for me?

YOU   Yes, I do, Miss _____. You received a fax message from
                   <small>LAST NAME</small>

_____ thanking you for accepting
          <small>FIRST NAME, LAST NAME</small>

the assignment as the keynote speaker at the convention in

_____.
  <small>CITY</small>

CALLER   Very good. I am glad he was so prompt in answering. Did he confirm at what time and on which day I am to speak?

YOU   Yes, you will speak at ———— p.m. on ——————————.
                              TIME   DAY

CALLER   Thank you. Were there any other messages?

YOU   Yes, you had a telephone call from ————————————at
                                        PERSON'S FIRST AND LAST NAME

the ————————————. She wants you to call her. Her telephone
              BUSINESS NAME

number is ——————————.

CALLER   Thank you. I'll be at the Sterling Street office in 15 minutes. Please forward all my calls to extension 925.

Note: Facsimile (fax) is a popular and inexpensive form of electronic mail. A fax machine transmits exact copies of letters, memorandums, or other messages electronically over telephone lines to another fax machine.

    Call forwarding is a feature of today's modern telephone systems. This feature allows you to use the keypad of your telephone to enter a numeric code to send Miss Umeki's calls to another telephone extension. When she gets a call, her desk telephone will not ring. Her calls will go directly to extension 925 at the Sterling Street office.

    These are very popular time-saving features available with many telephone systems.

EXERCISE 44
Goal: To index titles in personal and in business names for filing.

RULE 5a A title (Miss, Mr., Mrs., Ms.) is the *last* indexing unit when it is used with a personal name. If a seniority title (II, III, Jr., Sr.) is used, it also is the *last* indexing unit. Numeric titles (II, III) are filed *before* alphabetic titles (Jr., Sr.). Professional titles (M.D., Ph.D., D.D.S.) are also the *last* units and are filed alphabetically as written. Royal and religious titles with either a given name or a surname only (Father Mark, Queen Anne, Princess Julianna) are indexed and filed as written.

Table 2-2 Examples of Rule 5a

	INDEXING ORDER			
Name Before Indexing	**Key Unit**	**Unit 2**	**Unit 3**	**Unit 4**
Brother Paul	Brother	Paul		
Senator Paula M. Brother	Brother	Paula	M	Senator
Paul Jas. Brotherton, Jr.	Brotherton	Paul	Jas	Jr
Paul Jas. Brotherton, Sr.	Brotherton	Paul	Jas	Sr
Mrs. Carrie L. Dowd	Dowd	Carrie	L	Mrs
Major Compton W. Dowd	Dowd	Compton	W	Major
Rev. Constance K. Dowd	Dowd	Constance	K	Rev
Father Thomas	Father	Thomas		
G. Paul Fatherton	Fatherton	G	Paul	
G. Paul Fatherton, II	Fatherton	G	Paul	II
G. Paul Fatherton, III	Fatherton	G	Paul	III
T. Cederick Fatherz, Ph.D.	Fatherz	T	Cederick	PhD
Brother Paul Luke Flanders	Flanders	Paul	Luke	Brother
Mayor Jan Barnes Flint	Flint	Jan	Barnes	Mayor
Father Thomas J. Forbes	Forbes	Thomas	J.	Father
Terry R. Foster, D.D.S.	Foster	Terry	R	DDS
Rabbi Isaac Greenberg	Greenberg	Issac	Rabbi	
Colonel Thos. O. Greenburg	Greenburg	Thos	O	Colonel
Wallace C. Gunnells, M.D.	Gunnells	Wallace	C	MD

RULE 5b Businesses use titles as part of their names to make the business names different. Titles in business names are filed as written.

Table 2-3 Examples of Rule 5b

Name Before Indexing	INDEXING ORDER			
	Key Unit	Unit 2	Unit 3	Unit 4
Doctors' Hospital	Doctors	Hospital		
Dr. Dino Health Spa	Dr	Dino	Health	Spa
Mister Mighty Shock Absorbers	Mister	Mighty	Shock	Absorbers
Mr. Music Specialty Store	Mr	Music	Specialty	Store
Mrs. Joleen's Beauty Balm	Mrs	Joleens	Beauty	Balm
Ms. Luggage	Ms	Luggage		
Professor Loo Lotions	Professor	Loo	Lotions	
Professors' Shopping Service	Professors	Shopping	Service	
Senator Walters Golfwear	Senator	Walters	Golfwear	
Senator's Choice Campers	Senators	Choice	Campers	

Follow the same steps you used in Exercise 34 to finish this exercise. On the front of each group of cards is the exercise number. Use this number in the *Answers* column for each exercise. Before the name shown on each card is a letter (*A, B, C, D,* or *E*). Use these steps to finish this exercise:

1. Put the five cards in correct alphabetic order by the name on each card.
2. Write the letters found in the left corner of the card (*A, B, C, D, E*) in the order in which the names come in alphabetic order.
3. Write the letters in the *Answers* column.
4. Follow the same steps for the other nine groups.

An example is shown.

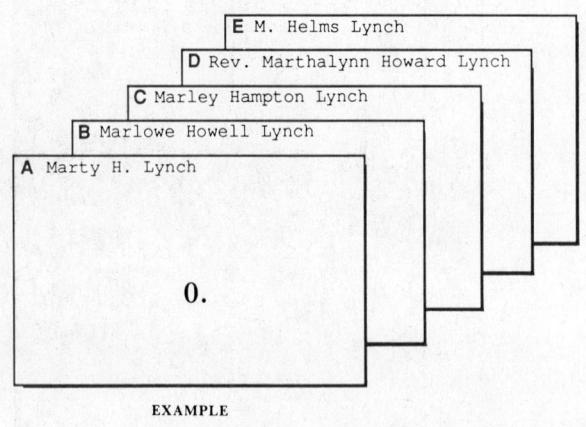

E M. Helms Lynch
D Rev. Marthalynn Howard Lynch
C Marley Hampton Lynch
B Marlowe Howell Lynch
A Marty H. Lynch

0.

EXAMPLE

ANSWERS

Example 0.   E, C, B, D, A

Group 1.   _____

Group 2.   _____

Group 3.   _____

Group 4.   _____

Group 5.   _____

Group 6.   _____

Group 7.   _____

Group 8.   _____

Group 9.   _____

Group 10.   _____

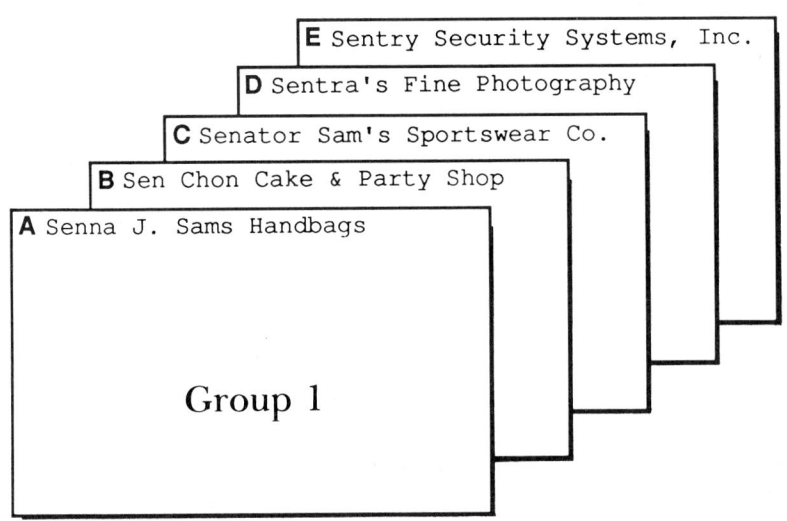

E Sentry Security Systems, Inc.
D Sentra's Fine Photography
C Senator Sam's Sportswear Co.
B Sen Chon Cake & Party Shop
A Senna J. Sams Handbags

Group 1

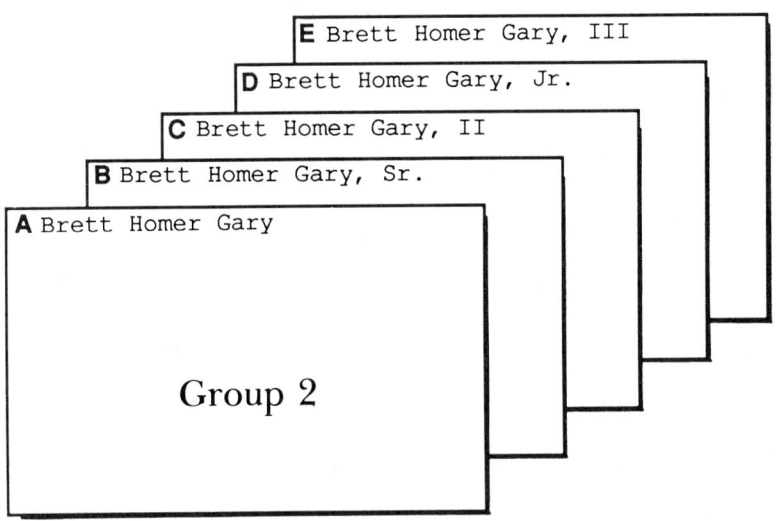

E Brett Homer Gary, III
D Brett Homer Gary, Jr.
C Brett Homer Gary, II
B Brett Homer Gary, Sr.
A Brett Homer Gary

Group 2

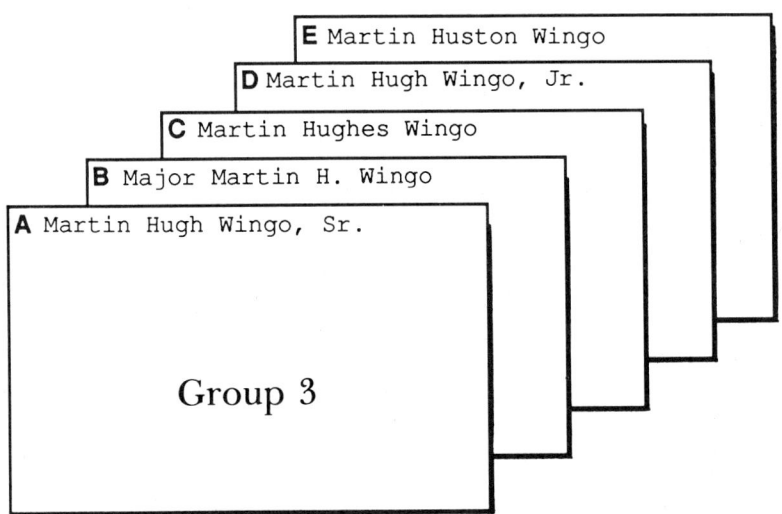

E Martin Huston Wingo
D Martin Hugh Wingo, Jr.
C Martin Hughes Wingo
B Major Martin H. Wingo
A Martin Hugh Wingo, Sr.

Group 3

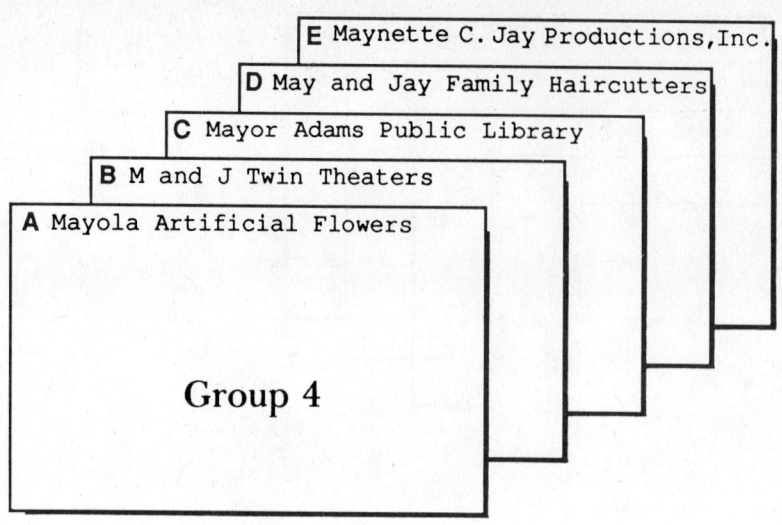

Group 4

- **E** Maynette C. Jay Productions, Inc.
- **D** May and Jay Family Haircutters
- **C** Mayor Adams Public Library
- **B** M and J Twin Theaters
- **A** Mayola Artificial Flowers

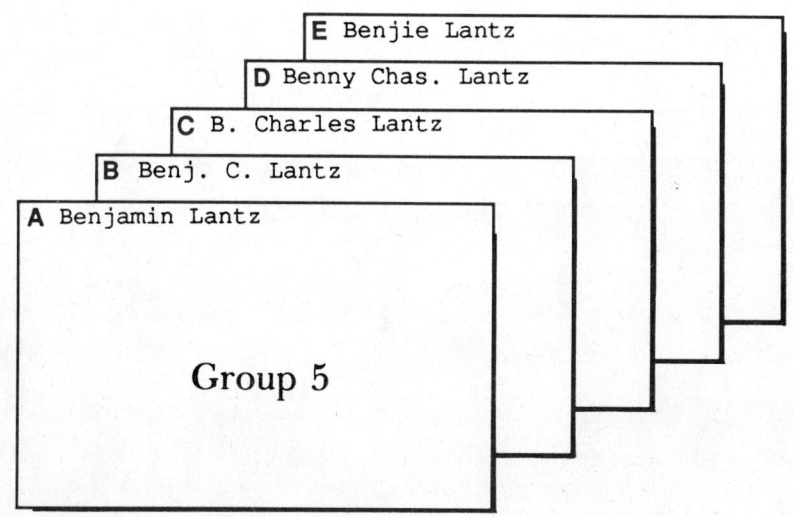

Group 5

- **E** Benjie Lantz
- **D** Benny Chas. Lantz
- **C** B. Charles Lantz
- **B** Benj. C. Lantz
- **A** Benjamin Lantz

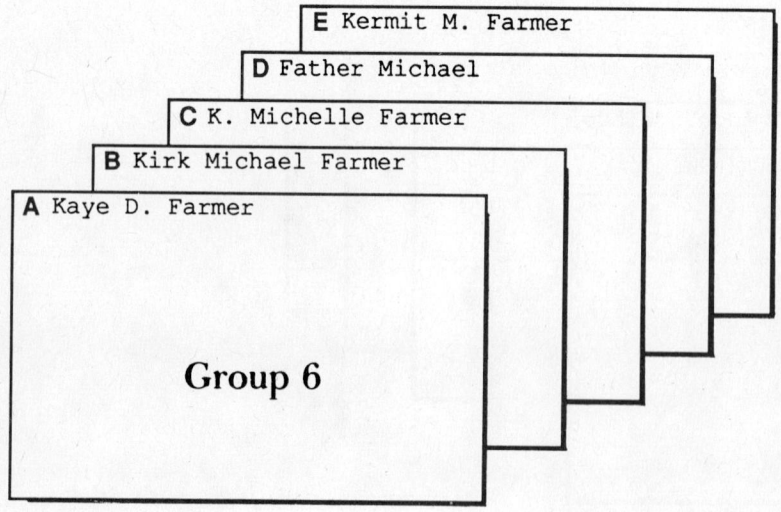

Group 6

- **E** Kermit M. Farmer
- **D** Father Michael
- **C** K. Michelle Farmer
- **B** Kirk Michael Farmer
- **A** Kaye D. Farmer

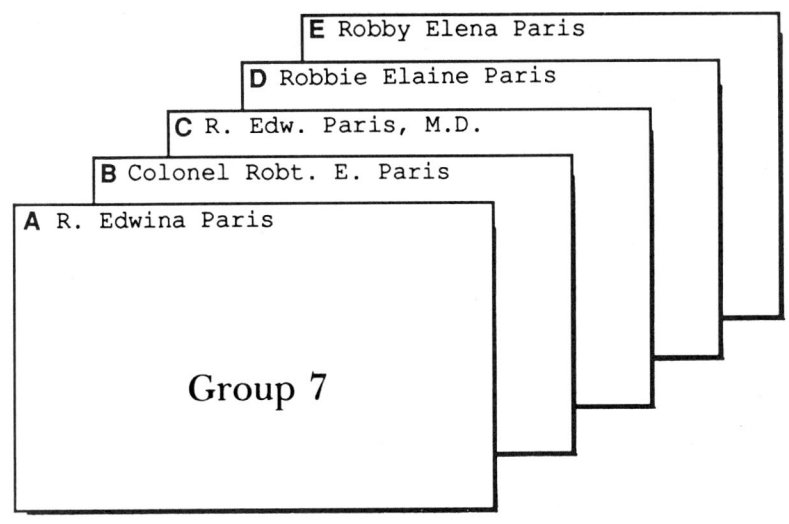

E Robby Elena Paris
D Robbie Elaine Paris
C R. Edw. Paris, M.D.
B Colonel Robt. E. Paris
A R. Edwina Paris

Group 7

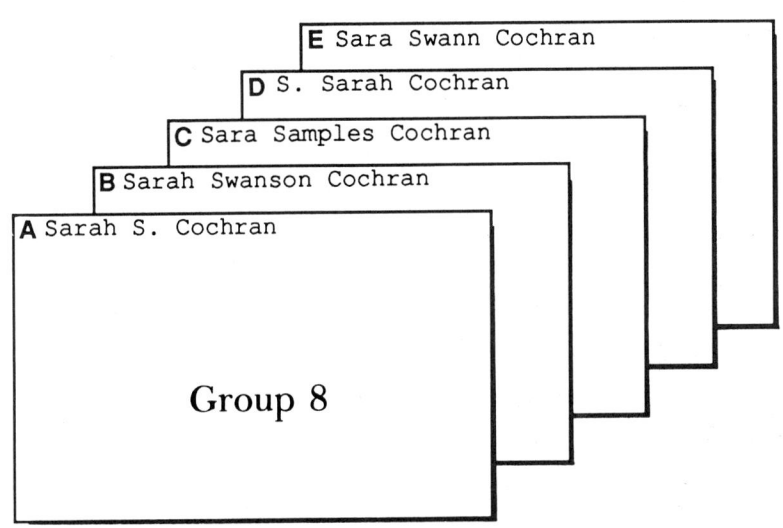

E Sara Swann Cochran
D S. Sarah Cochran
C Sara Samples Cochran
B Sarah Swanson Cochran
A Sarah S. Cochran

Group 8

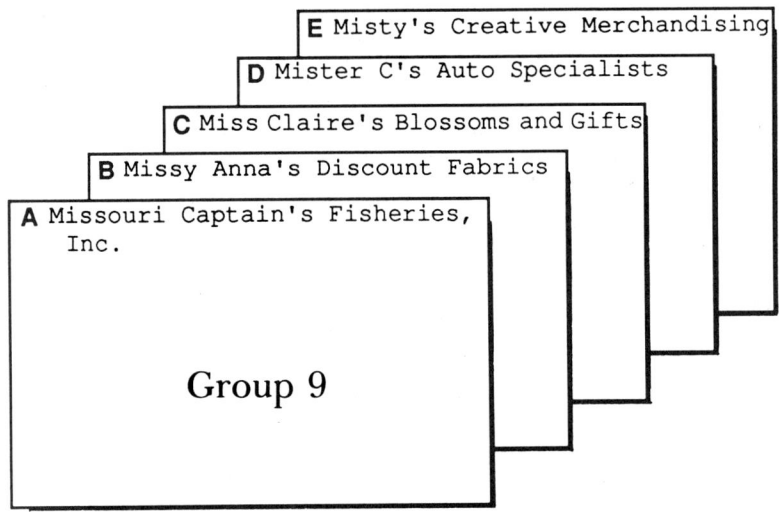

E Misty's Creative Merchandising
D Mister C's Auto Specialists
C Miss Claire's Blossoms and Gifts
B Missy Anna's Discount Fabrics
A Missouri Captain's Fisheries, Inc.

Group 9

Exercise 44

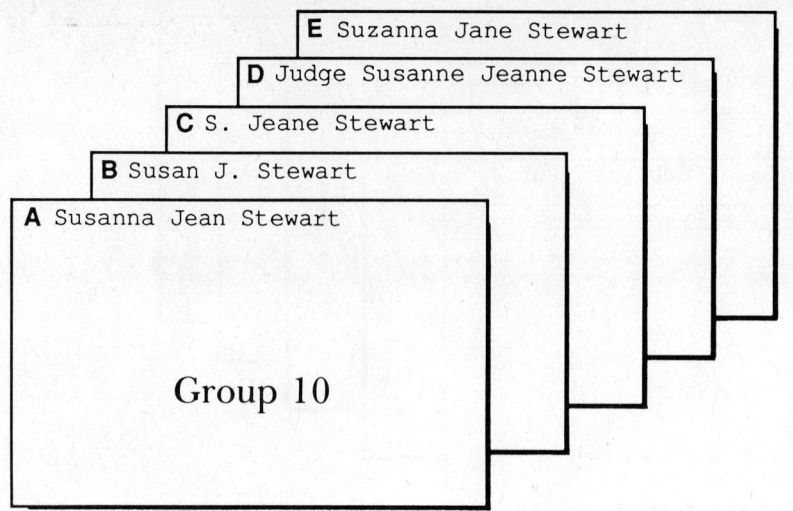

E Suzanna Jane Stewart

D Judge Susanne Jeanne Stewart

C S. Jeane Stewart

B Susan J. Stewart

A Susanna Jean Stewart

Group 10

EXERCISE 45
Goal: To make change using the count-back method when the customer gives you extra coins.

In Exercise 10 you learned how to make change using the count-back method. You learned to begin with the amount of the purchase and, beginning with the smallest coin in your cash drawer, "count" the change to add up to the bill the customer gave you.

Sometimes, a sale will add up to an amount that would result in the customer receiving pennies or receiving almost a dollar's worth of change. Customers may not always want to receive these extra pennies or coins. The customer may give you another coin to reduce the amount of change he or she will receive.

Study the example shown below to see how to "count" back the change when you are given extra coins.

Example: You work at the checkout counter of a drugstore. A customer brings his purchases to you to ring up. The total bill is $15.02. The customer gives you a $20 bill and a nickel (.05 or 5 cents).

The change for the $15 will be counted from the $20 bill given to you. The change for the 2 cents will be counted from the nickel.

Counting money from the cash drawer:

- take from the drawer .01 (1 penny)   and say to yourself <u>3 cents</u>
- take from the drawer .01 (1 penny)   and say to yourself <u>4 cents</u>
- take from the drawer .01 (1 penny)   and say to yourself <u>5 cents</u>
- take from the drawer a $5 bill   and say to yourself <u>$20.00</u>

Counting money to the customer:

Count the change to the customer just as you counted it when taking it from the drawer. The change you should give the customer will be three pennies and one five dollar bill.

In this exercise write in the *Take from cash drawer* column each coin or bill you would remove from your cash drawer to make the change for the sale. In the *Say to the customer* column, write what you would say to the customer. An example is shown.

	TOTAL OF SALE	CUSTOMER GIVES YOU	TAKE FROM CASH DRAWER	SAY TO CUSTOMER
0.	$5.03	$10.05	.01	.04
			.01	.05
			5.00	10.00
1.	$9.15	$10.25		
2.	$12.74	$15.75		
3.	$15.21	$20.25		
4.	$23.18	$30.20		
5.	$43.68	$50.75		

EXERCISE 46
Goal: To add words to your vocabulary.

The words in Column 1 are among those words most frequently mispronounced and misspelled. Spend time in study and in drill before you finish the exercise. In your home study, pronounce the words as they are divided in Column 2. Drill on the correct spelling and meanings. You will find the words and meanings on the unit test.

COLUMN 1	COLUMN 2	COLUMN 3
1. **agenda**	a-gen-da	program, schedule, order of business, timetable, docket
2. **bequeath**	be-queath	hand down, leave, give, endow, will
3. **congregate**	con-gre-gate	get together, gather, meet, assemble, convene
4. **dictionary**	dic-tion-ar-y	wordbook, glossary, thesaurus, concordance, reference book
5. **extremely**	ex-treme-ly	very, terribly, exceedingly, intensely, quite
6. **gratitude**	grat-i-tude	appreciation, thankfulness, gratefulness, recognition
7. **impartial**	im-par-tial	fair, just, unprejudiced, equitable, unbiased
8. **knowledge**	knowl-edge	learning, education, ability, wisdom, awareness
9. **museum**	mu-se-um	gallery, exhibition hall, treasure hall, institute, repository
10. **normal**	nor-mal	usual, typical, regular, general, traditional
11. **oblige**	o-blige	accommodate, provide, assist, furnish, aid
12. **privilege**	priv-i-lege	right, benefit, birthright, advantage, freedom
13. **separate**	sep-a-rate	cut, break, split, individual, single
14. **trespass**	tres-pass	go too far, break the law, violate, intrude, overstep
15. **valid**	val-id	genuine, official, legal, lawful, proven

Look at the meanings in Column 1. Write or print in the blank space in Column 2 the word in today's lesson that correctly matches the meanings in Column 1.

COLUMN 1	COLUMN 2
1. very, terribly, quite	1. _____
2. accommodate, provide, aid	2. _____
3. go too far, break the law, overstep	3. _____
4. fair, just, unbiased	4. _____
5. hand down, give, will	5. _____
6. gallery, institute, exhibition hall	6. _____
7. cut, break, split	7. _____
8. get together, meet, convene	8. _____
9. genuine, official, legal	9. _____
10. appreciation, thankfulness, gratefulness	10. _____
11. right, benefit, advantage	11. _____
12. program, schedule, order of business	12. _____
13. learning, education, awareness	13. _____
14. usual, typical, regular	14. _____
15. wordbook, glossary, reference book	15. _____

EXERCISE 47
Goal: To write petty cash receipts.

Most companies pay bills by writing checks. Many offices use cash to pay amounts too small to write a check. Examples of small expenses are a roll of tape, one postage stamp, the fee to have a small package delivered, or gas for a company car.

Offices usually have one person in charge of the **petty cash fund**—the office cashier, petty cash clerk, secretary, or another office worker. Petty means *little or small.* The cost of these petty cash items is too small to write a check. The fund is usually kept in one place, such as a metal box, and has an amount of bills and coins for ready use when a petty cash item is needed. The person who receives money from the petty cash fund has spent his or her money for a petty item. The company owes that person. The person is paid back the money from the petty cash fund. The person who spent his or her money will give the person in charge of the petty cash fund the receipt for the money spent.

A **petty cash book** is kept as a record of all money paid. You will not use this book in this exercise. You will only learn how to write a **receipt.** Some offices use a **voucher,** another type of business form. Both the cash register receipt for a petty cash item and a business form (voucher or receipt) are used with the petty cash fund in some offices.

Fig. 2-5 Petty Cash Receipt

```
     Industrial Supplies Co.
     PETTY CASH RECEIPT

 ①  No. 202                    Date ____ 7-22 __ 19 --    ②

     Received of Industrial Supplies Co.    $ 5.68          ③

 ④  Five and 69/100 _____ Dollars

     For paper clips, index cards, and

 ⑤     rubber cement _____

     Account Charged: Office Supplies Signed _____
            ⑥                                ⑦
```

1. Each receipt has a different number. Write receipt numbers in consecutive order, such as 1, 2, 3, 4, and so forth. The sample receipt is number 202. The next receipt will be 203.
2. The date on the receipt is always the date on which you write the receipt.
3. The amounts of a petty cash receipt are written in numbers and in words like the amounts you wrote on other receipts and on checks.

4. Write the amounts in words the same way you wrote other receipts and checks.
5. After *For,* write the item bought or the reason the money was spent.
6. *Account Charged* is one of the column headings on the petty cash receipt. The office manager usually tells the petty cash person which account to charge.
7. The person receiving money for petty cash items will sign the receipt to show that he or she was paid the money.

Fill in the two petty cash receipt forms that follow. Use this information.

Form 1: Use today's date. Write Receipt 203 for $25.96 for gas for a company car. The account charged is Sales Expense. Sign the name of Thelma Green, the person who would receive the receipt and the money.

Industrial Supplies Co.
PETTY CASH RECEIPT

No. _____   Date _____ 19 _____

Received of Industrial Supplies Co. $_____

_____Dollars

For _____

_____

Account Charged: _____ Signed _____

Form 2: Use today's date. Write receipt 204 for 65 cents for postage due on a package. The account charged is Postage. Sign the name of Sally Logan. You may wish to look at the example on page 17 to see how receipts for less than one dollar are written.

Industrial Supplies Co.
PETTY CASH RECEIPT

No. _____   Date _____ 19 _____

Received of Industrial Supplies Co. $_____

_____Dollars

For _____

_____

Account Charged: _____ Signed _____

EXERCISE 48
Goal: To use reference sources to find information.

To find the answers to the questions below, use the Reference Sources of this text-workbook. Write or print your answers in the space at the end of the line.

ANSWERS

1. What is the number of the section in *The Sun* for each of the services listed below (in the Reference Sources, numbers are on the *left* of each column):

   a. Kennel Service

   1a. _____

   b. Tutoring

   1b. _____

   c. Word Processing Service

   1c. _____

2a. What is the name of the publisher of *Vocabulary for Competency, Book 1*?

   2a. _____

2b. Who is the author of *The Successful Woman?*

   2b. _____

2c. In which city is *Charlotte Ford's Book of Modern Manners* published?

   2c. _____

3a. What is the telephone number of the Necco Sewing Center on Light Circle?

   3a. _____

3b. What is the name of the CPA on Tara Circle?

   3b. _____

3c. What is the telephone number of the Personnel office at the Postal Service?

   3c. _____

4. What are the address abbreviations for the following words:

   a. Lakes

   4a. _____

   b. Freeway

   4b. _____

   c. Plaza

   4c. _____

5a. What was the amount of the March 15 deposit in the checkbook?

   5a. _____

5b. What was the balance brought forward on check stub 1323?

   5b. _____

5c. What was the balance *before* check 1317 was written?

   5c. _____

EXERCISE 49
Goal: To make decisions about printing on business forms.

Use the following information to fill in the form. Make your own decisions about correct printing, abbreviations, and placement.

Form 1: On January 28 (current year), Jeff Hayashi, who lives at 2286 Brighton Avenue, Apartment 86, New Britain, Connecticut 06051-2936, received Policy No. ANA 0538459 from the Upton Company.

PRINT POLICY NO. BELOW	PRINT COMPANY NAME BELOW	MO.	DAY	YR.

PRINT LAST NAME BELOW	PRINT FIRST NAME BELOW	M.I.

PRINT STREET NO. BELOW	PRINT STREET NAME, ROUTE, OR P.O. BOX NO. BELOW	PRINT APT. NO. BELOW

PRINT CITY OR TOWN BELOW	STATE	ZIP CODE

Use the following information to fill in the parcel post labels. Make your own decisions about correct printing, abbreviations, and placement.

Form 2: Address a parcel post label to Madeline Carroll who lives at 186 Ranger Drive, Saginaw, Michigan 48603-4348. The parcel is from Eleanora Watkins who lives at 3 Spencer Drive, Aspen, Colorado 81612-1254.

PARCEL POST | CONTENTS: MERCHANDISE RETURN REQUESTED

FROM

TO

Form 3: Address a parcel post label to David Prather who lives at 9112 E. Central Street, Wichita, Kansas 67206-9638. The parcel is from William King who lives at 700 Main Street, Deadwood, South Dakota 57732-5421.

PARCEL POST | CONTENTS: MERCHANDISE RETURN REQUESTED

FROM

TO

UNIT 2C

EXERCISE 50
Goal: To improve handwriting and spelling.

Follow the same steps that you used in other handwriting and spelling exercises. *Do not write too fast.* Pronounce the word in syllables and as a word. Your goal is to improve your handwriting and your spelling.

1. *ad ja cent* _____

2. *bul le tin* _____

3. *cam paign* _____

4. *del e gate* _____

5. *es pe cial ly* _____

6. *fa vor ite* _____

7. *hes i tate* _____

8. *li cense* _____

9. *max i mum* _____

10. *no tice* _____

11. *o mit ted* _____

12. *par al lel* _____

13. *qual i fy* _____

14. *ri dic u lous* _____

15. *val u a ble* _____

EXERCISE 51
Goal: To use dates to file business forms.

Another way to file business forms is to use *chronological* order. The word *chronological* means that happenings or events are put in order of time. Dates are used to put the business forms in file drawers.

The two file cabinets in Fig. 2-6 each have four drawers, for a total of eight drawers. In the corner of each drawer is a letter (*A, B, C, D, E, F, G,* or *H*). Each drawer has a label with the dates of the forms filed in that drawer. For example, the label on Drawer A shows that forms with dates between January 1, 1990 and April 30, 1990, are filed in that drawer. Drawer B has dates between May 1, 1990 and August 31, 1990. Use the letter of the alphabet and the dates on each drawer to finish this exercise.

Fig. 2-6 File Cabinets for Chronological Filing

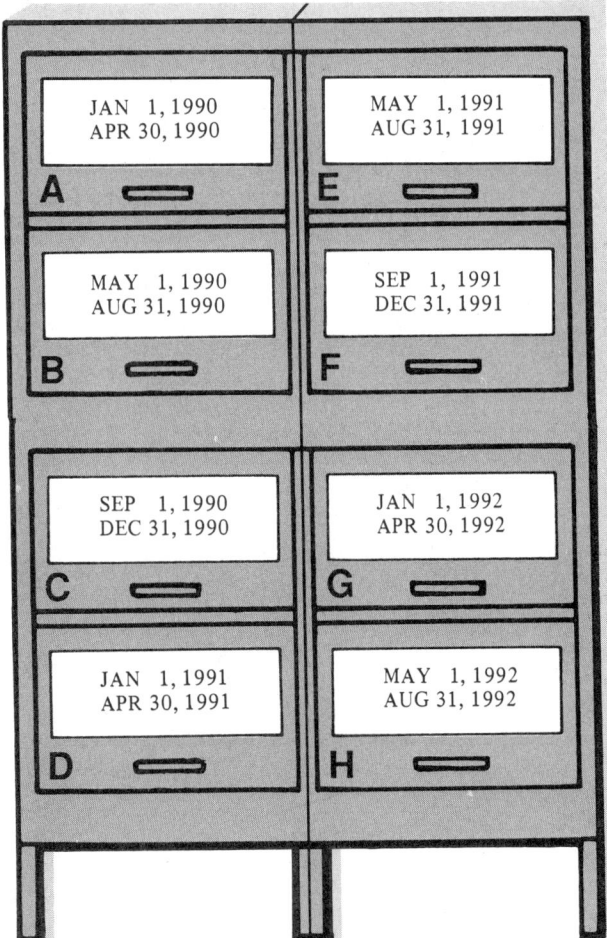

Look at the date in Column 1. Find the drawer (*A, B, C, D, E, F, G,* or *H*) where you would file a form with this date. Write the letter of the file drawer in Column 2. An example is shown.

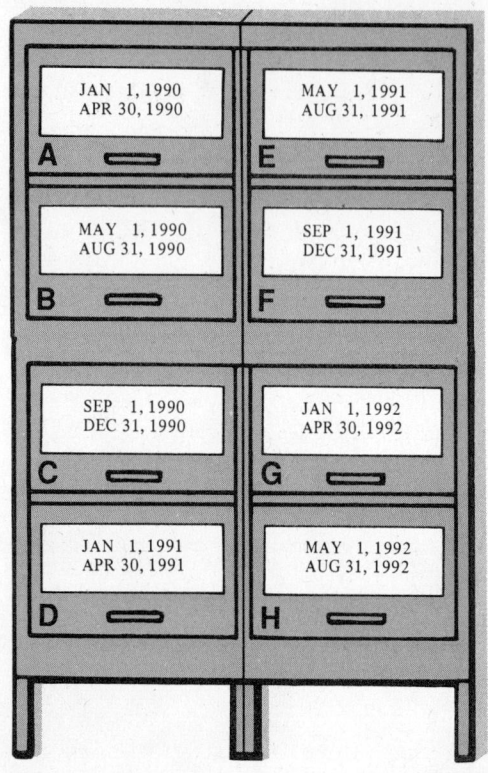

	COLUMN 1		COLUMN 2
0.	November 3, 1990	0.	C
1.	October 11, 1991	1.	_____
2.	March 3, 1992	2.	_____
3.	November 18, 1991	3.	_____
4.	May 19, 1990	4.	_____
5.	July 22, 1990	5.	_____
6.	February 12, 1990	6.	_____
7.	May 5, 1992	7.	_____
8.	April 1, 1991	8.	_____
9.	December 14, 1990	9.	_____
10.	August 30, 1990	10.	_____
11.	June 8, 1991	11.	_____
12.	July 24, 1992	12.	_____
13.	April 18, 1990	13.	_____
14.	January 3, 1991	14.	_____
15.	September 18, 1990	15.	_____

EXERCISE 52
Goal: To prepare a cash drawer count report.

At the end of the work day, a cashier must count the money in the cash drawer. Each value (denomination) is shown on the *Cash Drawer Count Report* on a separate line. Values are either bills or coins.

Bills (or currency) are $20, $10, $5, or $1. **Coins** are half-dollars (.50), quarters (.25), dimes (.10), nickels (.05), or pennies (.01).

Use Fig. 2-7 as a guide as you fill in the reports in this exercise.

Fig. 2-7 Cash Drawer Count Report

Column 1   Column 2   Column 3

Quantity	X Value (Denomination)	= Amount
30	$20.00 Bills	6 0 0 00
50	10.00 Bills	5 0 0 00
75	5.00 Bills	3 7 5 00
180	1.00 Bills	1 8 0 00
8	.50 Coins	4 00
60	.25 Coins	1 5 00
50	.10 Coins	5 00
80	.05 Coins	4 00
200	.01 Coins	2 00
	Total in Cash Drawer	1, 6 8 5 00

Complete Reports 1 and 2 by following these steps:

1. Look at Report 1 line by line. Multiply the number in Column 1 (Quantity) times the denomination in Column 2 (Value). Write the total value in Column 3 (Amount).
2. Find the total of Column 3. Write the total on the last line of the report.
3. Finish Report 2 by following the same steps you used to finish Report 1.

Report 1

Column 1	Column 2		Column 3
Quantity	X	Value (Denomination)	= Amount
40		$20.00 Bills	
40		10.00 Bills	
50		5.00 Bills	
100		1.00 Bills	
6		.50 Coins	
40		.25 Coins	
70		.10 Coins	
60		.05 Coins	
300		.01 Coins	
		Total in Cash Drawer	

Report 2

Column 1	Column 2		Column 3
Quantity	X	Value (Denomination)	= Amount
20		$20.00 Bills	
25		10.00 Bills	
30		5.00 Bills	
80		1.00 Bills	
4		.50 Coins	
30		.25 Coins	
60		.10 Coins	
70		.05 Coins	
100		.01 Coins	
		Total in Cash Drawer	

EXERCISE 53
Goal: To learn about telephone answering services and to use office files/databases to find answers to questions.

A telephone answering service is a way to answer telephone calls when you are away from the telephone. One kind of answering service is an **automatic answering machine** which you turn on before leaving the office at the end of the workday. You may also turn on the machine if you leave the office for lunch or a brief trip. Telephone calls are answered automatically with a recorded message and a request for the caller to leave his or her name, telephone number, and a brief message after the sound of a tone. The machine then records the message. When you return, you rewind the message tape. You can listen to each message and answer each call quickly. Some machines also record the time of day the call was made to your telephone.

A business, such as A to Z Answering Service, is another kind of answering service. The business has several operators who answer calls for many different businesses or persons. A doctor may have this service for all calls he or she receives after office hours. If an emergency call comes in, the operator can call the doctor at home, on a mobile telephone, or use a beeper number throughout the night.

Illus. 2-3 Automatic Answering Machine

Courtesy of AT&T Archives

You work for the Goza Marketing Group, a clothing business in Louisville, Kentucky. You are Mrs. Goza's secretary. At the end of the workday, you turn on the automatic answering machine. As soon as you arrive the next morning, you listen to the messages on the machine.

Message 1

This is Aldo Marquardt in Santa Fe, New Mexico. My telephone number is 505-555-3920, Extension 290. I would like some information about North Carolina businesses.

    You can answer his call. Find the North Carolina section of the rotary file on your desk. To call him back, use a person-to-person call. If he is not at his office, you will not have to pay for the call.

Illus. 2-4 Rotary File

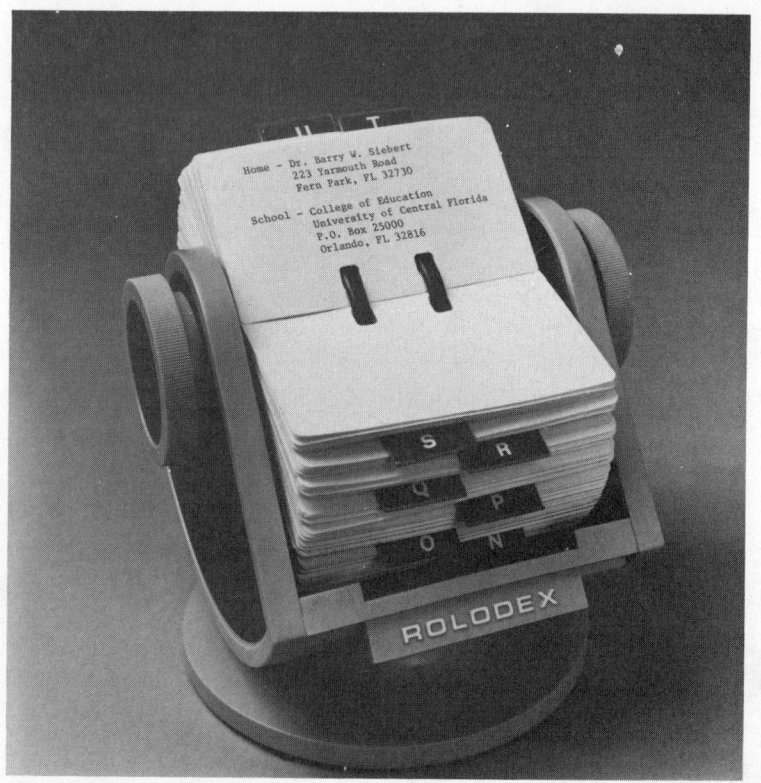

    You may use direct dialing for a long-distance, person-to-person call. You will dial the number and Operator 1 in Louisville (the city where you place the call) will help you. Operator 2 will be the switchboard operator at the business that you call in Santa Fe, New Mexico.

    Dial 0-505-555-3920. The "0" signals that you need an operator to complete your call. You hear a beep.

OPERATOR 1   May I help you?

YOU   Yes. I want to place a person-to-person call to Aldo Marquardt at Extension 290.

OPERATOR 1   Thank you. I am ringing his number.

OPERATOR 2	Navajo Distributors, may I help you?
OPERATOR 1	Long distance calling Aldo Marquardt at Extension 290.
OPERATOR 2	One moment, please.
SECRETARY	Mr. Marquardt's office, Miss McKee speaking. May I help you?
OPERATOR 1	Long distance calling Mr. Marquardt.
SECRETARY	May I ask who is calling?
YOU	_____, with Goza Marketing Group YOUR TITLE, FIRST, LAST NAME in Louisville, Kentucky.
SECRETARY	Will you hold, please?
MARQUARDT	Aldo Marquardt speaking. How are you, _____? TITLE, LAST NAME *Operators hang up.* Thank you for returning my call so promptly. I was talking to Mrs. Goza about some North Carolina businesses I want to visit. I remember one of them was in Brevard and the other in Waynesville. Can you give me the names of those businesses and the owners?
YOU	Yes, I can. Will you hold, please?
(PAUSE)	(Look in the rotary file for the answers. You found the North Carolina section *before* you placed the call. You did not waste time looking for it after you dialed the number.) Thank you for waiting. In Brevard, you may like to visit _____ at _____. OWNER'S NAME BUSINESS NAME In Waynesville, visit _____ at OWNER'S NAME _____. BUSINESS NAME
MARQUARDT	Thank you for this information. Tell Mrs. Goza I hope to see her at the Apparel Mart Show in Atlanta next month. Good-bye.
YOU	You are welcome. I will give Mrs. Goza your message. Good-bye.

Note: Mr. Marquardt's secretary asked who was calling. She *screened* the call. To screen a call is to ask the caller's name and sometimes the purpose of the call. When Mr. Marquardt was told the caller's name and purpose of the call, he was able to handle the call faster and more efficiently.

Message 2

This is Gretchen Zimmer at City General Hospital. My number is 555-0039, Extension 134. I need to talk to Mrs. Goza about volunteers for the Med-Fund campaign.

You can answer her call. Find the Med-Fund volunteer file. Her questions about the campaign can be answered from the names in the file.

You dial the number. The telephone rings.

OPERATOR   City General Hospital

YOU   Extension 134, please.

             The telephone rings.

ZIMMER   Good morning, Gretchen Zimmer speaking.

YOU   Ms. Zimmer, I am _____ at Goza Marketing
                                  TITLE, LAST NAME

             Group returning your call. May I help you?

ZIMMER   You probably can. I need to know the names of a volunteer in

             Bardstown and another in Shepherdsville. Also, do you have busi-

             ness telephone numbers for them?

YOU   Will you hold, please?

(PAUSE)   (Look in the Office Files/Databases for the answers to her

             questions.)

             Thank you for holding. In Bardstown, call _____ at
                                                          FIRST, LAST NAME

             _____. In Shepherdsville, call _____
                 NUMBER   FIRST, LAST NAME

             at _____.
                   NUMBER

ZIMMER   Thank you very much. Give my regards to Mrs. Goza. Good-bye.

YOU   You are welcome. I will tell Mrs. Goza that you send your regards. Good-bye.

Note: You **screened** the calls and answered for your employer, Mrs. Goza.

EXERCISE 54
Goal: To add words to your vocabulary.

The words in Column 1 are among those words most frequently mispronounced and misspelled. Spend time in study and in drill before you finish the exercise. In your home study, pronounce the words as they are divided in Column 2. Drill on the correct spelling and meanings. You will find these words and meanings on the unit test.

COLUMN 1	COLUMN 2	COLUMN 3
1. adjacent	ad-ja-cent	next to, near, close, neighboring, beside
2. bulletin	bul-le-tin	report, message, statement, memorandum, communication
3. campaign	cam-paign	crusade, project, drive, movement, program
4. delegate	del-e-gate	ambassador, agent, representative, appoint, authorize
5. especially	es-pe-cial-ly	particularly, chiefly, specially, unusually, principally
6. favorite	fa-vor-ite	choice, preferred, popular, preference
7. hesitate	hes-i-tate	pause, falter, delay, tarry, balk
8. license	li-cense	permit, charter, right, franchise, authority
9. maximum	max-i-mum	most, highest, largest, greatest, top
10. notice	no-tice	see, observe, be aware of, call attention to, point out
11. omitted	o-mit-ted	left out, ignored, bypassed, disregarded, excluded
12. parallel	par-al-lel	equal, matching, similar, like, counterpart
13. qualify	qual-i-fy	prepare, equip, train, fit, define
14. ridiculous	ri-dic-u-lous	crazy, foolish, absurd, laughable, unbelievable
15. valuable	val-u-a-ble	expensive, high-priced, exorbitant, costly, worthwhile

Read each sentence carefully. Look at the meaning under the space with the number. In the *Answers* space, write or print the word from today's word list that matches the meaning.

ANSWERS

Which ice cream flavor is your _____(1)_____ ?
preference

The Parents Club started a _____(2)_____to stop
crusade
child abuse.

The stock person _____(3)_____ Item 305M from the
left out
shipment.

The new science building is _____(4)_____to the
next to
agriculture building.

_____(5)_____the footnotes before you key the report.
see

If you expect to _____(6)_____for the receptionist's
prepare
job, include Speech 201 in your class schedule.

Be _____(7)_____careful when you proofread the
particularly
printouts.

Two _____(8)_____lines marked the spaces in the
equal
parking lot.

The latest news _____(9)_____contained the names of
message
the missing campers.

A _____(10)_____is a requirement before marriage.
permit

Do not _____(11)_____to report any errors in your order.
delay

The _____(12)_____ number of persons allowed in the
largest
conference hall is 250.

Keep _____(13)_____jewels in a safe deposit box.
expensive

Whom did the Student Council elect as a _____(14)_____
representative
to the Washington conference?

Some college students regret their _____(15)_____
crazy
omission of a keyboarding course in high school.

1. _____
2. _____
3. _____
4. _____
5. _____
6. _____
7. _____
8. _____
9. _____
10. _____
11. _____
12. _____
13. _____
14. _____
15. _____

144

EXERCISE 55
Goal: To identify the main points in a paragraph.

It is important for you to be able to identify the main points when writing or reading a paragraph, a letter, or an article. The *main point* of a paragraph, a letter, or an article is the single most important idea in that group of words. Identifying these main points as you read will make your understanding of what you are reading much easier.

Read the paragraphs shown below. As you read pay particular attention to the underlined sentences. The underlined sentences are the main points of these paragraphs.

The Kentucky Derby is run every year at Churchill Downs in Kentucky. Two-year old colts from all over the country will be attempting to add this "Run for the Roses" crown to their list of horse races won. This exciting horse race will be run next Saturday at 2:00 p.m.

The New York Giants won the 1990 Super Bowl! The game against the Buffalo Bills was hard fought and tough. Both teams wanted to win, but the Giants were not to be denied this victory.

Disneyland's Main Street Electric Parade is very exciting to see. Thousands of little light bulbs are used to light up floats. You will see Alice in Wonderland, Donald Duck, and Mickey Mouse, of course. The very last float is a huge eagle with the American Flag.

After you have read the above paragraphs, read them once again. Notice that the sentences that are NOT underlined give additional information about the sentence that is underlined. Notice also that all sentences in a paragraph must pertain to the same subject.

Read the paragraphs below and underline the main points.

1. Mariel is an accomplished horsewoman. She has won four championship titles since she began showing her horse, Stryker. Next year she hopes to compete in the Olympics.

2. Pyramids were built as burial tombs for Egyptian kings. Egyptians believed in life after death. Because of these beliefs they built burial tombs for their kings and filled them with treasures for their next life. The most famous pyramid was built for King Tutankhamen—King Tut.

3. The violinist practiced her solo for weeks before her recital. On the night of the recital, she played beautifully without making a single mistake.

4. Bill finally learned to type. He has been working hard all semester to master this skill. When he began his typing class in September, he was sure he would never learn to type.

5. Our football team was undefeated this year. The entire school is proud of this team's accomplishment. They played magnificently together with no one player trying to "steal the show."

6. The installation of FBLA officers will be held Friday night. The newly elected president is excited about the activities planned for the coming year. If you are interested in becoming a member, see any of the officers for an application.

7. Dr. Charles Mannes has announced the addition of Dr. Marcia Brunner to his staff. Dr. Brunner has just completed her residency at Mt. Pinion General Hospital. She is trained in plastic surgery and general surgery. Dr. Brunner will replace Dr. John Westin who has retired from practice.

8. Word processing is a skill everyone should know. The ability to run a word processing program in today's office is a necessity. In order to be better prepared for work after schooling is completed, you should learn to run the most popular word processors.

9. The annual school musical was a wonderful success. Ben Logan sang the lead part of Billy. The female lead was sung by Suzie Fernandez. All the chorus parts and dances were well rehearsed, which made this musical so successful.

10. The Annual Fourth of July picnic and parade will begin at 10:00 a.m. Be sure to bring your chairs and your picnic baskets for this exciting event. The day will climax with a fireworks show in the stadium.

EXERCISE 56

Goal: To index the names of married women and the names of persons and businesses with foreign spellings for filing.

RULE 6 A married woman's name is indexed and filed as written. Follow Rule 1a as you index her name. If more than one form of a name is known, the second or third name may be cross-referenced.

Note: A married woman's name in a business is indexed and filed as written.

Table 2-4 Examples of Rule 6

	INDEXING ORDER			
Name Before Indexing	Key Unit	Unit 2	Unit 3	Unit 4
Mrs. Anne Thorpe Martin *(Mrs. Darwin C. Martin)	Martin	Anne	Thorpe	Mrs
Mrs. Annette Marie Martin	Martin	Annette	Marie	Mrs
Mrs. Anthony H. Martin	Martin	Anthony	H	Mrs
Mrs. Antoinette Wills Martin *(Ms. Antoinette Wills)	Martin	Antoinette	Wills	Mrs
Ms. Anwanda Martin *(Mrs. Anwanda Martin Newby) *(Mrs. Barney Newby)	Martin	Anwanda	Ms	
Mrs. Darwin C. Martin	Martin	Darwin	C	Mrs
Mrs. Anne Martin's Boutique	Mrs	Anne	Martins	Boutique
Mrs. Anwanda Martin Newby	Newby	Anwanda	Martin	Mrs
Mrs. Barney Newby	Newby	Barney	Mrs	
Ms. Antoinette Wills	Wills	Antoinette	Ms	

*These names are cross-referenced.

RULE 7 An article or particle (first part of a name) in the beginning of the name of a foreign person or a foreign business is used with the part of the name coming after the article to form one indexing unit. No space is left in the name. For example, the last name De La Rue is indexed DeLaRue.

Examples of articles and particles are: a la, D', Da, De, Del, De la, Della, Den, Des, Di, Dos, Du, El, Fitz, Il, L', La, Las, Le, Les, Lo, Los, M', Mac, Mc, O', Per, Saint, San, Santa, Santo, St., Ste., Te, Ten, Ter, Van, Van de, Van der, Von, Von der.

Table 2-5 Examples of Rule 7

		INDEXING ORDER		
Name Before Indexing	**Key Unit**	**Unit 2**	**Unit 3**	**Unit 4**
Professor Louisa M. Dando	Dando	Louisa	M	Professor
Louis Edwin D'Andrea	DAndrea	Louis	Edwin	
Dandria Lawncare Products	Dandria	Lawncare	Products	
Dr. Christiana J. De la Cruz	DelaCruz	Christiana	J	Dr
Delamar Electric Corp.	Delamar	Electric	Corp	
Del la Mar Printers, Inc.	Dellamar	Printers	Inc	
Ms. Charlotte Del la Rosa	DellaRosa	Charlotte	Ms	
Prof. C. Marvin DeNio	DeNio	C	Marvin	Prof
Glenna Mae D'Hollosey	DHollosey	Glenna	Mae	
Gregorio Diaz, D.D.S.	Diaz	Gregorio	DDS	
Sister Anna Maria du Pont	duPont	Anna	Maria	Sister
Charles W. MacFarland	MacFarland	Charles	W	
Rev. Josefina C. Martinez	Martinez	Josefina	C	Rev
McCue Nurseries, Inc.	McCue	Nurseries	Inc	
Miss Paula Gayle Mimms	Mimms	Paula	Gayle	Miss
Nina J. O'Day	ODay	Nina	J	
Alex W. Saints	Saints	Alex	W	
Andrea Elaine San Angelo	SanAngelo	Andrea	Elaine	
Joanna Cloe St. Amour	StAmour	Joanna	Cloe	
Vernon T. St. John	StJohn	Vernon	T	
Van Allyn Florists	VanAllyn	Florists		
T. Oliver van Dyke	vanDyke	T	Oliver	
Brother Julio Velez	Velez	Julio	Brother	
Ouida J. von Borg, Ph.D.	vonBorg	Ouida	J	PhD

In Column 1 are names *to be* indexed and filed. In Column 2 the same names *have been* indexed and filed. Use these steps to finish this exercise:

1. Look at the folders in Column 2. Find the *one* folder in Column 2 that is out of order.
2. In the *Answers* column, write the corresponding letter (*A, B, C, D, E*) of the name that is out of order.
3. Follow the same steps for the ten names.

Look at the example. Miss Alice B. Adam is out of order. The letter *B* is written in the *Answers* column.

COLUMN 1		COLUMN 2	

Ms. Angela B. Adams
Mrs. A. Bonnie Adams
Mrs. Arlene Boone Addams
Miss Alice B. Adam
Ms. Arlisa Bea Adamms

E Addams Arlene Boone Mrs

0.

D Adamms Arlisa Bea Ms

C Adams Angela B Ms

B Adam Alice B Miss

A Adams A Bonnie Mrs

ANSWERS

0.   B

6. _____

1. _____

7. _____

2. _____

8. _____

3. _____

9. _____

4. _____

10. _____

5. _____

Santa Fe Guided Tours
Alberto Santos Drug Store
San Carlos Barber College
Manuel Santana CPA
San Marcos Community Church

E Santos Alberto Drug Store

1.

D Santana Manuel CPA

C Santa Fe Guided Tours

B San Marcos Community Church

A San Carlos Barber College

Ms. Tillie A. Teale
Mrs. T's Tearoom
Ms. Tammy C. Teare
Ms. Tommi Lynne Teal
Mrs. Thelma B. Teaque

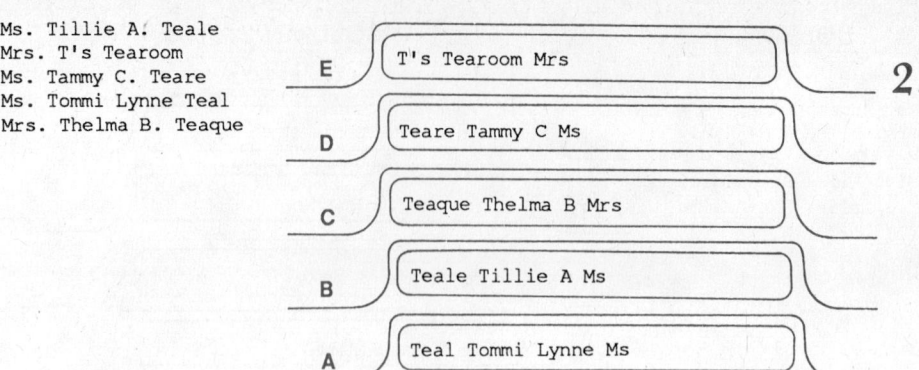

2.

E — T's Tearoom Mrs

D — Teare Tammy C Ms

C — Teaque Thelma B Mrs

B — Teale Tillie A Ms

A — Teal Tommi Lynne Ms

Garry Franc St. Cyr
Glenda Faye Saint Louis
Gregory F. Saine
Gary & Floy Saint, Inc.
Gigi Faith St. Pierre, M.D.

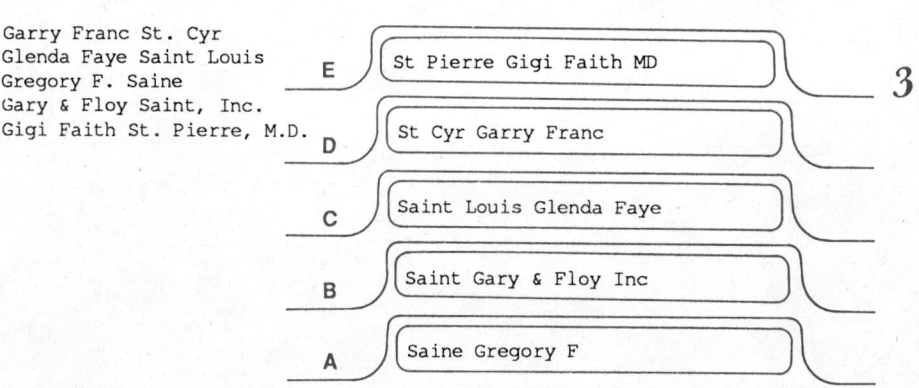

3.

E — St Pierre Gigi Faith MD

D — St Cyr Garry Franc

C — Saint Louis Glenda Faye

B — Saint Gary & Floy Inc

A — Saine Gregory F

Mrs. Hortense D. Holley
Mrs. Holly Kaye Hollen
Miss Hallie Kate House
Ms. Helen's House of Flowers
Miss Heather K. Hollar

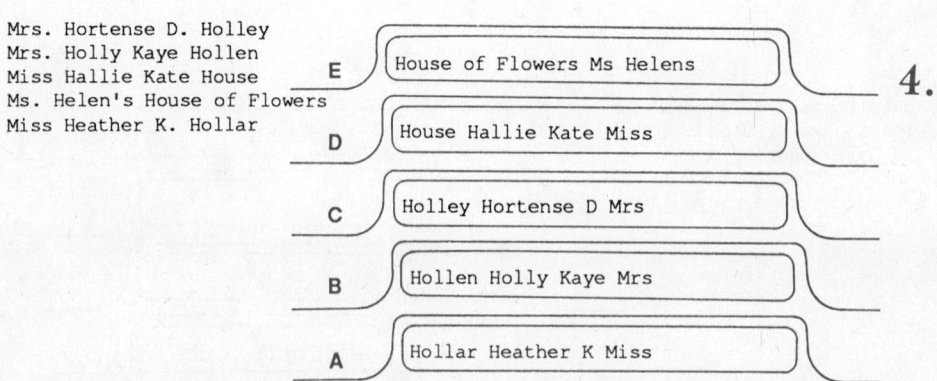

4.

E — House of Flowers Ms Helens

D — House Hallie Kate Miss

C — Holley Hortense D Mrs

B — Hollen Holly Kaye Mrs

A — Hollar Heather K Miss

Miss Marjorie B. O'Frank
Ms. May Ella Office
Miss Main's Office Temps,
   Inc
Ms. Marie Willene Off
Ms. Michelle N. O'Galvin

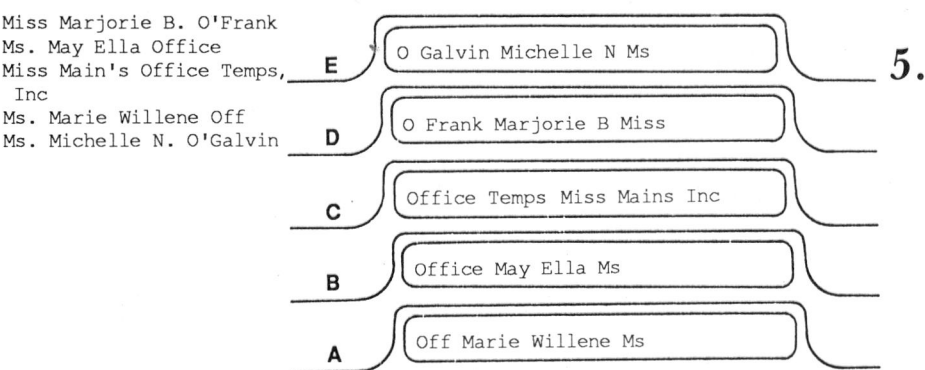

5.

E — O Galvin Michelle N Ms

D — O Frank Marjorie B Miss

C — Office Temps Miss Mains Inc

B — Office May Ella Ms

A — Off Marie Willene Ms

Opal Anne De Moss
Orville Frank Delamor
Otto Karl Del Motte
Olivia Camille De La Mor
Otha Paul Delamore

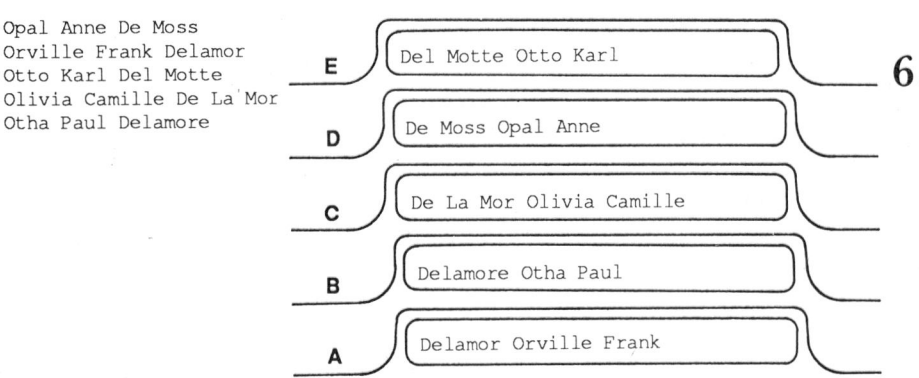

6.

E — Del Motte Otto Karl

D — De Moss Opal Anne

C — De La Mor Olivia Camille

B — Delamore Otha Paul

A — Delamor Orville Frank

Almira Lois Van de Veer
Allie Lee Von der Lynn
Alvin Louis Van der Griffe
Alston Lowe Vande Berg
Alf Loye Von Derlage

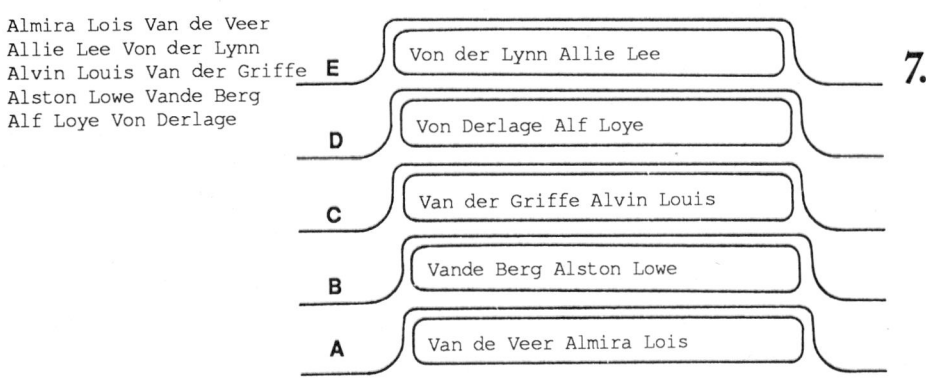

7.

E — Von der Lynn Allie Lee

D — Von Derlage Alf Loye

C — Van der Griffe Alvin Louis

B — Vande Berg Alston Lowe

A — Van de Veer Almira Lois

Barbara FitzGerald Pet Shop
B & W Pawn Shop
Brenda Jo Fitzgerald
Byron Joseph Fitzmaurice
Bruce Fitzgerald Discount
  Cars

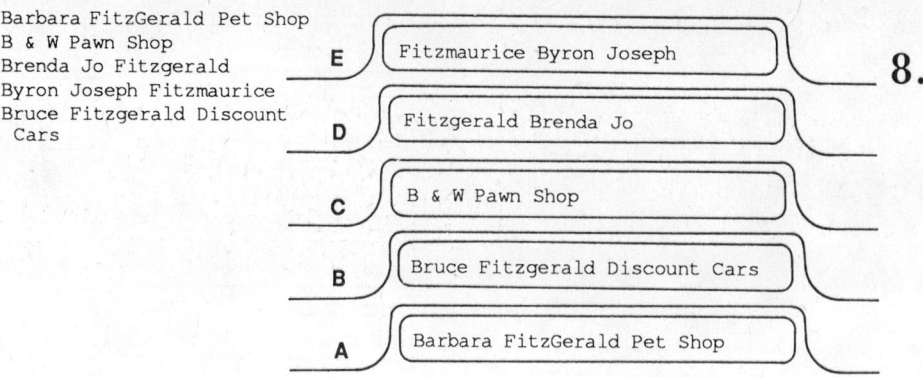

8.

E Fitzmaurice Byron Joseph

D Fitzgerald Brenda Jo

C B & W Pawn Shop

B Bruce Fitzgerald Discount Cars

A Barbara FitzGerald Pet Shop

Wayne Wray La Mott
Wanda F. Le Claire
Willard Drew Las Palmas
Waldo R. Los Gollas
Willa Jane L'Estrange

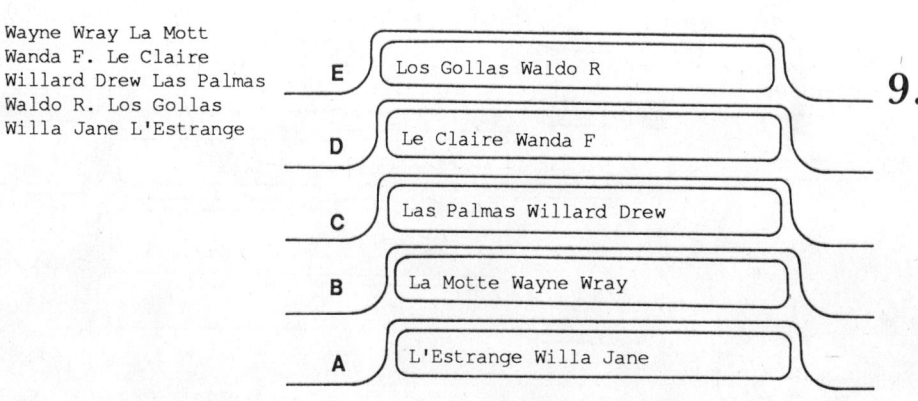

9.

E Los Gollas Waldo R

D Le Claire Wanda F

C Las Palmas Willard Drew

B La Motte Wayne Wray

A L'Estrange Willa Jane

Jeff K. De Shazo
Jules Keyes Dos Pappas
Joy Kim De Savieu
Janelle Kane Des Jardins
Joshua Kevin De Santose

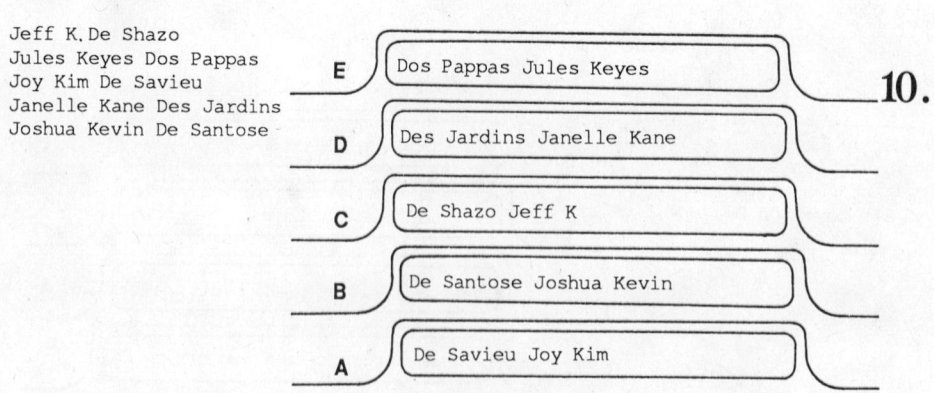

10.

E Dos Pappas Jules Keyes

D Des Jardins Janelle Kane

C De Shazo Jeff K

B De Santose Joshua Kevin

A De Savieu Joy Kim

EXERCISE 57
Goal: To use reference sources to find information.

To find the answers to the questions below, use the Reference Sources of this text-workbook. Write or print your answers in the space at the end of the line.

ANSWERS

1a. To whom did Danny Lavant place a telephone call on 7/6?   1a. _____

1b. During July, one call was placed to what telephone number in Abilene, TX?   1b. _____

1c. On which date was a call placed to Sumter, SC?   1c. _____

2a. What is the proofreader's mark meaning to *close up*?   2a. _____

2b. What is the mark for a *new paragraph*?   2b. _____

2c. What is the mark for *capitalize*?   2c. _____

3a. On the freight shipping form on 09/02, what was the fee for shipping the parcel to Grand Isle, LA?   3a. _____

3b. What were the contents of the parcel shipped on 09/02 to Dr. Mary A. Lane?   3b. _____

3c. To what city was Shipment 516 sent on 09/02?   3c. _____

4a. What is the amount of income tax withheld for a single person on a monthly payroll whose wages were $880 with zero allowances?   4a. _____

4b. What is the amount of income tax withheld for a married person on a monthly payroll whose wages were $1,600 with five allowances?   4b. _____

4c. What is the amount of income tax withheld for a single person on a monthly payroll whose wages were $975 with one allowance?   4c. _____

5a. What are the cities served by Flight 825? (Use names, not codes.)   5a. _____

5b. For which city is EWR the three-letter code?   5b. _____

5c. What two cities are served by Flight 100?   5c. _____

EXERCISE 58
Goal: To see if the names of businesses are exactly the same.

Look at the handwritten name in Column 1 and the typewritten name in Column 2. If the two names are exactly the same, circle the *S* in Column 3. If the two names are different, circle the *D* in Column 3.

COLUMN 1	COLUMN 2	COLUMN 3
1. *Greta Electric Authority*	Gretna Electric Authority	1. S D
2. *Daffodil Tours, Inc.*	Daffodil Tours, Inc.	2. S D
3. *Rosenwald Reality Group*	Rosenwald Realty Group	3. S D
4. *Tocca Research Institute*	Toca Research Institute	4. S D
5. *Freemont Data Services*	Freemont Data Service	5. S D
6. *Viceroy Square Apts.*	Viceroy Square Apts.	6. S D
7. *A-1 Radiator Works*	A-1 Radiator Works	7. S D
8. *Peniston Tractor Co.*	Peniston Tractor Co.	8. S D
9. *Earlma Bakery, Inc.*	Earlma Bakery, Inc.	9. S D
10. *Copernicus Tree Surgeons*	Copernicus Tree Surqeons	10. S D
11. *Loran Floral Products*	Loran Floral Products, Inc.	11. S D
12. *Diaz Dance Expressions, Ltd.*	Diaz Dance Expressions, Ltd.	12. S D
13. *Jay Medical - Dental Labs*	Jay Medical-Dental Lab	13. S D
14. *Waterbeds for Chilton*	Waterbeds for Chilton	14. S D
15. *J & W Developement Co.*	J & W Development Co.	15. S D

UNIT 2D

EXERCISE 59
Goal: To index identical names of persons or businesses for filing.

RULE 8   Addresses are used to index identical (alike) names of persons, businesses, institutions, and organizations. Cities are indexed first. Then, index states or provinces, street names, house numbers, or building numbers in that order.

Note 1: When the first units of street names are written as numbers (such as 12th Street), the names are put in ascending (smallest number to largest number) order and put *before* alphabetic street names (such as Arnold Street). For example, 12th Street comes before 18th Street. All numbered streets (such as 12th Street and 18th Street) come *before* named streets (such as Alamo Street, Alexander Street, Barnes Street).

Note 2:   Street names with compass directions (North, East, South, West) are indexed as written. Numbers after compass directions are indexed before alphabetic names (North 4th, North Main, NE Fourth, Northeast Fourth).

Note 3:   House and building numbers written as figures are indexed in ascending (smallest number to largest number) order and put before spelled-out building names (704 The Maxwell Building). If a street address and a building name are shown in an address, do not use the building name. Use only the street address. Do not use ZIP Codes in indexing.

Note 4:   Seniority titles (II, III, Jr., Sr.) are indexed as shown in Rule 5a and are put *before* addresses.

Table 2-6   Examples of Rule 8

	INDEXING ORDER			
Name Before Indexing	Key Unit	Unit 2	Unit 3	Unit 4 Address
(Names of Cities Used to Determine Filing Order)				
Ace Automation Center Des Moines, Iowa	Ace	Automation	Center	Des Moines Iowa
Ace Automation Center Waterloo, Iowa	Ace	Automation	Center	Waterloo Iowa
(Names of States and Provinces Used to Determine Filing Order)				
Bayshore Country Club Brunswick, Georgia	Bayshore	Country	Club	Brunswick Georgia
Bayshore Country Club Brunswick, Maine	Bayshore	Country	Club	Brunswick Maine
Cloudland Ranch Victoria, Arkansas	Cloudland	Ranch		Victoria Arkansas

Name Before Indexing	Key Unit	Unit 2	Unit 3	Unit 4	Address
Cloudland Ranch Victoria, British Columbia	Cloudland	Ranch			Victoria British Columbia

(Names of Streets and Building Numbers Used to Determine Filing Order)

Name Before Indexing	Key Unit	Unit 2	Unit 3	Unit 4	Address
Discount Pharmacy 65-15 Street Boise, Idaho	Discount	Pharmacy			65 - 15 Street
Discount Pharmacy 18-41 Street Boise, Idaho	Discount	Pharmacy			18 - 41 Street
Discount Pharmacy 379 Amboy Street Boise, Idaho	Discount	Pharmacy			379 Amboy Street
Discount Pharmacy 636 Amboy Street Boise, Idaho	Discount	Pharmacy			636 Amboy Street
Discount Pharmacy 825 SE 22 Street Boise, Idaho	Discount	Pharmacy			825 SE 22 Street
Discount Pharmacy 18 SE Ninth Street Boise, Idaho	Discount	Pharmacy			18 SE Ninth Street
Discount Pharmacy 955 Tell Road Boise, Idaho	Discount	Pharmacy			955 Tell Road

(Seniority Titles Used to Determine Filing Order Before Addresses)

Name Before Indexing	Key Unit	Unit 2	Unit 3	Unit 4	Address
Henry G. Evans 398 Barley Drive Topeka, Kansas	Evans	Henry	G		
Henry G. Evans, II 701 Alma Circle Dallas, Texas	Evans	Henry	G	II	
Henry G. Evans, III 194 Victory Place Lima, Ohio	Evans	Henry	G	III	
Henry G. Evans, Jr. 220 Herman Court Arvada, Colorado	Evans	Henry	G	Jr	Arvada Colorado
Henry G. Evans, Jr. 550 Lyric Lane Durham, North Carolina	Evans	Henry	G	Jr	Durham North Carolina

Index the following cards in the correct order according to the rules just provided you. After the cards are in the correct order, enter the letter from the upper left corner of each card in the *Answers* column. Notice that the column begins with Number 1 at the bottom.

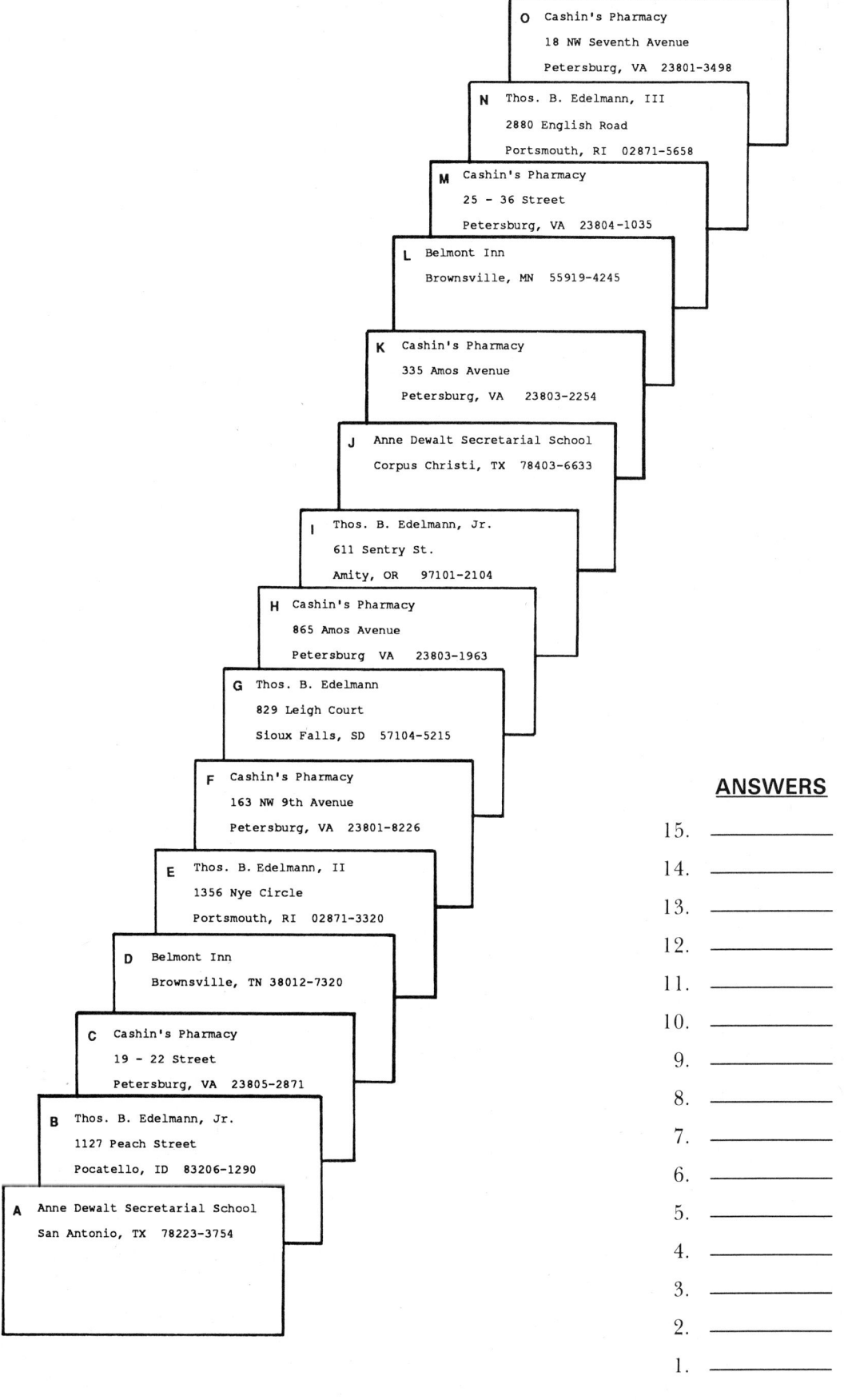

O   Cashin's Pharmacy
    18 NW Seventh Avenue
    Petersburg, VA 23801-3498

N   Thos. B. Edelmann, III
    2880 English Road
    Portsmouth, RI 02871-5658

M   Cashin's Pharmacy
    25 - 36 Street
    Petersburg, VA 23804-1035

L   Belmont Inn
    Brownsville, MN 55919-4245

K   Cashin's Pharmacy
    335 Amos Avenue
    Petersburg, VA 23803-2254

J   Anne Dewalt Secretarial School
    Corpus Christi, TX 78403-6633

I   Thos. B. Edelmann, Jr.
    611 Sentry St.
    Amity, OR 97101-2104

H   Cashin's Pharmacy
    865 Amos Avenue
    Petersburg VA 23803-1963

G   Thos. B. Edelmann
    829 Leigh Court
    Sioux Falls, SD 57104-5215

F   Cashin's Pharmacy
    163 NW 9th Avenue
    Petersburg, VA 23801-8226

E   Thos. B. Edelmann, II
    1356 Nye Circle
    Portsmouth, RI 02871-3320

D   Belmont Inn
    Brownsville, TN 38012-7320

C   Cashin's Pharmacy
    19 - 22 Street
    Petersburg, VA 23805-2871

B   Thos. B. Edelmann, Jr.
    1127 Peach Street
    Pocatello, ID 83206-1290

A   Anne Dewalt Secretarial School
    San Antonio, TX 78223-3754

ANSWERS

15. _____

14. _____

13. _____

12. _____

11. _____

10. _____

9. _____

8. _____

7. _____

6. _____

5. _____

4. _____

3. _____

2. _____

1. _____

EXERCISE 60
Goal: To see if ZIP Codes are exactly the same.

Look at the ZIP Code in Column 1 and the ZIP Code in Column 2. If the two codes are exactly the same, circle the *S* in Column 3. If the two codes are different, circle the *D* in Column 3.

COLUMN 1	COLUMN 2	COLUMN 3
1. 30354-1120	30354-1120	1. S D
2. 65442-0485	65442-0435	2. S D
3. 17709-0384	17109-0384	3. S D
4. 80229-3170	80229-3170	4. S D
5. 02173-6034	02173-6034	5. S D
6. 70129-0823	70129-0823	6. S D
7. 20028-3412	20028-3472	7. S D
8. 52720-0176	52720-0176	8. S D
9. 79420-2245	79490-2245	9. S D
10. 00918-0406	00918-0406	10. S D
11. 44142-2258	44142-2258	11. S D
12. 60646-1275	60646-1275	12. S D
13. 96820-3089	96820-3089	13. S D
14. 27108-0276	27108-0276	14. S D
15. 33040-7795	33040-1795	15. S D

EXERCISE 61
Goal: To make a bank deposit with only currency and coins.

Some businesses (such as fast-food restaurants or gas stations) receive more bills (currency) and coins each day than checks. A bank deposit usually is made each day with only currency and coins. Bills are counted and a wrapper is put around the stack. Coins are also counted and put in a special wrapper from the bank.

Look at the samples below. The wrappers around the bills have a certain value ($1,000 and $500, for example) printed on them. The coins are in wrappers with a certain value ($10, $5, and $2, for example).

Follow these steps to complete the deposit slip on page 164.

1. Write the current date and year on the date line of the deposit slip.
2. Add the amounts (in dollars) shown on the bundles of bills. Find the total value of all bills. Write this amount on the deposit slip on the line beside *Currency*. Notice the dollars and cents amounts are divided by a line.
3. Add the amounts (in dollars and cents) shown on the rolls of coins. Find the total value of all coins. Write this amount on the deposit slip on the line beside *Coins*.
4. Add the total values of all the bills and coins. Find the total. Write the total value of all bills and coins on the deposit slip on the last line after *Total*.

DEPOSIT SLIP

95th Street Car Wash, Inc.
14-95th Street, SW
Yakima, WA 98902-0373

DATE _____ 19 _____

91-7429
————
3241

CHECKS AND OTHER ITEMS ARE RECEIVED FOR DEPOSIT SUBJECT
TO THE RULES AND REGULATIONS OF THIS FINANCIAL INSTITUTION

2Y *SECOND YAKIMA*

The Second National Bank of Yakima, WA 98901-1148

⑆324174290⑈ 13 289 247⑆

	DOLLARS	CENTS
CURRENCY		
COINS		
CHECKS 1.		
List Singly 2.		
● Be sure 3.		
each item is endorsed 4.		
Total From Other Side		
Total Items **TOTAL**		

Use reverse side for additional listing or attach tape.

  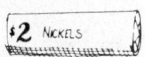 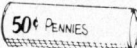

  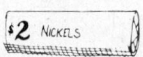 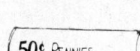

 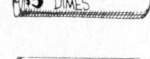 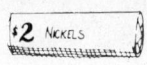 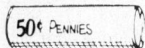

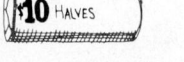   

EXERCISE 62
Goal: To use reference sources to find information.

To find the answers to the questions below, use the Reference Sources of this text-workbook. Write or print your answers in the space at the end of the line.

ANSWERS

1a. In San Diego, (1) on which day was the temperature the lowest?

(2) What was the lowest temperature?

1a. (1)_____

(2)_____

1b. In Buffalo, (1) on which day was the temperature the highest?

(2) What was the highest temperature?

1b. (1)_____

(2)_____

1c. Of the three cities, Austin, Dallas, and El Paso, (1) which city had the lowest temperature forecast on Thursday?

(2) What was the forecast temperature?

1c. (1)_____

(2)_____

2a. What is the closing inventory number of information processing labels?

2a. _____

2b. What is the inventory value of these labels?

2b. _____

2c. What is the total value of the entire inventory?

2c. _____

3a. What river flows through the states of Kentucky, Tennessee, and Alabama?

3a. _____

3b. What four states come together at one point?

3b. _____

3c. What country borders the United States to the north?

3c. _____

4a. What is the area code for Alabama?

4a. _____

4b. In which time zone is Utah?

4b. _____

4c. Which Canadian province is in the Pacific time zone?

4c. _____

5a. In which county is Delaware City, DE, located?

5a. _____

5b. What is the ZIP Code for 563 Chapel St. S in Newark, DE?

5b. _____

5c. What is the ZIP Code for the Newark, DE, Medical Building?

5c. _____

6a. What is the 6 percent sales tax on an $8.85 purchase?

6a. _____

6b. What is the 4½ percent sales tax on an $11.75 purchase?

6b. _____

6c. What is the 5 percent sales tax on a $53.55 purchase?

6c. _____

Unit 2D

EXERCISE 63
Goal: To add words to your vocabulary.

The words in Column 1 are among those words most frequently mispronounced and misspelled. Spend time in study and in drill before you finish the exercise. In your home study, pronounce the words as they are divided in Column 2. Drill on the correct spelling and meanings. You will find these words and meanings on the unit test.

COLUMN 1	COLUMN 2	COLUMN 3
1. adequate	ad-e-quate	enough, fit, suitable, ample, sufficient
2. burden	bur-den	load, weight, cargo, responsibility, exert
3. conference	con-fer-ence	meeting, assembly, discussion, seminar, consultation
4. decoration	dec-o-ra-tion	trimming, ornament, medal, award, adornment
5. excellent	ex-cel-lent	superior, great, outstanding, choice, superb
6. hindrance	hin-drance	handicap, difficulty, blockage, restriction, obstruction
7. independent	in-de-pen-dent	separate, free, unattached, self-supporting, self-governing
8. locality	lo-cal-i-ty	place, region, neighborhood, zone, site
9. minimum	min-i-mum	least, lowest, smallest, slightest, bottom
10. obsolete	ob-so-lete	out of date, old-fashioned, outworn, ancient, old
11. punctual	punc-tu-al	on time, prompt, reliable, precise, dependable
12. quantity	quan-ti-ty	amount, number, size, volume, sum
13. sacrifice	sac-ri-fice	give up, surrender, yield, forfeit, part with
14. violence	vi-o-lence	wildness, roughness, fury, rage, tumult
15. warehouse	ware-house	storehouse, depot, stockroom, depository, building

Look at the meanings in Column 1. Circle the *correctly spelled* word in Column 2 that matches the meanings in Column 1.

	COLUMN 1	COLUMN 2
1.	great, superior	excellant excelent excellent excellunt
2.	obstruction, difficulty	hindrance hinderence hinderance hindrence
3.	on time, prompt	punctuial punctul punctual puntial
4.	meeting, seminar	confernce conferrence conferance conference
5.	yield, give up	sacrafice sacrefice sacrefise sacrifice
6.	least, lowest	minimum minamum minimun minnimum
7.	amount, number	quanity quannity quantity quontity
8.	responsibility, load	burden burdon berdun burrden
9.	wildness, roughness	vilence vialense vialonce violence
10.	place, region	locallity localaty locality locolity
11.	trimming, award	decration decaration decorattion decoration
12.	outworn, out of date	obsolete obsalete obsoleat obsoleet
13.	enough, fit	adequate adaquit adequitte adoquite
14.	unattached, free	independant indipendent indopendent independent
15.	storehouse, depot	wearhouse warhouse warehouse wearhouce

EXERCISE 64
Goal: To make decisions about printing on business forms.

Use the information below. Fill in the return address space on the envelopes shown below. Make your own decisions about correct printing, abbreviations, and placement.

Form 1: Cassandra Quiroz lives at 2728 Del Monte Street, Sacramento, California 95801-4483. Her account number is 6947-23-9621.

Name		Place Stamp here
Number Street		P.O. will not deliver without postage
City or Town	State	Zip	
Account No.		

Form 2: Henry Salinas lives at 448 North Main Street, Fond du Lac, Wisconsin 54934-2644. His account number is 397 44 937 66.

Name		Place Stamp here
Number Street		P.O. will not deliver without postage
City or Town	State	Zip	
Account No.		

Form 3: Carroll Cartwright lives at 229 East Colfax Avenue, Denver, Colorado 80222. His account number is 4474 6320 8742.

Name		Place Stamp here
Number Street		P.O. will not deliver without postage
City or Town	State	Zip	
Account No.		

NAME _____ CLASS _____

EXERCISE 65
Goal: To improve spelling and handwriting of proper names of states and capital cities.

As you write and spell the proper names in this exercise, follow the same steps that you used in the other handwriting and spelling exercises of proper names. *Do not write too fast.* You will have these same proper names on the unit test. Spend time during your home study to review these proper names.

Raleigh, North Carolina   *Little Rock, Arkansas*

_____   _____

_____   _____

_____   _____

Olympia, Washington   *Honolulu, Hawaii*

_____   _____

_____   _____

_____   _____

Helena, Montana   *Annapolis, Maryland*

_____   _____

_____   _____

_____   _____

Exercise 65   **171**

Car son Cit y, Ne vad a

_____

_____

_____

Mont gom er y, Al a bam a

_____

_____

_____

Rich mond , Vir gin ia

_____

_____

_____

EXERCISE 66
Goal: To learn about personal paging systems and to use office files/databases to find answers to questions.

Earlier you talked to someone with a mobile (cellular) telephone. Like the cellular telephone, a **personal paging system** can be used by persons away from their business telephones. The tiny boxlike device may be called by different names, such as beeper, signaler, or pager.

A beeper is very valuable to an executive who wishes to keep in touch with the office. Each beeper has a seven-digit telephone number. A nurse at the hospital may dial the beeper number of a doctor who is at a football game. The doctor hears a beep (or buzz) sound from the beeper. From the nearest telephone the doctor may call the number shown on the lighted end of the beeper.

Illus. 2-5   A Beeper Is Used to Get in Touch with Someone not in the Office

You are working for Bozeman Marketing Research. Beepers are used by employees who leave the office to call on clients throughout the city. Cedric Reish asked you to let him know when the envelopes arrive from Ellis Paper Products. Jenny Mize will be visiting clients all afternoon. She can be reached on her beeper.

Call 1 📞 *The telephone rings.*

YOU   Bozeman Marketing Research, —————— speaking.
YOUR FIRST NAME

CALLER   ——————, this is Cedric answering your beep.
YOUR FIRST NAME

YOU   Yes, Cedric, the envelopes arrived from Tampa.

CALLER   Very good! How many did we receive?

(PAUSE)   (Look in the Office Files/Databases. You have displayed the Receiving Report on your computer screen.)

YOU   ——————. That is five boxes fewer than we ordered.

(PAUSE)   (From the Remarks column on your screen, you should be able to tell why the five boxes were missing. You look at the Remarks column to find the code and the reason for the missing boxes.)

YOU   —————————————— is the reason for the missing boxes.

CALLER   We can get by with the shipment. I will report the missing boxes. Thank you for paging me. Good-bye.

YOU   You are welcome. Good-bye.

Call 2 📞 *The telephone rings.*

YOU   Bozeman Marketing Research, —————— speaking.
YOUR FIRST, LAST NAME

CALLER   Jenny Mize, please.

YOU   Miss Mize is away from the office. May I help you?

CALLER   Yes, this is Herb Terry at Key Air. Jenny and I are serving on the Advisory Committee for the Business Education Clubs. I need some judges for the events at the State Leadership Conference.

YOU	I do not have that information, but I can page Miss Mize. How many judges do you need?
CALLER	I need one each for Public Speaking, Parliamentary Procedure, and Job Interview.
YOU	May I have your telephone number, Mr. Terry?
CALLER	555-3472, Extension 45.
YOU	That was 555-3472, Extension 45. You should hear from Miss Mize or me within an hour.
CALLER	I will be in the office all day. Thank you. Good-bye.
YOU	You are welcome. Good-bye.
(PAUSE)	(In the Office Files/Databases, find the Bozeman Marketing Research files. Stored on your computer is a data file of the names, addresses, and telephone numbers of the speakers and judges. You display the first screen which is the beginning of the alphabetic list of speakers and judges. You dial 555-0328, the number of Jenny Mize's beeper. Jenny's beeper signals her, and she sees your number on the lighted end of her beeper. She dials your telephone number.)

Call 3   *The telephone rings.*

YOU	Bozeman Marketing Research, _____ speaking. YOUR FIRST, LAST NAME
CALLER	_____, this is Jenny answering your beep. YOUR FIRST NAME
YOU	Miss Mize, Mr. Herb Terry at Key Air called. He needs judges for the three events at the State Leadership Conference of the Business Education Clubs.
CALLER	What are the three events?
YOU	Public Speaking, Parliamentary Procedure, and Job Interview.

CALLER   In the data file, find the telephone numbers of Billie Burdett, Jacob Carlton, and Linda Paul. Call Herb and give him their names and telephone numbers. Tell him that these people will accept any judging assignment. They have served many times. Thank you for your beep. Good-bye.

YOU   You are welcome. Good-bye.

(PAUSE)   (You find that you will have to display another screen to find the names and numbers of the three persons. When you find the information, dial Mr. Terry's number.)

Call 4   *The telephone rings.*

OPERATOR   Key Air Public Relations, Angelica Vadillo speaking.

YOU   Extension 45, Mr. Herb Terry, please.

OPERATOR   One moment, please.

HERB   Herb Terry speaking.

YOU   Mr. Terry, I am _____ , calling for Miss
             YOUR FIRST, LAST NAME
       Mize in regard to the judges you need for the State Leadership Conference. Miss Mize suggested Billie Burdett, whose telephone number is _____; Jacob Carlton, at _____; and Linda Paul, at _____.

HERB   Thank you very much, _____.
             TITLE, LAST NAME

YOU   Miss Mize said that these people will accept any judging assignment. They have served many times. You are welcome. Good-bye.

Note: For both calls you had to make decisions. You were a help to both Cedric and Jenny because you could use the paging system to reach both of them. You then used your desk telephone to talk to them. The computer data files were a quick way to find the information needed for both calls.

Congratulations! You have now finished the exercises for Unit 2. Before you ask your teacher for the unit test, study the vocabulary, spelling, and filing exercises in this unit. You will also need to know the states and capitals. Ask your teacher for instructions for turning in your work. Do not begin work on the exercises in Unit 3 until your teacher tells you to do so.

NAME _____ CLASS _____

UNIT 3A

Follow the same steps you used in other handwriting and spelling exercises. *Do not write too fast.* Pronounce the word in syllables and as a word.

1. *ac tu al ly* _____
2. *be gin ning* _____
3. *com plete ly* _____
4. *dis ap point ed* _____
5. *e mer gen cy* _____
6. *jew el ry* _____
7. *lab o ra to ry* _____
8. *nu mer ous* _____
9. *out ra geous* _____
10. *pros per ous* _____
11. *rec om mend* _____
12. *sum mon* _____

13. *thor ough* _____

14. *va ri e ty* _____

15. *worth while* _____

EXERCISE 68
Goal: To keep a tally and take a grand total.

A **tally** is a count made by using a slash mark (/) to represent one of something. For example, a count may be kept of how many customers come into a cafeteria at a certain time. If two customers come into the cafeteria at 11:00 a.m., two slash marks (//) would be written on the report. Five slash marks (////) show that five customers came into the cafeteria.

On the following report, the tallies for the entire day are written. Look at Line 0 for 11:00 a.m. Notice that the number 37 (representing the number of lunch customers) is written at the end of the line under *Total*. If you count the tally marks *across* the line as 5, 10, 15, and so forth, you will find that the tally marks on Line 0 add up to 37.

Count the tally marks for the other lines. Write the total number of marks at the end of each line. Find the Grand Total of the *Total* column. Write the Grand Total at the bottom of the *Total* column.

NUMBER OF LUNCH CUSTOMERS

Time		Total	
11:00	///// ///// ///// ///// ///// ///// ///// //	37	0.
11:15	///// ///// ///// ///// ///// ///// ///// ///// ///// ////		1.
11:30	///// ///// ///// ///// ///// ///// ///// ///// ///// ///// /// /////		2.
11:45	///// ///// ///// ///// ///// ///// ///// ///// ///// ///// ///// ///// ///// ///		3.
12:00	///// ///// ///// ///// ///// ///// ///// ///// ///// ///// ///// ///// ///// /////		4.
12:15	///// ///// ///// ///// ///// ///// ///// ///// ///// ///// ///// ///		5.
12:30	///// ///// ///// ///// ///// ///// ///// ///// ///// ///// /////		6.
12:45	///// ///// ///// ///// ///// ///// ///// ///// ///// ///// ///// /		7.
1:00	///// ///// ///// ///// ///// ///// ///// ///// ///// ///// ///// //		8.
1:15	///// ///// ///// ///// ///// ///// ///// ///// /////		9.
1:30	///// ///// ///// ///// ///// ///		10.
1:45	///// ///// ///// ///// ///		11.
2:00	///// ///// ///// /		12.
2:15	///// ///// ///// /		13.
2:30	///// ///// /////		14.
2:45	///// ///// //		15.
Date 8-20-19--		Grand Total	16.

EXERCISE 69
Goal: To index numbers in business names for filing.

RULE 9 Numbers spelled out in a business name (fifty-five) are indexed as written and filed alphabetically. Numbers written in number form (55) are indexed as *one* unit. Names with numbers in the first unit are indexed in ascending order (smallest to largest) *before* alphabetic names. Arabic numbers (1, 2, 3, . . .) are filed before Roman numbers (4 and 5 come before IV and V). Names with inclusive numbers (55–59) are indexed by the first number only (55). Names with numbers coming after the first unit (Route 55 Theater) are filed alphabetically before a similar name without a number (Route Planners Tours).

> **Note:** In indexing numbers written as numbers that end with st, d, and th (1st, 2d, 3d, 4th, 5th), do not use the endings. Use only the numbers (1, 2, 3, 4, 5).

Table 3-1 Examples of Rule 9

	INDEXING ORDER			
Name Before Indexing	Key Unit	Unit 2	Unit 3	Unit 4
6th & Elm Warehouse	6	and	Elm	Warehouse
6th & Harmes Washerette	6	and	Harmes	Washerette
6 Day Photo Developers	6	Day	Photo	Developers
6 Pence Cafe	6	Pence	Cafe	
6th Quarter Hotel	6	Quarter	Hotel	
650-675 Bartels Blvd.	650	Bartels	Blvd	
The 650 Bartels Boutique	650	Bartels	Boutique	The
1667 Realty Company	1667	Realty	Company	
The 16000 Condominiums	16000	Condominiums	The	
Six Zero Six Motel	Six	Zero	Six	Motel
The Sixth State Resort	Sixth	State	Resort	The
Six-Thousand Toy Museum	Six Thousand	Toy	Museum	
Sixty Minutes Cleaners	Sixty	Minutes	Cleaners	
Trail 15 Nature Club	Trail	15	Nature	Club
Trail 28 Nature Society	Trail	28	Nature	Society
Trail Blazers Hiking Club	Trail	Blazers	Hiking	Club

In Column 1 are the names of businesses with a letter (*A, B, C, D,* etc.) before them. In Column 2 is a file drawer. Five of the names from Column 1 are already printed on cards and filed. In Column 3 are the letters that are before the names in Column 1. For example, the first card in the drawer is *4 and Barnes Apothecary.* In Column 3 on the first line is the letter *J,* which is the letter before the *4th & Barnes Apothecary* in Column 1.

Use these steps to finish this exercise:

1. Using Rule 9, decide which card comes after *4 and Barnes Apothecary.*
2. Print the name on the card in the file drawer.
3. Write the letter in Column 3.
4. Repeat Steps 1–3. File all the cards. Write the letters in Column 3.

COLUMN 1	COLUMN 2	COLUMN 3
A. 4th Precinct Bug Specialists	Highway By-Way Seafood	--15. _D_
B. Four Seasons Travel Service		--14. _____
C. 4 Maids Tearoom		--13. _____
D. Highway By-Way Seafood	Fourth Street Framer The	--12. _G_
E. 1492 Americana Museum		--11. _____
F. 4th and Sorrento Market		--10. _____
G. The Fourth Street Framer	14000 Office Park The	--9. _N_
H. Highway 45 Buggyworks		--8. _____
I. 400-425 Harris Plaza		--7. _____
J. 4th & Barnes Apothecary		--6. _____
K. The Four Sons Dairy	4 Precinct Bug Specialists	--5. _A_
L. Highway 7 Radio & TV Doctor		--4. _____
M. 4 Minutes Heel Repair Bar		--3. _____
N. The 14000 Office Park		--2. _____
O. The 400 Fruit & Vegetable Bin	4 and Barnes Apothecary	--1. _J_

F - H

EXERCISE 70
Goal: To learn about the centrex telephone system and to use office files/databases to find answers to questions.

Centrex (central exchange) is another kind of telephone system. Illustration 3-1 shows a centrex system. Incoming calls do not go through a switchboard operator with this system. Instead, each **extension** (telephone) has its own seven-digit number. Incoming calls can be dialed directly to your extension.

Assume you need to call the financial aid office of a large university that has a centrex system. First, look in the telephone directory under the name of the university. Next, you would look for the number of the financial aid office. You would then dial the number and your call would go directly to the financial aid office. A switchboard operator is not needed to connect your call. If a number for the financial aid office is not shown in the telephone directory, you would dial the number in the directory for university information. Tell the operator you need the extension of the financial aid office. The operator may give you the number of the extension or may send the call to the financial aid office extension. Write the number in a place where you can find it easily if you need to call the financial aid office again.

Outgoing calls from a centrex system are made by dialing "9" (or some other number), waiting for the dial tone, and dialing the number you want to call.

Illus. 3-1 A Centrex System

You work at Heintzelman Communication Systems. You work in the travel department, where you make airline and hotel reservations for Heintzelman executives who travel on business. Your telephone extension is connected to the centrex system.

Call 1 📞   *The telephone rings.*

YOU   Travel Department, _____ speaking. May I
                               _{YOUR TITLE, LAST NAME}

help you?

CALLER   Yes, _____. This is Rosalynn Ferris, secretary to Alex
                     _{YOUR FIRST NAME}

Lambros in the Legal Department. Will you look on his Flight Log to

see how many miles Mr. Lambros flew in May?

YOU   Yes, _____, I will be happy to look. Will you hold,
               _{CALLER'S FIRST NAME}

please?

(PAUSE)   (You find Heintzelman Communication Systems in the Office

Files/Databases.)

Thank you for holding, _____. Mr. Lambros had a
                              _{CALLER'S FIRST NAME}

total of _____ miles in May. Is there anything else I may find

for you?

CALLER   Yes. I am preparing Mr. Lambros' expense report for last month. I

cannot find his airline ticket receipt for the trip he made on June 6. He

visited two cities and returned the same day.

YOU   I can find those city names for you. Will you hold, please?

(PAUSE)   (You find the Flight Log in the Office Files/Databases. You will have

to look in the References Sources for the names of the two cities.)

Thank you for waiting, _____. Mr. Lambros visit-
                          _{CALLER'S FIRST NAME}

ed _____ and _____ on June 6. Do

you need the flight numbers?

CALLER   No, thank you. I will ask him for the receipt now that I know the name

of the cities. Thank you. Good-bye.

YOU   You are welcome. Good-bye.

Call 2 🕿   *The telephone on Randall Hattaway's desk rings.*

Randall asked you to answer his calls. He also gave you the vacation schedule because so many persons wanted to know if their vacation dates had been set. You can answer his telephone calls because your telephone equipment has the **call pickup** feature.

YOU   Mr. Hattaway's desk. _____ speaking.
                                         YOUR TITLE, LAST NAME

CALLER   This is Rebecca Hardison in Accounts Receivable. Can you tell me the two weeks I have been given for vacation?

(PAUSE)   (Look in the Office Files/Databases for the answers.)

YOU   I can help you, _____. Mr. Hattaway left the
                           HER TITLE, LAST NAME
schedule with me. You have the week beginning _____
                                                 MONTH, DAY
and the week beginning _____.
                           MONTH, DAY

CALLER   Thank you very much. Can you tell me the dates that Suzann Pasquale will be on vacation?

YOU   No, I am sorry, but I am not allowed to give personal information about a co-worker to you. Ms. Pasquale will have to call for her own vacation dates.

CALLER   I understand. Thank you. Good-bye.

YOU   You are welcome. Good-bye.

Note: In large businesses you use a person's title and last name unless you know a caller well enough to use a first name. You never answer personal questions about someone else because personal information is *confidential*. You tell Rebecca her vacation dates, but Suzann may not want anyone to know her vacation dates.

EXERCISE 71
Goal: To see if street addresses are exactly the same.

Look at the street address in Column 1 and the street address in Column 2. If the two addresses are the same, fill in the space under the *a* in Column 3. If the two addresses are not the same, fill in the space under the *b* in Column 3. Look carefully at the example to see how to fill in your answer.

COLUMN 1	COLUMN 2	COLUMN 3
		a b
0. 12403 Olive Place	12043 Olive Pl.	0. ‖ ▌
		a b
1. 3622 Georgia Avenue	3622 Georgia Avenue	1. ‖ ‖
		a b
2. 17389 S.W. 121st Terrace	17889 S.W. 121st Terrace	2. ‖ ‖
		a b
3. 838 Karo Blvd., Apt C-4	838 Karo Blvd., Apt G-4	3. ‖ ‖
		a b
4. 2155 Francisco Ave., S	2155 Francisco Ave., S	4. ‖ ‖
		a b
5. 3629 Longmeadow St., N	3629 Longmeadow St.	5. ‖ ‖
		a b
6. 19878 Seven Mile Rd., W	19818 Seven Mile Rd., W	6. ‖ ‖
		a b
7. 2849 Will Rogers Lane	2849 Will Rogers Lane	7. ‖ ‖
		a b
8. 4824 Confederate Hwy. W	4824 Confederate Hy., W	8. ‖ ‖
		a b
9. 871 Drabbington Way	871 Drabbington Wy	9. ‖ ‖
		a b
10. 14287 2nd Ave., NW	14287 2d Ave., NW	10. ‖ ‖
		a b
11. 2339 Massasoit Ct.	2339 Massasoit Ct.	11. ‖ ‖
		a b
12. 11384 E. Central Pkwy	11384 Central Pkwy	12. ‖ ‖
		a b
13. 113885 Ponderosa Dr.	13885 Bonderosa Dr.	13. ‖ ‖
		a b
14. 831 N.E. 115th St., Apt. 4C	831 N.E. 115th St., Apt. 4C	14. ‖ ‖
		a b
15. 723 St. Ignatius Place	728 St. Ignatius Place	15. ‖ ‖

EXERCISE 72
Goal: To put disks in correct numeric order.

Floppy disks are used by many office workers today. These disks are filed in subject, geographic, numeric, or alphabetic order. Containers for filing disks are shown in Illus. 3-2. These storage containers make it quick and easy to find the correct disk.

Illus. 3-2   Containers for Filing Floppy Disks

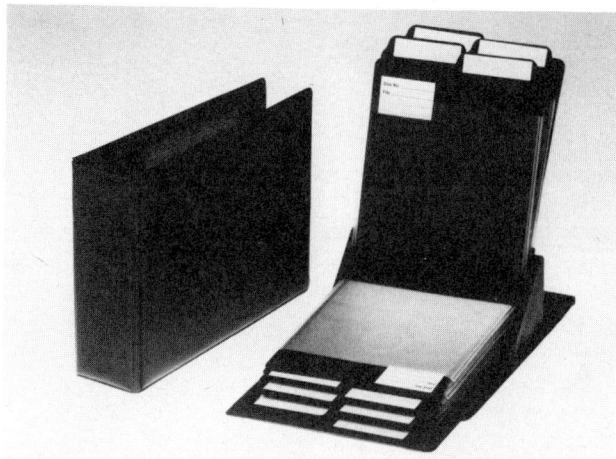

Ring King Visibles, Inc.

Ring King Visibles, Inc.

The disks shown on page 192 are not in correct numeric order. Put the disks in correct order so that the numbers are consecutive from the lowest number to the highest number. The letter (*A, B, C,* or *D*) is shown beside each number. After you have the disks in correct numeric order, write the letters for the disks in the *Answers* column. The letter for the first disk (lowest number) will be on Line 1. The letter for the last disk (highest number) will be on Line 15.

O NO. 13876

N NO. 12534

M NO. 13844

L NO. 13561

K NO. 12840

J NO. 12196

I NO. 12480

H NO. 13345

G NO. 12407

F NO. 12774

E NO. 13288

D NO. 12993

C NO. 13117

B NO. 12405

A NO. 13028

DEPARTMENT: *LEGAL*

DICTATOR: *CHARLENE LANE*

DATES: *03/-- TO 04/--*

15. _____

14. _____

13. _____

12. _____

11. _____

10. _____

9. _____

8. _____

7. _____

6. _____

5. _____

4. _____

3. _____

2. _____

1. _____J_____

EXERCISE 73
Goal: To add words to your vocabulary.

The words in Column 1 are among those words most frequently mispronounced and misspelled. Spend time in study and in drill before you finish the exercise. In your home study, pronounce the words as they are divided in Column 2. Drill on the correct spelling and meanings. You will find these words and meanings on the unit test.

COLUMN 1	COLUMN 2	COLUMN 3
1. **abrupt**	a-brupt	sudden, short, curt, unexpected, surprising
2. **boundary**	bound-a-ry	border, limits, edge, margin, bounds
3. **confidential**	con-fi-den-tial	secret, classified, private, honest, faithful
4. **deficiency**	de-fi-cien-cy	lack, need, scarcity, shortage, inadequacy
5. **elementary**	el-e-men-ta-ry	simple, easy, clear, understandable, basic
6. **familiar**	fa-mil-iar	well known, frequent, friendly, acquainted, customary
7. **history**	his-to-ry	story, annals, background, chronicle, record
8. **juvenile**	ju-ve-nile	youthful, childlike, immature, minor, teenager
9. **language**	lan-guage	communication, speech, tongue, voice, jargon
10. **probably**	prob-a-bly	very likely, possibly, presumable, conceivably, apparently
11. **reputation**	rep-u-ta-tion	name, standing, fame, regard, estimation
12. **sufficient**	suf-fi-cient	enough, adequate, ample, plentiful, abundant
13. **tentative**	ten-ta-tive	indefinite, possible, proposed, conditional, unconfirmed
14. **urgent**	ur-gent	important, immediate, pressing, crucial, demanding
15. **vaguely**	vague-ly	confusingly, indefinitely, unclearly, uncertainly, ambiguously

Look at the meanings in Column 1. Write or print in the blank space in Column 2 the word in today's lesson that correctly matches the meanings in Column 1.

COLUMN 1	COLUMN 2
1. youthful, childlike, teenager	1. _____
2. secret, classified, private	2. _____
3. very likely, possibly, presumable	3. _____
4. confusingly, unclearly, uncertainly	4. _____
5. well known, friendly, acquainted	5. _____
6. name, standing, fame	6. _____
7. lack, need, shortage	7. _____
8. important, immediate, pressing	8. _____
9. communication, speech, voice	9. _____
10. border, limits, edge	10. _____
11. story, annals, record	11. _____
12. indefinite, proposed, unconfirmed	12. _____
13. sudden, unexpected, surprising	13. _____
14. enough, adequate, abundant	14. _____
15. simple, easy, understandable	15. _____

UNIT 3B

EXERCISE 74
Goal: To tell time using analog and digital clocks.

In Exercise 31 you learned about analog clocks. Analog clocks have faces and two hands that move around the face of the clock. A *digital* clock does not have a face. A digital clock uses only numbers to tell you the time. Digital clocks may be found on wrist watches, VCRs, in your bedroom, or in an automobile dashboard.

Look at Fig. 3-1 and identify the parts of a digital clock.

Fig. 3-1 Digital Clock

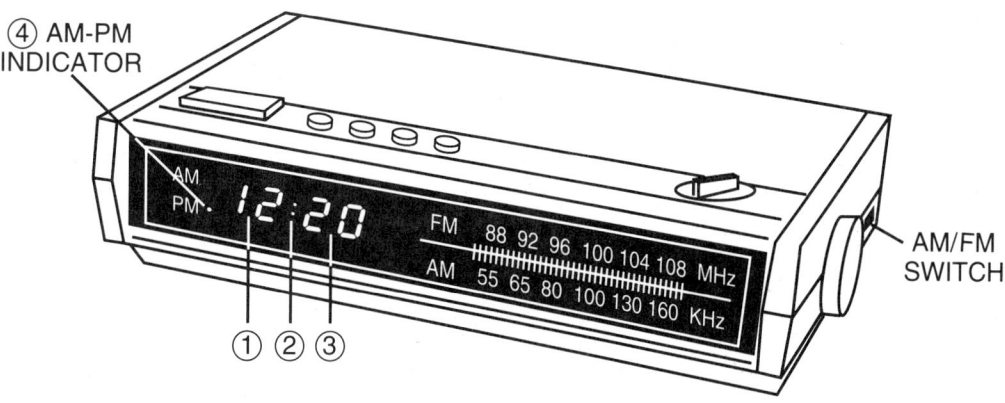

1. The first two numbers represent the hour of the day.
2. The colon divides the hour from the minutes.
3. The last two numbers represent the minutes of the hour.
4. A light will indicate whether the time is a.m. or p.m.

In Fig. 3-2 you will see a digital clock and an analog clock that show the same time. However, the analog clock cannot show whether it is a.m. or p.m.

Fig. 3-2 Digital and Analog Clocks Showing the Same Time

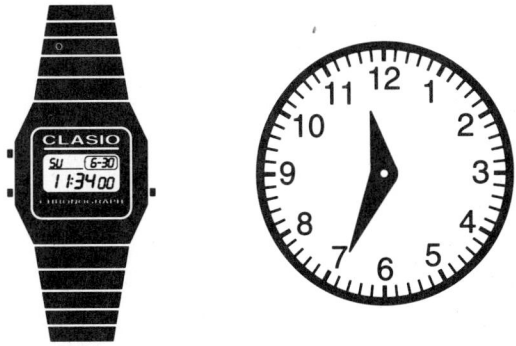

Look at each of the digital clocks below to determine the time. Draw the hands on the analog clock to the right of each digital clock. Figure 3-2 on page 195 will help you.

1.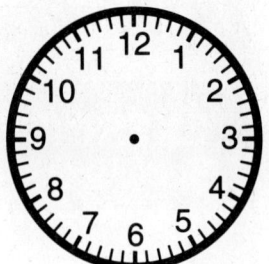

2.

3.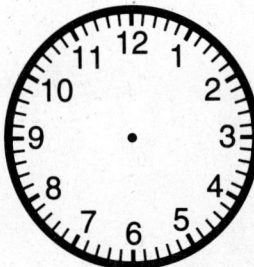

4.

5.

EXERCISE 75
Goal: To use reference sources to find information.

To find the answers to the questions below, use the Reference Sources of this text-workbook. Write or print your answers in the space at the end of the line.

ANSWERS

1a. What is the amount of income tax withheld for a single person on a weekly payroll whose wages were $216 with one allowance?

1a. _____

1b. What is the amount of income tax withheld for a married person on a weekly payroll whose wages were $315 with four allowances?

1b. _____

1c. What is the amount of income tax withheld for a single person on a monthly payroll whose wages were $950 with one allowance?

1c. _____

2a. When it is 1 p.m. in San Francisco, what time is it in Washington, DC?

2a. _____

2b. What is the area code for Manitoba, Canada?

2b. _____

2c. If you left Tampa, Florida, at 5 p.m., what time would it be in New Orleans, Louisiana, when you arrived after a 1-hour-23-minute flight?

2c. _____

3a. What state is the farthest north?

3a. _____

3b. What are the names of the five Great Lakes?

3b. _____

_____

_____

_____

_____

_____

3c. What is the capital of the United States?

3c. _____

4a. What was the amount of Check 1321?

4a. _____

4b. To whom was Check 1324 written?

4b. _____

4c. For what was Check 1319 written?

4c. _____

5a. What is the telephone number of the regional commissioner of the Bureau of Labor Statistics?

5a. _____

5b. What is the street address of the attorney whose last name is Nations?

5b. _____

5c. In what kind of business is George C. Needle?

5c. _____

EXERCISE 76
Goal: To make decisions about printing on business forms.

Alex Leffingwall works in sales zone ALM037. He opens a new account (number 0029517328) for Marguerite H. Boyanton who lives at 3774 Heritage Springs Circle, Hattiesburg, Mississippi 39402-3386. Fill in the new account form below. Make your own decisions about correct printing, abbreviations, and placement.

New Account 1

NEW ACCOUNT

Account Number | Salesperson's Last Name | Sales Zone

Mr. Mrs. Ms. | First Name | Middle Initial | Last Name

Address | Apt. No.

City | State | ZIP

You also work for the same company as Alex Leffingwall. You are employed in sales zone RKQ449. Use the information shown on the next page to open two new accounts. Make your own decisions about correct printing, abbreviations, and placement.

Open account number 459657125 for Robin Ellithorpe who lives at 1985 Whittier Circle, Boulder, Colorado 80321-1344.

New Account 2

NEW ACCOUNT

Account Number	Salesperson's Last Name	Sales Zone

Mr. Mrs. Ms.	First Name	Middle Initial	Last Name

Address	Apt. No.

City	State	ZIP

Open account number 459456921 for Steven Lindhorst who resides at 3603 Riverside Drive, Boulder, Colorado 80321-1344.

New Account 3

NEW ACCOUNT

Account Number	Salesperson's Last Name	Sales Zone

Mr. Mrs. Ms.	First Name	Middle Initial	Last Name

Address	Apt. No.

City	State	ZIP

EXERCISE 77
Goal: To improve spelling and handwriting of proper names of states, capitals, and territories.

As you write and spell the proper names in this exercise, follow the same steps that you used in the other handwriting and spelling exercises of proper names. *Do not write too fast.* You will have these same proper names on the unit test. Spend time during your home study to review these proper names.

San ta Fe, New Mex i co

Con cord, New Hamp shire

_____

_____

_____

_____

_____

_____

Jef fer son City, Mis sou ri

Hart ford, Con nect i cut

_____

_____

_____

_____

_____

_____

Har ris burg, Penn syl va nia

San Juan, Puer to Ri co

_____

_____

_____

_____

_____

_____

Bismarck, North Dakota

———————————————

———————————————

———————————————

Springfield, Illinois

———————————————

———————————————

———————————————

Baton Rouge, Louisiana

———————————————

———————————————

———————————————

EXERCISE 78
Goal: To add words to your vocabulary.

The words in Column 1 are among those words most frequently mispronounced and misspelled. Spend time in study and in drill before you finish the exercise. In your home study, pronounce the words as they are divided in Column 2. Drill on the correct spelling and meanings. You will find these words and meanings on the unit test.

COLUMN 1	COLUMN 2	COLUMN 3
1. **actually**	ac-tu-al-ly	really, truly, certainly, genuinely, positively
2. **beginning**	be-gin-ning	origin, starting point, outset, birth, commencement
3. **completely**	com-plete-ly	wholly, entirely, totally, fully, thoroughly
4. **disappointed**	dis-ap-point-ed	let down, discouraged, frustrated, saddened, displeased
5. **emergency**	e-mer-gen-cy	crisis, predicament, difficulty, tension, urgency
6. **jewelry**	jew-el-ry	gems, jewels, trinkets, treasure, valuables
7. **laboratory**	lab-o-ra-to-ry	workshop, workroom, testroom, experiment station
8. **numerous**	nu-mer-ous	many, plentiful, abundant, countless, innumerable
9. **outrageous**	out-ra-geous	excessive, inhuman, brutal, improper, immoderate
10. **prosperous**	pros-per-ous	successful, well-off, rich, wealthy, flourishing
11. **recommend**	rec-om-mend	approve, endorse, applaud, suggest, urge
12. **summon**	sum-mon	send for, call, ask, invite, urge
13. **thorough**	thor-ough	complete, careful, precise, entire, full
14. **variety**	va-ri-e-ty	difference, change, diversity, variation, mixture
15. **worthwhile**	worth-while	beneficial, rewarding, helpful, useful, invaluable

Look at the meanings in Column 2. Find the word in Column 1 that correctly matches the meanings. In Column 3 write the *letter* of the matching word from Column 1.

COLUMN 1	COLUMN 2	COLUMN 3
A. actually	1. complete, careful, full	1. _____
B. beginning	2. gems, valuables, trinkets	2. _____
C. completely	3. rich, wealthy, successful	3. _____
D. disappointed	4. entirely, wholly, totally	4. _____
E. emergency	5. difference, diversity, change	5. _____
F. jewelry	6. let down, discouraged, saddened	6. _____
G. laboratory	7. send for, call, invite	7. _____
H. numerous	8. helpful, beneficial, rewarding	8. _____
I. outrageous	9. really, truly, certainly	9. _____
J. prosperous	10. workroom, testroom, workshop	10. _____
K. recommend	11. approve, suggest, endorse	11. _____
L. summon	12. difficulty, crisis, predicament	12. _____
M. thorough	13. excessive, inhuman, improper	13. _____
N. variety	14. origin, outset, starting point	14. _____
O. worthwhile	15. many, plentiful, countless	15. _____

NAME _____ CLASS _____

EXERCISE 79
Goal: To index names of organizations and institutions for filing.

RULE 10 Names of organizations and institutions are indexed and filed the same way as the name is shown on the company's **letterhead.** The letterhead is at the top of the paper used for writing letters and has the name of the organization, the address, and sometimes the telephone number. If *the* is part of the name on a letterhead, put *the* as the last indexing unit in filing.

Examples of organizations and institutions are: banks and other financial institutions, clubs, colleges, hospitals, hotels, lodges, motels, museums, religious institutions, schools, unions, and universities.

Table 3-2 Examples of Rule 10

Name Before Indexing	Key Unit	Unit 2	Unit 3	Unit 4
Assembly of Truth Tabernacle	Assembly	of	Truth	Tabernacle
The Association for Beekeepers	Association	for	Beekeepers	The
Atlanta Pet Hospital	Atlanta	Pet	Hospital	
Atlantic Antiques Exchange	Atlantic	Antiques	Exchange	
Atlantic Shell Collectors Club	Atlantic	Shell	Collectors	Club
Bacon County Academy	Bacon	County	Academy	
Bank of Bakersfield	Bank	of	Bakersfield	
Bismarck Weavers Union	Bismarck	Weavers	Union	
Carolton Museum of Art	Carolton	Museum	of	Art
Church of Deliverance	Church	of	Deliverance	
Danville Mental Health Association	Danville	Mental	Health	Association
Denver School for Deaf	Denver	School	for	Deaf
Eagan Allergy Clinic	Eagan	Allergy	Clinic	
Ebsen Board of Realtors	Ebsen	Board	of	Realtors
Fairview Public Speaking Institute	Fairview	Public	Speaking	Institute
Fargo Motor Hotel	Fargo	Motor	Hotel	
Galveston Commission on Pollution	Galveston	Commission	on	Pollution
Georgetown Community College	Georgetown	Community	College	

Exercise 79

205

INDEXING ORDER

Name Before Indexing	Key Unit	Unit 2	Unit 3	Unit 4
Helen Hayes Middle School	Helen	Hayes	Middle	School
Hotel Gatlinburg	Hotel	Gatlinburg		
Midwest Order of Police	Midwest	Order	of	Police
Motel Miami Palms	Motel	Miami	Palms	
National Federation for Diabetes	National	Federation	for	Diabetes
National Music Lovers Society	National	Music	Lovers	Society
University of Hawaii	University	of	Hawaii	

Use three steps to finish the exercise for filing names of organizations and institutions:

1. Follow Rule 10. Put the names of the organizations and institutions in Column 1 in correct alphabetic order.
2. On the cards in the file drawer in Column 2 print in ALL CAPITAL LETTERS, *in correct alphabetic order,* the names from Column 1. The first name is printed on the first card. Go from the front of the file drawer to the back of the drawer as you print the names on the cards.
3. In Column 3 write the number shown before each name in Column 1, where the name is printed in Column 2. The first answer is shown.
4. Follow Steps 1–3 to show the ten cards in correct alphabetic order in the file drawer.

COLUMN 1	COLUMN 2	COLUMN 3
1. Alamo Clinic of Chiropractors		-- 10. _____
2. Association of Legal Secretaries		-- 9. _____
3. Assembly of Holiness Church		-- 8. _____
4. All The Time Answering Service		-- 7. _____
5. American Alliance on Patriotism		-- 6. _____
6. Alamos City Hospital		-- 5. _____
7. All Around Austin Couriers		-- 4. _____
8. Allentown Alliance Against Hunger		-- 3. _____
9. Albany Commission for Clean Air		-- 2. _____
10. Akron Library for the Blind	AKRON LIBRARY FOR THE BLIND	-- 1. *10* _____

A

RULE 11 When a single word in a business name has two or more parts (Inter-State), the parts are indexed in separate units. InterState would be two parts. If a name has two compass directions with a space between them (North West), each compass direction is a separate unit in indexing. However, *north-west* and *northwest* are indexed as one unit. Cross-reference if you wish. For example, North West; SEE ALSO Northwest, North-West.

Table 3-3 Examples of Rule 11

	INDEXING ORDER			
Name Before Indexing	**Key Unit**	**Unit 2**	**Unit 3**	**Unit 4**
Broad Way Publishers, Inc.	Broad	Way	Publishers	Inc
Broadway Car Rentals	Broadway	Car	Rentals	
Down Town Apothecary	Down	Town	Apothecary	
Tyler J. Down, D.V.M.	Down	Tyler	J	DVM
Downtown Merchants Mart	Downtown	Merchants	Mart	
Rev. Murray B. Downtrey	Downtrey	Murray	B	Rev
North East Caterers	North	East	Caterers	
North Woods Health Center	North	Woods	Health	Center
Miss Yola Jane North	North	Yola	Jane	Miss
Northeast Wedding Planners	Northeast	Wedding	Planners	
River View Country Club	River	View	Country	Club
Riverview Motor Inn	Riverview	Motor	Inn	
Ms. Natashia Riverview	Riverview	Natashia	Ms	

Use the same steps for this exercise for filing separated single words that you used for the last exercise for filing names of organizations and institutions:

1. Put the names in Column 1 in correct alphabetic order.
2. On the cards in the file drawer in Column 2 print in ALL CAPITAL LETTERS, in correct alphabetic order, the names from Column 1.

3. In Column 3 write the number shown before each name in Column 1, where the name is printed in Column 2. The first answer is shown.
4. Follow Steps 1–3 to show the ten cards in correct alphabetic order.

<table>
<tr><th>COLUMN 1</th><th>COLUMN 2</th><th>COLUMN 3</th></tr>
</table>

COLUMN 1

1. Ridgeview Dancenter
2. Ridgepoint Produce Mart
3. Ridge and Ridge Ceramic Creations
4. Ridgemont Wayside Inn
5. Ms. Berthajean W. Ridge
6. Ridge View Cinema
7. Ridge City Canoe Rentals
8. Robin Ridge House of Travel
9. Ridge View Home for the Aged
10. Ridgecrest State College

COLUMN 3

10. _____
9. _____
8. _____
7. _____
6. _____
5. _____
4. _____
3. _____
2. _____
1. ___3___

NAME _____ CLASS _____

EXERCISE 80
Goal: To use reference sources to find information.

To find the answers to the questions below, use the Reference Sources of this text-workbook. Write or print your answers in the space at the end of the line.

ANSWERS

1a. What was the name of the person called on 7/18?

1a. _____

1b. To which city was a call placed in the afternoon on 7/26?

1b. _____

1c. At what time was the morning call placed on 7/30?

1c. _____

2a. What is the capital of Florida?

2a. _____

2b. How many states border Tennessee?

2b. _____

2c. What river runs along Oregon's eastern boundary?

2c. _____

3a. What is the ZIP Code for Viola, DE?

3a. _____

3b. What is the ZIP Code for the Delaware Department of Labor (government offices)?

3b. _____

3c. What is the general delivery ZIP Code in Newark, DE?

3c. _____

4. What are the Postal Service abbreviations for the following words:

  a. Harbor

4a. _____

  b. Bypass

4b. _____

  c. Village

4c. _____

5. In which section of the *Daily News* will you find (give the number shown at the right of the section name):

  a. Career Services

5a. _____

  b. Musical Merchandise

5b. _____

  c. Mountain Property

5c. _____

EXERCISE 81
Goal: To learn about the automatic dialing features of telephone equipment and to use office files/databases to answer questions.

Many push-button telephones have the one-touch automatic dialing feature. Automatic dialing telephones save much time since you do not have to dial the number each time. This popular feature allows you to dial a telephone number once and store it in the telephone's "memory." First, you dial 9 (or some other number) to get an outside line. Then you press the button on the telephone for the previously stored number you wish to call. You do not dial any numbers. The telephone automatically dials for you!

If you have a telephone with the automatic dialing feature to use at work, you will need to decide which numbers you will store or "program" into the telephone. First, program in emergency numbers, such as the police and fire departments. Next, program in business numbers that are called frequently. These numbers may be the bank, post office, and important customers of your company.

Speed calling may be used in some parts of the country. On a magnetic memory device in push-button telephones, you may store up to 30 telephone numbers that you call often. To call a number, you dial a one-, two-, or three-digit code.

Illus. 3-3 Telephone with an Automatic Dialing Feature

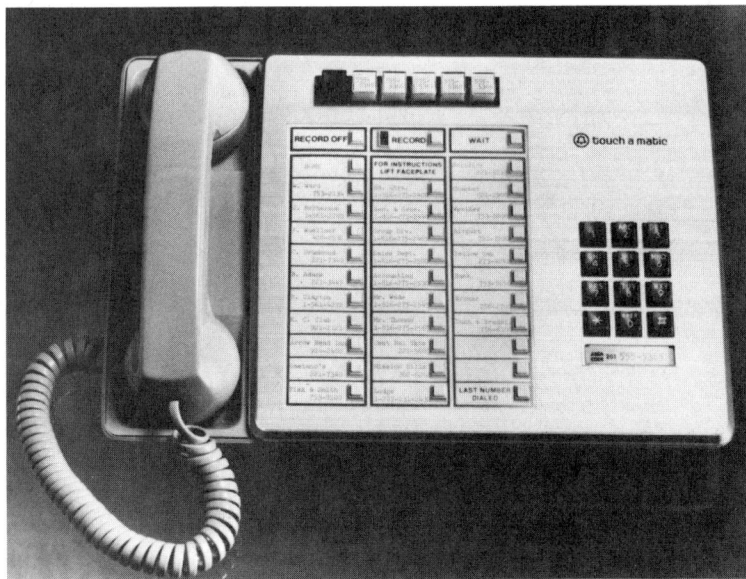

Courtesy of AT&T Archives

You work for Alaniz Bookkeeping Service. Mrs. Alaniz asks you to call Darrell Newby at Just Jeans, a clothing manufacturer. She also wants you to make a reservation for her on Key Air. She wants to fly to Memphis on the earliest flight on Wednesday, June 5. She wants to return to Little Rock on the latest flight on the same day. You use the automatic dialing feature for both calls.

Call 1

You press a button on your telephone for an outside line. You press a button for Just Jeans on your telephone equipment.

 *The telephone rings.*

OPERATOR	Good morning, Just Jeans.
YOU	Darrell Newby, please.
OPERATOR	One moment, please.

The telephone rings.

NEWBY	Darrell Newby speaking.
YOU	Mr. Newby, this is _____ at Alaniz Bookkeeping

<small>YOUR TITLE, LAST NAME</small>

Service. Mrs. Alaniz asked me to call you. How may I help you?

NEWBY   Thank you for calling. I need to know about my accounts receivable. I want to visit those accounts that are at least three months behind in payments.

YOU   One moment, please, Mr. Newby.

(PAUSE)   (Find Alaniz Bookkeeping Service in the Office Files/Databases. Display the schedule of accounts receivable for Just Jeans on your computer screen.)

Thank you for waiting. I have your schedule on my screen. Do you have a particular account in mind?

NEWBY   I know that McRae Clothing Depot is already in the hands of a collection agency. Do you see any other accounts that are at least three months behind in payments?

YOU   Yes, _____ is now overdue _____ days with
<small>NAME OF ACCOUNT</small>   <small>NUMBER</small>
a balance of _____.
<small>AMOUNT</small>

NEWBY   Thank you. I will visit this account today. Your monthly reports

	are here on my desk. I am behind in clearing my stack of mail. Good-bye.
YOU	You are welcome. Call us whenever we can serve you. Good-bye.

> **Note:** Mrs. Alaniz let you make the decisions about Mr. Newby's call. She depended on you to find the information he needed.

Call 2

Each month you receive two copies of the Key Air Flight Schedule. You file one copy in the subject file in your desk-drawer file under Travel. Mrs. Alaniz keeps the other schedule in her briefcase.

Plan the trip on Key Air *before* you call the reservations office. Be able to give the agent flight information without loss of time. Mrs. Alaniz prefers a window seat in the coach section. Her business telephone number is 555-0207. Her home telephone number is 555-5399. The tickets should be mailed to Mrs. Nina Alaniz, Alaniz Bookkeeping Service, 1780 Milton Parkway, Searcy, Arkansas 72143-3027.

 *The telephone rings.*

AMBROSE	Key Air, Reginald Ambrose speaking.
YOU	Mr. Ambrose, I would like to make a reservation for one person on Wednesday, June 5, from Little Rock on Flight _____ to Memphis, and a return flight the same day on Flight _____.
(PAUSE)	(The agent is checking his computer screen.)
AMBROSE	Do you prefer first-class or coach service?
YOU	_____.
AMBROSE	Yes, I can confirm Flight _____ on Wednesday, June 5, leaving Little Rock at _____ TIME, arriving in Memphis at _____ TIME. I can also confirm Flight _____ leaving Memphis at _____ TIME, arriving in Little Rock at _____ TIME. What is the name of the person?

YOU   _____.
                    HER TITLE, FIRST NAME, LAST NAME

AMBROSE   Do you prefer a window or aisle seat?

YOU   A/an _____ seat, please.

AMBROSE   What are your business and home telephone numbers?

YOU   The business telephone number is _____ and the

                  home telephone number is _____.

AMBROSE   Your seat assignment on both flights is 12A. May I mail your tickets?

YOU   Yes, mail them to Mrs. Alaniz at _____
                                     NUMBER, STREET NAME

         _____.
         CITY, STATE, ZIP CODE

AMBROSE   May I help you with other reservations?

YOU   No, thank you. Please bill the Alaniz Bookkeeping Service account.

AMBROSE   Thank you for calling Key Air. Enjoy your flight. Good-bye.

YOU   You are welcome. Good-bye.

Note: You kept the schedule in the file nearest the telephone. You did not keep the agent waiting for information. You did not need to give your name because the flight was for only Mrs. Alaniz. Business telephone calls, such as making an airline reservation, should be brief.

EXERCISE 82
Goal: To see if stock numbers are the same.

Look at the stock number in Column 1 and the stock number in Column 2. If the two stock numbers are the same, fill in the space under the *a* in Column 3. If the two stock numbers are not the same, fill in the space under the *b* in Column 3.

	COLUMN 1	COLUMN 2	COLUMN 3
			a b
1.	BCJ0934	BCJ0934	1. ‖ ‖
2.	RSE3402	RSE3402	2. ‖ ‖
3.	PZH0403	PZH0403	3. ‖ ‖
4.	MVE7645	MYE7645	4. ‖ ‖
5.	PJW0817	PJW0817	5. ‖ ‖
6.	BWV1530	BWV1530	6. ‖ ‖
7.	QEU6639	QEU6639	7. ‖ ‖
8.	KLA6037	KLA6031	8. ‖ ‖
9.	WIY3306	WIY3306	9. ‖ ‖
10.	VQO6171	VQC6171	10. ‖ ‖
11.	EMS2953	EMS2953	11. ‖ ‖
12.	AHW3026	AHW3026	12. ‖ ‖
13.	GRM5917	GRN5917	13. ‖ ‖
14.	BDA9052	BDA9052	14. ‖ ‖
15.	EBB4583	EPB4583	15. ‖ ‖

EXERCISE 83
Goal: To make decisions about setting priorities.

To set priorities, you put activities in the order of their importance. You decide which activity must be finished first, second, third, etc. In this exercise you will use activities that are done early in the morning, before you leave for work or school, to decide which activity has priority over the other activities.

Make your own decisions about setting priorities for the activities you write on the Things to Do form on page 218. *Read all ten activities before you fill in the form.* Put only the necessary information about each activity on the form. *You need not copy the activity word for word as it is shown in the list.* Put the most important (or first) activity on Line 1. The last activity should be shown on Line 10. Use the current date.

Each morning before you leave for work, there are a number of things that you need to do at home. Listed below are some of those things you might do. Put the items in order as you would do them. Complete the Things to Do form on page 218.

1. Lock the front door.
2. Get dressed.
3. Clean up the breakfast dishes.
4. Take a shower.
5. Fix and eat your breakfast.
6. Shut off the alarm clock.
7. Put the cat outside.
8. Feed the cat.
9. Make sure you have the keys to the house.
10. Get out of bed.

THINGS TO DO
TODAY

DATE: _____

1. _____

2. _____

3. _____

4. _____

5. _____

6. _____

7. _____

8. _____

9. _____

10. _____

UNIT 3C

EXERCISE 84
Goal: To use the terminal digit method for filing numbers.

In Exercise 5 you put numbers in **consecutive** order. In this exercise you will learn **terminal digit filing,** another method of numeric filing. In the terminal digit method, the numbers are filed in the same way as in consecutive filing (small number to high number) except there is a different way of reading numbers. In terminal digit filing, the numbers are read from *right to left* in small groups beginning with the terminal (last) group.

A **digit** is one number. Terminal digit filing is used when numbers have five or more digits. In the number 412336, the digits could be separated into two groups of three digits each (412 336) or three groups of two digits each (41 23 36). You may find the groups divided by a hyphen (41-23-36). See the sample below.

<table>
<tr><td align="center"><u>3</u></td><td align="center"><u>2</u></td><td align="center"><u>1</u></td></tr>
<tr><td align="center">Last</td><td align="center">Second</td><td align="center">First</td></tr>
<tr><td align="center">41</td><td align="center">23</td><td align="center">36</td></tr>
</table>

Use Fig. 3-3 to help you find the folder 412336. Follow these steps:

1. Look at the terminal digit, 36. This is the drawer number.
2. Look for the file guide in the file drawer with the number, 23, the second digit in the terminal digit group.
3. Look for the folder after the number, 40, because 41 is the last digit group you are looking for.

Fig. 3-3 Example of Terminal Digit Filing

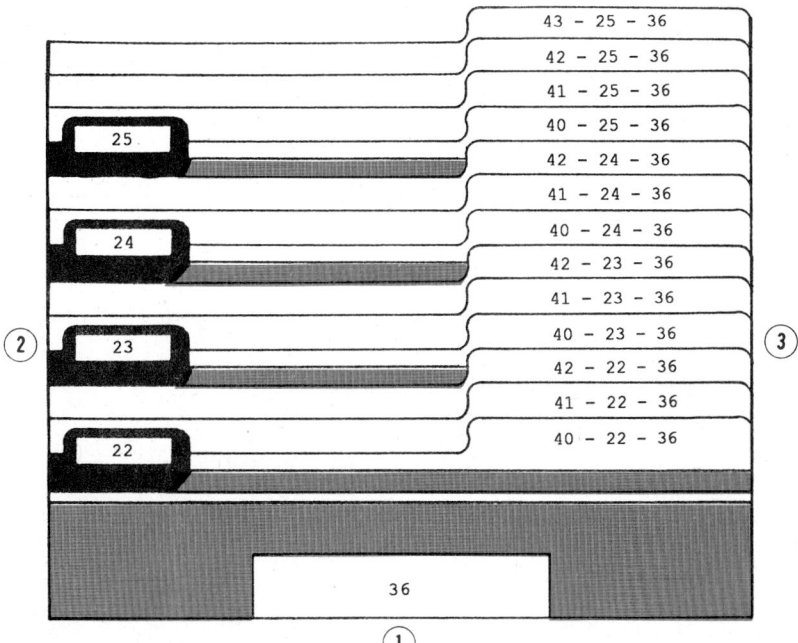

Look closely at the file drawer on page 219 to see the correct way to put folders in order. You see that the *first* group of numbers for the entire drawer is 36, which represents the file drawer number.

The file guides are in consecutive order: 22, 23, 24, and 25. Look at the digits in the second group. *Move from right to left.* All the 22 digits are behind the 22 guide; all the 23 digits are behind the 23 guide, and so on.

Look at the last group. *Move from right to left.* The digits 40, 41, and 42 are in consecutive order behind guide 22. Then the same digits, 40, 41, and 42 are in consecutive order behind guide 23.

Look at the file drawer on page 219 to help you with this exercise. Start at the bottom of the file drawer. Read to the top of the drawer. Put an X in the *Answers* column for a file folder out of order. The first X is shown as an example.

ANSWERS

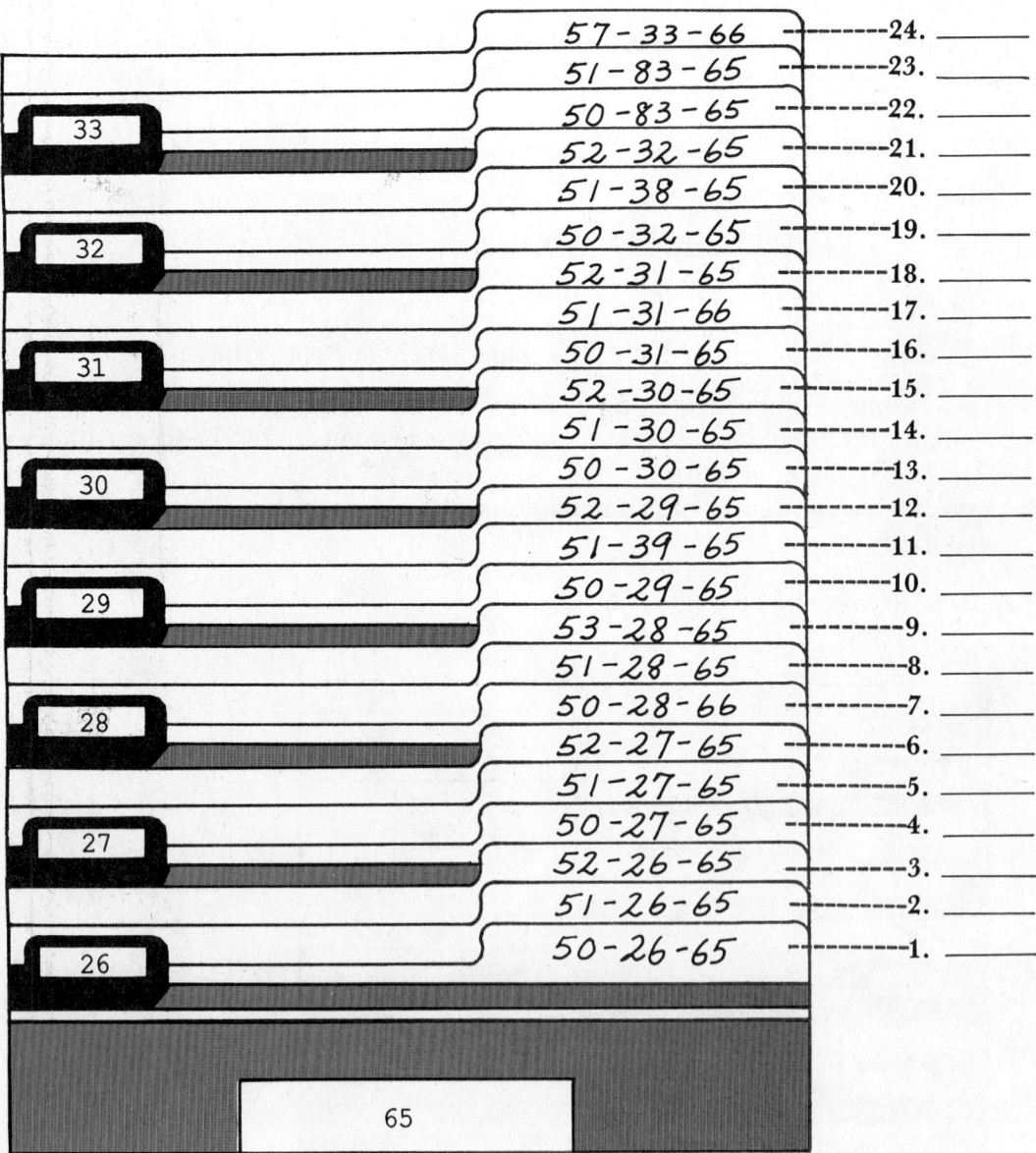

Folder	Answer
57 – 33 – 66	24. _____
51 – 83 – 65	23. _____
50 – 83 – 65	22. _____
52 – 32 – 65	21. _____
51 – 38 – 65	20. _____
50 – 32 – 65	19. _____
52 – 31 – 65	18. _____
51 – 31 – 66	17. _____
50 – 31 – 65	16. _____
52 – 30 – 65	15. _____
51 – 30 – 65	14. _____
50 – 30 – 65	13. _____
52 – 29 – 65	12. _____
51 – 39 – 65	11. _____
50 – 29 – 65	10. _____
53 – 28 – 65	9. _____
51 – 28 – 65	8. _____
50 – 28 – 66	7. _____
52 – 27 – 65	6. _____
51 – 27 – 65	5. _____
50 – 27 – 65	4. _____
52 – 26 – 65	3. _____
51 – 26 – 65	2. _____
50 – 26 – 65	1. _____

Guides: 33, 32, 31, 30, 29, 28, 27, 26 — 65

EXERCISE 85
Goal: To use reference sources to find information.

To find the answers to the questions below, use the Reference Sources of this text-workbook. Write or print your answers in the space at the end of the line.

ANSWERS

1a. The state of Alaska lies between which two countries?

1a. _____

1b. The Hawaiian Islands are in which ocean?

1b. _____

1c. Illinois is bordered on the north by which state?

1c. _____

2a. What is the total cost for one double sided, double density, 5.25″ disk, including 5 percent sales tax?

2a. _____

2b. What is the total cost for three WA77 Business Forms, including 6 percent sales tax?

2b. _____

2c. What is the total cost for three Auto Parts 00145573, including 4½ percent sales tax?

2c. _____

3a. What kind of aircraft is used on Flight 726?

3a. _____

3b. How many air miles are flown on Flight 304?

3b. _____

3c. What meal is served on Flight 304? (Use word, not letter.)

3c. _____

4a. What is the U.S. Postal Service fee for a 9-pound fourth-class, parcel to ZIP Code 75203? Also, add a charge for special handling.

4a. _____

4b. What is the cost to mail 12 single post cards?

4b. _____

4c. What is the fee for a 10-ounce, first-class letter sent special delivery?

4c. _____

5a. What is the number of miles from Raleigh to Dallas?

5a. _____

5b. What is the number of miles from New Orleans to Atlanta to Charleston?

5b. _____

5c. What is the number of miles from Jacksonville to Washington to Lexington?

5c. _____

EXERCISE 86
Goal: To improve handwriting and spelling.

Follow the same steps that you used in Exercise 2 as you finish this exercise. Your goal is to improve your handwriting and your spelling. *Do not write too fast.* Pronounce the word in syllables and as a word.

1. *ac cu ra cy* _____

2. *cau tious* _____

3. *de lin quent* _____

4. *e ven tu al ly* _____

5. *fail ure* _____

6. *guar an tee* _____

7. *im mense* _____

8. *jo vi al* _____

9. *li a bil i ty* _____

10. *ne go ti ate* _____

11. *oc ca sion* _____

12. *pos ses sion* _____

13. *sub mit* _____

14. *ter mi nate* _____

15. *wit ness* _____

EXERCISE 87
Goal: To see if cities and ZIP Codes are exactly the same.

Look at the cities and ZIP Codes in Column 1 and the cities and ZIP Codes in Column 2. If the two cities and codes are the same, fill in the space under the *a* in Column 3. If the two cities and codes are not the same, fill in the space under the *b* in Column 3.

COLUMN 1	COLUMN 2	COLUMN 3
		a b
1. Fort Devens, MA 01433-2874	Fort Devens, MA 01433-2874	1. || ||
2. Fontana, WI 53125-9327	Fontana, WS 53125-9327	2. || ||
3. Myakka City, FL 33551-8347	Myakka City, Fl 33551-8347	3. || ||
4. Hueytown, AL 35020-6693	Hueytown, AL 35020-6693	4. || ||
5. Pittsburg, CA 94565-2828	Pittsburgh, CA 94565-2828	5. || ||
6. New Salem, IL 62357-4593	New Salem, IL 62375-4593	6. || ||
7. Clitherall, MN 56524-8349	Clitherall, MN 56524-8349	7. || ||
8. Medford, OK 73759-2913	Medford, OH 73759-2913	8. || ||
9. Henrieville, UT 84736-1634	Henrieville, UT 84786-1634	9. || ||
10. Grand Glaise, AR 72056-6217	Grand Glaise, AR 72056-6217	10. || ||
11. Maurepas, LA 70449-3182	Maurapas, LA 70449-3182	11. || ||
12. Woonsocket, RI 02895-1437	Woonsocket, RI 02895-1437	12. || ||
13. Scottsdale, AZ 85253-4177	Scottdale, AZ 85253-4177	13. || ||
14. Elmendorf, TX 78112-3976	Elmendorf, TX 781112-3976	14. || ||
15. Quilcene, WA 98376-4731	Quilcene, WA 98367-4731	15. || ||

EXERCISE 88
Goal: To add words to your vocabulary.

The words in Column 1 are among those words most frequently mispronounced and misspelled. Spend time in study and in drill before you finish the exercise. In your home study, pronounce the words as they are divided in Column 2. Drill on the correct spelling and meanings. You will find these words and meanings on the unit test.

COLUMN 1	COLUMN 2	COLUMN 3
1. accuracy	ac-cu-ra-cy	correctness, exactness, precision, reliability, evenness
2. cautious	cau-tious	careful, vigilant, watchful, guarded, leery
3. delinquent	de-lin-quent	late, negligent, faulty, remiss, in the wrong
4. eventually	e-ven-tu-al-ly	finally, ultimately, in the end, at last, after all
5. failure	fail-ure	decline, defeat, lapse, loser, falling short
6. guarantee	guar-an-tee	security, token, pledge, warranty, vouch for
7. immense	im-mense	huge, great, vast, mighty, enormous
8. jovial	jo-vi-al	merry, happy, jolly, cheerful, lively
9. liability	li-a-bil-i-ty	something owed, obligation, drawback, handicap, disadvantage
10. negotiate	ne-go-ti-ate	bargain, transact, arrange, settle
11. occasion	oc-ca-sion	event, occurrence, happening, festival, celebration
12. possession	pos-ses-sion	ownership, title, custody, monopoly, control
13. submit	sub-mit	give up, offer, propose, surrender, present
14. terminate	ter-mi-nate	stop, end, cease, cut off, complete
15. witness	wit-ness	see, observe, viewer, bystander, observer

Read each sentence carefully. Look at the meaning under the space with the number. In the *Answers* space, write or print the word from today's word list that matches the meaning.

ANSWERS

_____(1)_____ in keyboarding is a necessary skill for
correctness
employment in the electronic office.

1. _____

The young children created a _____(2)_____ atmo-
happy
sphere.

2. _____

Does the tournament _____(3)_____ before the winter
                          end
holidays?

3. _____

Did Judge Roane call more than one _____(4)_____?   4. _____
                                      observer

Lack of rain was a cause of the _____(5)_____ of the
                               falling short
farmers' peach crops.

5. _____

The flu epidemic was a _____(6)_____ to our good
                        handicap
attendance record.

6. _____

Take _____(7)_____steps when you mountain-climb.   7. _____
       careful

Attitude is a trait of _____(8)_____importance in job
                        great
success.

8. _____

Do not be _____(9)_____in returning the library books.   9. _____
           late

A bud will _____(10)_____ develop into a beautiful
            finally
flower.

10. _____

Use an apostrophe and an *s* to show _____(11)_____ of
                                      ownership
nouns.

11. _____

The company offered a one-year _____(12)_____ on all
                                warranty
repairs.

12. _____

_____(13)_____ your suggestions for improving service to
 offer
the cafeteria manager.

13. _____

High school graduation is a special _____(14)_____ in
                                     happening
life.

14. _____

The employees and management will _____(15)_____ a
                                   bargain
new union contract next month.

15. _____

EXERCISE 89
Goal: To learn about speakerphones and to use office files/databases to find answers to questions.

A **speakerphone** is a phone you can use without holding a receiver in your hand. A speakerphone is connected to a desk telephone. When the telephone rings, you answer by pressing a button that turns on the speakerphone. You may talk from anywhere in the room since you talk and listen without the telephone receiver in your hand. A microphone inside the speakerphone receives the conversation. The person on the other line can hear you as you usually sound over the telephone.

You may also have a conference using a speakerphone. Three or more persons may use the speakerphone as a way of holding a conference with individuals located outside the company. In this exercise you will answer questions in a conference call.

You are working for the Convention Planners Bureau, a business that sets up meetings, conferences, and conventions for large groups, such as the Southwestern Automation Association.

Illus. 3-4 Conference Call with a Speakerphone

Call 1

You have arranged a conference call with the switchboard operator at the Bureau. Your call includes four persons.

The long-distance call comes through the switchboard. The switchboard operator rings the telephone on the desk of Jeff Holt, your supervisor. You press the button on the speakerphone. You, Jeff Holt, and Amanda Feld are in Jeff Holt's office to hold a conference with the long-distance callers, Madeline Tipton and Mary Ellen Walker.

Madeline used the WATS (Wide Area Telephone Service) line to call from New Orleans. Persons call long distance on WATS without the service of a telephone company operator. Convention Planners Bureau pays for the WATS line as a special service. You could also use the WATS line to call Madeline in New Orleans.

You are ready for the conference. The speakerphone is turned on. The operator has Madeline and Mary Ellen waiting on the WATS line.

YOU	Good morning, Madeline and Mary Ellen. I have Jeff Holt and Amanda Feld with me to make plans for the Southwestern Automation Conference.
MADELINE	Thank you. I have Mary Ellen Walker here with me also. We need to select two persons for the session on Thursday at 9:30 a.m. We already have three members of the panel.
AMANDA	May I suggest Dr. Steven Naylon? He has registered for the conference.
MARY ELLEN	Yes, he is excellent on a panel. Is he still in Lafayette?
(PAUSE)	(Find the answer to her question.)
YOU	No, Dr. Naylon's address is _____ NUMBER AND STREET NAME in _____. The ZIP Code is _____. CITY, STATE
MADELINE	Jeff, do you have any suggestions for the other panelist?
JEFF	Yes, I think Delores Ingram is always in demand as a speaker. She is also registered for the conference.
MADELINE	May I have her telephone number?
(PAUSE)	(Find the number for her.)
YOU	Her number in Houma, Louisiana, is _____. AREA CODE NUMBER
MADELINE	Thank you, _____. We have two more YOUR FIRST NAME sessions where we need a speaker. Does anyone have suggestions?
AMANDA	The microfiche files should have subjects and persons to help us.
MARY ELLEN	Yes, that is a good idea. Barbi Orr will speak for us. How is she listed on the microfiche list?

(PAUSE)	(Look in the Office Files/Databases for the answer to her question.)
YOU	Her specialty is _____.
JEFF	We need someone for a session on laser printing. Whose name do we have on file?
(PAUSE)	(Find the answer to his question.)
YOU	_____. FIRST NAME, LAST NAME
AMANDA	In case someone cannot speak, we need to have two persons to call. We always find networking and computer security as two popular sessions at an automation conference. Whom do you have for those specialties?
(PAUSE)	(Find the answer to her question.)
YOU	_____ is an expert in networking and FIRST NAME, LAST NAME _____ is an expert in computer security. FIRST NAME, LAST NAME
MADELINE	I thank each of you for helping me with these names. I will call you after I have more information on the conference. Good-bye.
YOU	Thank you, Madeline and Mary Ellen. Good-bye.

Note: You used the first names of everyone in the conference. Only one person spoke at a time. Your answers were brief. You started and ended the conference.

Call 2

Russ Olla uses the COM line on his desk telephone to dial your telephone. You answer his call on the speakerphone.

RUSS	Good afternoon, _____. I am Russ Olla in the YOUR FIRST NAME Special Events office. Do you have a microfiche list I could use for a computer conference that I am planning for high school students?

YOU   Yes, I do, _____. Do you want a particular person or
                       HIS FIRST NAME
             subject?

RUSS   Yes, we have used Jenny Kite as a speaker. Students always like her. I

             also think the education and training list would have good speakers.

             Can you find Jenny's specialty and the speakers from education?

YOU   Yes, I can. I have the microfiche list on the rotary file on my desk.

(PAUSE)   (You did not put Russ on hold because you are talking to him on the

             speakerphone. Find the answers to his questions.)

             Jenny Kite is an expert in _____. For

             education   and   training   speakers,   you   should   call

             _____.

RUSS   Thank you very much. Good-bye.

YOU   You are welcome. Good-bye.

EXERCISE 90
Goal: To see if credit card numbers are exactly alike.

Look at the credit card number in Column 1 and the credit card number in Column 2. If the two numbers are exactly alike, fill in the space under the *a* in Column 3. If the two numbers are not alike, fill in the space under the *b* in Column 3.

COLUMN 1	COLUMN 2	COLUMN 3
		a b
1. 4000 8901 2345 6789	4000 8901 2345 6789	1. ‖ ‖
2. 5380 1368 2004 0217	4380 1368 2004 0217	2. ‖ ‖
3. 2453 1080 7732 9038	2453 1080 7132 9038	3. ‖ ‖
4. 8865 5395 2018 2539	8865 5395 2018 2539	4. ‖ ‖
5. 1167 3060 5737 2435	1176 3060 5737 2435	5. ‖ ‖
6. 6030 1815 5348 8234	6030 1815 5348 8234	6. ‖ ‖
7. 9914 6748 8003 3553	9974 6748 8003 3553	7. ‖ ‖
8. 3276 6151 4020 9926	3276 6151 4020 9926	8. ‖ ‖
9. 5603 3771 4003 9296	5603 3771 4003 9296	9. ‖ ‖
10. 7274 9294 7740 3015	7274 9294 7740 3075	10. ‖ ‖
11. 6395 5682 1173 5942	6395 5682 1173 5942	11. ‖ ‖
12. 2118 4438 2773 5558	2118 4438 2773 5558	12. ‖ ‖
13. 9003 6762 2654 9174	9008 6762 2654 9174	13. ‖ ‖
14. 3490 2007 2836 5529	3490 2007 2386 5529	14. ‖ ‖
15. 7682 3279 9448 2001	7682 3279 9443 2001	15. ‖ ‖

EXERCISE 91
Goal: To index hyphenated names and compound names for filing.

RULE 12   The name of a person separated with a hyphen (Allen-White) is indexed as one unit. The hyphen is not used. *Allen-White* is indexed as one unit with no hyphen—*AllenWhite*. The name of a business or place separated with hyphens (Shop-N-Save) is indexed as one unit. The hyphen is not used. *Shop-N-Save* is indexed as one unit with no hyphens—*ShopNSave*.

Table 3-4   Examples of Rule 12

Name Before Indexing	INDEXING ORDER			
	Key Unit	Unit 2	Unit 3	Unit 4
Kimberly Jo Albright, RN	Albright	Kimberly	Jo	RN
All-Bright Car Wash	AllBright	Car	Wash	
Allbrighten Motor Express, Inc.	Allbrighten	Motor	Express	Inc
Allbrighton's Variety Stores	Allbrightons	Variety	Stores	
Miss San-li Sheng	Sheng	Sanli	Miss	
Father Amos South	South	Amos	Father	
South Way Bowling Lanes	South	Way	Bowling	Lanes
South's Best Bar-B-Que	Souths	Best	BarBQue	
Southway Graphics, Inc.	Southway	Graphics	Inc	
South-Way Lumber Co.	SouthWay	Lumber	Co	
South-West Messenger Taxi	SouthWest	Messenger	Taxi	
Verita Lucille South-Wester, CPS	SouthWester	Verita	Lucille	CPS
South-Western Video Center	SouthWestern	Video	Center	
Prof. E. Jonathan Southwesterny	Southwesterny	E	Jonathan	Prof

The cards shown below are *not* in correct alphabetic order. Use Rule 12 and finish this exercise. Follow these steps:

1. Put the cards in correct alphabetic order.
2. In the *Answers* column, print the letter before the name shown on the card.
3. The first card in correct order will be on Line 1. The last card will be on Line 10.

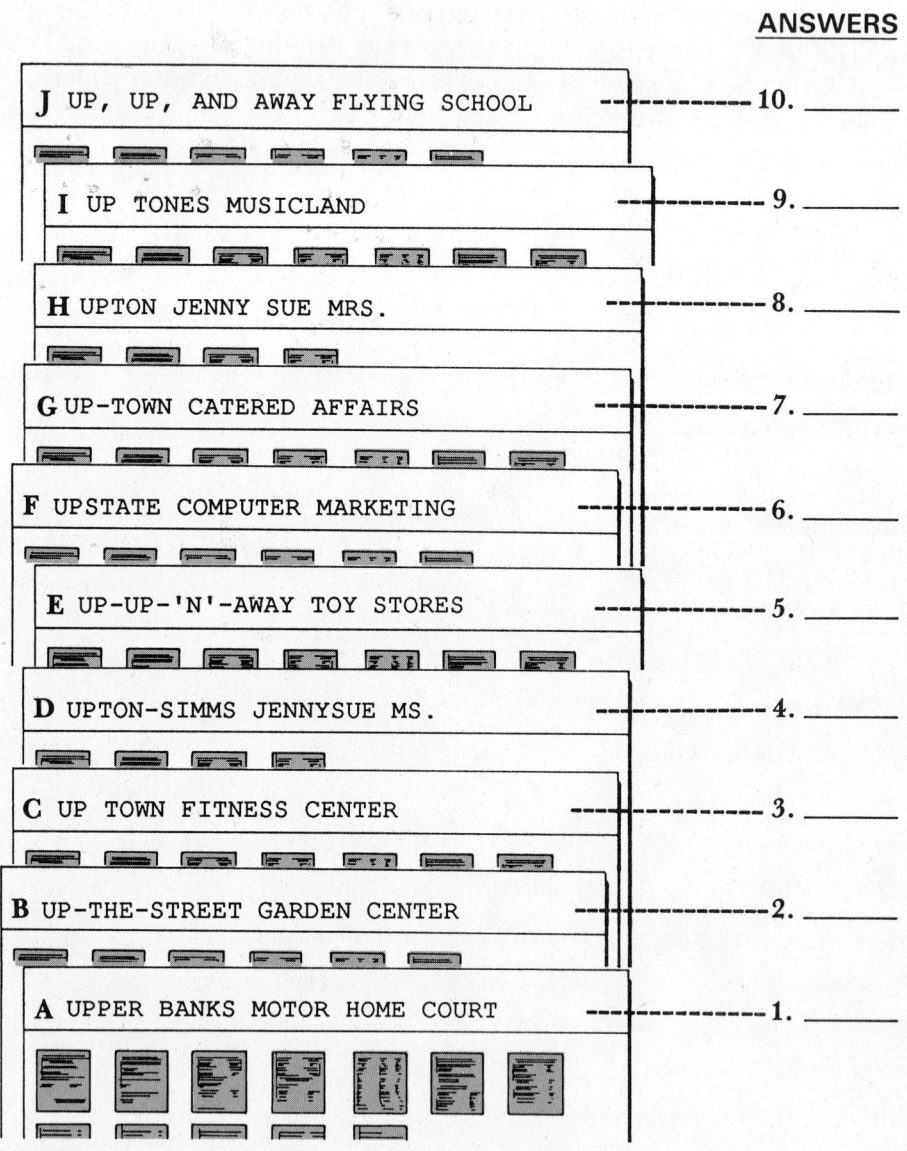

J UP, UP, AND AWAY FLYING SCHOOL --------------- 10. _____

I UP TONES MUSICLAND --------------- 9. _____

H UPTON JENNY SUE MRS. --------------- 8. _____

G UP-TOWN CATERED AFFAIRS --------------- 7. _____

F UPSTATE COMPUTER MARKETING --------------- 6. _____

E UP-UP-'N'-AWAY TOY STORES --------------- 5. _____

D UPTON-SIMMS JENNYSUE MS. --------------- 4. _____

C UP TOWN FITNESS CENTER --------------- 3. _____

B UP-THE-STREET GARDEN CENTER --------------- 2. _____

A UPPER BANKS MOTOR HOME COURT --------------- 1. _____

Unit 3C

RULE 13   A compound name has two words (Rose Marie). If a space comes between the two words, the names are two indexing units. *Rose Marie Cruz* is three units. Although *St. Mark* is a compound name, *St.* (Saint) is a word beginning. Follow Rule 7 and index *St. Mark* as one indexing unit (StMark). Compound business or place names with spaces between the parts of the names are separate indexing units. *North Carolina* and *Mid West* have two separate indexing units each.

Table 3-5   Examples of Rule 13

Name Before Indexing	INDEXING ORDER			
	Key Unit	Unit 2	Unit 3	Unit 4
Mid Western Hunting Preserve	Mid	Western	Hunting	Preserve
Ms. Annie Sue Midas	Midas	Annie	Sue	Ms
Mrs. Anniesue L. Midas	Midas	Anniesue	L	Mrs
Mid-Western Travel Agency	MidWestern	Travel	Agency	
North Dakota Iron-Art Works	North	Dakota	IronArt	Works
Timothy Jay Northard	Northard	Timothy	Jay	
Sainte Mary's Academy	SainteMarys	Academy		
Selmon D. Saint Louis	SaintLouis	Selmon	D	
Saint-Mori Fruit Shippers	SaintMori	Fruit	Shippers	
San Diego Botanical Gardens	SanDiego	Botanical	Gardens	
St. Augustine Book Nook	StAugustine	Book	Nook	
St. Charles Avenue Pet Store	StCharles	Avenue	Pet	Store

The cards shown in the file drawer below are *not* in correct alphabetic order. Use Rule 13 and finish this exercise. Follow these steps:

1. Put the cards in correct alphabetic order.
2. In the *Answers* column, print the letter before the name shown on the card.
3. The first card in correct order will be on Line 1. The last card will be on Line 10.

J SOUTH WAY TRUCKING LINES	10. ____
I SANI-FIRST CLEANING CONTRACTORS	9. ____
H SAN JUAN SWIMWEAR MAKERS	8. ____
G SAINT THOMAS COLLECTOR'S CORNER	7. ____
F SAYNE-WISE EDNAJO D MRS	6. ____
E SOUTH CAROLINA TEXTILES INC	5. ____
D S'N'S FACTORY OUTLET	4. ____
C ST JOSEPH SECOND-HAND STORE	3. ____
B SANTA ANA SOFTWARE HOUSE	2. ____
A SAN CARLOS EDNA JO MS	1. ____

S

S

238

Unit 3C

EXERCISE 92
Goal: To improve writing numbers.

Write the claim numbers in Column 1 in the boxes in Column 2. An example is shown.

COLUMN 1   ## COLUMN 2

488-27-3095-D   0.

Claim Number From Health Insurance Card

| 4 | 8 | 8 | 2 | 7 | 3 | 0 | 9 | 5 | D |

156-59-8703-K   1.

Claim Number From Health Insurance Card

714-02-3697-L   2.

Claim Number From Health Insurance Card

200-84-0172-P   3.

Claim Number From Health Insurance Card

618-35-9449-R   4.

Claim Number From Health Insurance Card

334-79-2741-S   5.

Claim Number From Health Insurance Card

809-47-6284-Y   6.

Claim Number From Health Insurance Card

UNIT 3D

EXERCISE 93
Goal: To improve spelling and handwriting of proper names of states, capitals, and territories.

As you write and spell the proper names in this exercise, follow the same steps that you used in the other handwriting and spelling exercises of proper names. *Do not write too fast.* You will have these same proper names on the unit test. Spend time during your home study to review these proper names.

Prov i dence, Rhode Is land

Tal la has see, Flor i da

O kla ho ma City, O kla ho ma

Charles ton, West Vir gin ia

Jack son, Mis sis sip pi

Bos ton, Mas sa chu setts

Sacramento, California   *Indianapolis, Indiana*

_____   _____

_____   _____

_____   _____

Charlotte Amalie, Virgin Islands

_____

_____

_____

EXERCISE 94
Goal: To make decisions about printing on business forms.

Use the information shown below and fill in the college housing application form. Make your own decisions about correct printing, abbreviations, and placement.

The instructions in the college catalog are: "Your dormitory assignment, room number, and adviser will be filled in by the Admissions Counselor." Alan Campbell Dorminey was born in Columbus, Franklin County, Ohio, on February 4, 1974. He now lives in Rhododendron, Oregon 97049-1006, at 378 West Fieldstone Drive. His telephone number is (503) 555-3419. In case of emergency, call Gertrude Ifeakanwa, M.D., whose office telephone number is (503) 555-3385 and whose telephone number after hours is (503) 555-3000.

PITTMAN UNIVERSITY
HOUSING APPLICATION

PITTMAN PANTHERS

LAST NAME   FIRST NAME   MIDDLE NAME

STREET ADDRESS   APT. NO.   CITY, STATE, ZIP

AREA CODE   TELEPHONE NO.   BIRTH DATE   CITY, COUNTY, STATE OF BIRTH

IN CASE OF EMERGENCY, PERSON TO BE NOTIFIED   AREA CODE   TELEPHONE NUMBER

DORMITORY ASSIGNMENT   ROOM NO.   ADVISER

Use the information shown below and fill in the application form. Make your own decisions about correct printing, abbreviations, and placement.

Ms. Carlene Marie B. Rossum is available nine hours between 8 a.m. and dusk. Her phone number is 555-2296. Her street (and mailing) address is 12850 West Wesley Parkway, Stone Mountain, Georgia 30083-2775, Apartment 212-W. She is insured by the Statesboro Group; her policy expires on December 30 of the current year. She drives a blue, 1991 Omega Sportster, with Georgia license plate number 225GWM. Her social security number is 244-30-9041.

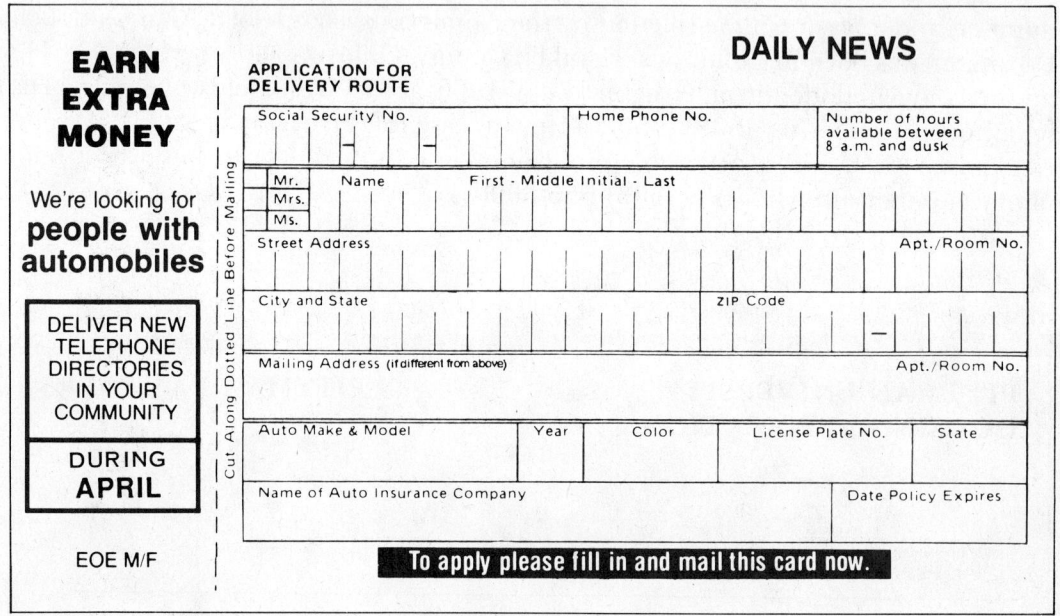

EXERCISE 95
Goal: To index government names for filing.

RULE 14

Federal The name of a federal government agency is indexed by the name of the government unit (United States Government) followed by the name of the office, bureau, department, etc., as written (Internal Revenue Service). The words "Office of," "Department of," "Bureau of," etc. are added *only if needed* for better understanding. The words are kept if they are already in the name. They are indexed as separate units.

> **Note:** If "of" is *not* a part of the name as written, it is *not* added.

State and Local The names of state, province, county, parish, city, town, township, and village governments or political divisions are indexed by their own names. The words "State of," "County of," "City of," "Department of," etc. are added *only if needed* for better understanding. The words are kept *if they are already in the name.* They are indexed as separate units.

Foreign The similar name in English is the first indexing unit for foreign government names. For example, *Estados Unidos Mexicanos* has the word, *Mexicanos,* which is close to the English word, Mexico. Mexico would be the first indexing unit. If needed, this English name is followed by the rest of the formal name of the government. Branches, departments, and divisions follow in order by their names. States, colonies, provinces, cities, and other divisions of foreign governments are followed by their names as spelled in English (Canada; Italy; or France, Paris). If necessary, cross-reference the written foreign name to the English name.

Table 3-6 Examples of Rule 14

NAME BEFORE INDEXING	INDEXING ORDER
Department of Commerce State of Florida Tallahassee, Florida	Florida State of 　Commerce Department of 　Tallahassee Florida
Department of Revenue State of Georgia Atlanta, Georgia	Georgia State of 　Revenue Department of 　Atlanta Georgia
Department of Labor State of Hawaii Honolulu, Hawaii	Hawaii State of 　Labor Department of 　Honolulu Hawaii

NAME BEFORE INDEXING	INDEXING ORDER
Bharat 　Rajya Sabha	India 　India Council of States
Sangamon County Department of Public Health Springfield, Illinois	Sangamon County 　Public Health Department of 　Springfield Illinois
Department of Safety Springfield, Illinois	Springfield 　Safety Department of 　Springfield Illinois
Animal and Plant Health Inspection 　Service Plant Protection and Quarantine U.S. Department of Agriculture	United States Government 　Agriculture Department of 　Animal and Plant Health Inspection 　　Service 　Plant Protection and Quarantine
Air Compliance Bureau Air, Pesticides, and Toxic 　Management Division U.S. Environmental Protection 　Agency	United States Government 　Environmental Protection Agency 　Air Pesticides and Toxic 　　Management Division 　Air Compliance Bureau
Atlanta Division Drug Enforcement Administration U.S. Department of Justice	United States Government Justice Department of 　Drug Enforcement Administration 　Atlanta Division

The index cards shown on page 247 are in *correct alphabetic* order. The indexing is *not* correct. Use the examples of Rule 14 and the sample shown below as a guide. Correct all indexing errors. Draw one line through the line on the card that is not correct. In the space at the right side of the card, write the correct indexing line. Not all cards have indexing errors.

San Bernardino County
~~Department of Children's Services~~ *Children's Services, Department of*
San Bernardino California

UNITED STATES GOVERNMENT
  Nuclear Regulatory Commission
  Division of Reactor Safety
  Operations Branch

UNITED STATES GOVERNMENT
  Labor Department of
  Bureau of Labor Statistics
  Operations Division of

UNITED STATES GOVERNMENT
  Refuges and Wildlife Division of
  Fish and Wildlife Service
  Department of Interior

PORTLAND MAINE
  Traffic Engineering Department of
  Portland

PONTIAC
  Parks and Recreation Department of
  Pontiac Michigan

PEORIA COUNTY
  Finance Department of
  Peoria Illinois

NEW JERSEY STATE OF
  Veterans Services Department of
  New Jersey Trenton

NEW HAMPSHIRE STATE OF
  Human Resources Department of
  Concord New Hampshire

NEVADA STATE OF
  Department of Corrections
  Carson City Nevada

NEBRASKA STATE OF
  Education Department of
  Lincoln Nebraska

EXERCISE 96
Goal: To make decisions about setting priorities.

In Exercise 83 you put activities into a list in the order of their importance. You decided which activity needed to be accomplished first.

In this exercise you will use the time of day to decide which activity has priority over the other activities. Make your own decisions about setting priorities for the activities you write on the Things to Do form on page 250. *Read all ten activities before you fill in the form.* Write or print the activities in their order of importance. Put only the necessary information about each activity on the form. *You need not copy the activity word for word as it is shown in the list.* Put the most important (or first) activity on Line 1. The last activity should be shown on Line 10. Use the current date. Working hours are from 8 a.m. until 5 p.m.

Listed below are the ten activities to be set in order:

1. Last thing before you leave office, remind night supervisor to set up conference room for meeting tomorrow.

2. Be at Peoples National Bank at 3 p.m. for closing of loan. Allow 30 minutes.

3. Just before lunch, call Carlos Fuentes of Del Rio Products at 555-2885.

4. When you leave the dentist, deliver the order to Daniels and Williams. Allow 25 minutes to drive.

5. Return to office by 4 p.m. to call Lillian Noble with the Visitors and Tourists Bureau at 555-0218.

6. First thing when you arrive at the office, call Sylvia Byrum with Wise Electronics in Winston-Salem, NC, at area code 704, telephone number 555-2300, extension 88.

7. At 1:45 meet Clare Lear to tour her new car dealership. Allow one hour.

8. At 6:30 this evening attend Desktop Publishing Seminar at Prescott Hotel.
9. Meet Captain Farrell of the Salvation Army at noon at United Way kick-off luncheon at Biltmore Plaza Hotel. Allow 1½ hours.
10. Be at dentist at 9:30 a.m. for a one-hour appointment.

THINGS TO DO
TODAY

DATE: _____

1. _____

2. _____

3. _____

4. _____

5. _____

6. _____

7. _____

8. _____

9. _____

10. _____

Unit 3D

EXERCISE 97
Goal: To make decisions about printing on forms.

Use the information shown below to complete the order form on page 252. Make your own decisions about correct printing, abbreviations, and placement.

Maddie Harris's friend, Ronald Martin, is planning a vacation in Florida. Maddie knows that Ronald has always wanted to go snorkeling to see the colorful fish in the Florida waters. So, as a surprise, Maddie has decided to send him an early birthday present—snorkeling equipment. Maddie will order this equipment from the Sports Spectrum catalog and mail it directly to Ronald.

Maddie orders one of each of the following items for Ronald:

Catalog Number	Description	Color	Price
1763-FMS	Standard Face Mask	Blue	$ 5.00
1985-FM	Medium Water Fins	Green	13.00
2001-S	Snorkel	Green	4.00

Maddie Harris lives at 498 Main Street, Cherokee, Iowa 51012-4002. Her daytime phone is (712) 555-6414. Her evening telephone number is (712) 555-1489. These items are to be shipped to Ronald Martin, 6888 Loras Avenue, Dubuque, Iowa 52001-4003. The gift card message should read "Have a great vacation." The card should read from Maddie. Be sure to add the shipping, packing, handling, and insurance charge of $4.25 to the total order. Maddie will pay for this purchase with her Americard. Her card number is 469-669-4095-783. Her card will expire on 9/94. Make sure you put Maddie's signature on the order form.

**Rainbow Circle
Daytona Beach, FL 32014-0143
(904) 555-1113**

Ordered by:

Name _____

c/o _____

Address _____

City _____ State _____ Zip _____

Daytime Phone ( ) _____ Evenings ( ) _____

Ship to: (Only if different from "Ordered by")

Name _____

c/o _____

Address _____

City _____ State _____ Zip _____

Gift Card Message _____

From _____

*Call us toll-free 24 hours a day, 7 days a week
to charge your order: 1-800-555-3110*

Catalog Number	Page No.	Description	Size	Color	Alternate Color Choice	Qty.	Price Total
| | |–| | | |							
| | |–| | | |							
| | |–| | | |							
| | |–| | | |							
| | |–| | | |							
| | |–| | | |							
| | |–| | | |							
| | |–| | | |							
					Shipping, Packing, Handling, and Insurance		4 25
						Total	

Method of payment:

☐ Charge to my *(circle one)*:

   AMERICARD

   NATIONAL EXPRESS

☐ Check or Money Order Enclosed

**Please include credit card number and
expiration date with charge orders!**

Expiration Date [Month / Year]

Thank You!

x _____
Signature (as shown on credit card)

EXERCISE 98
Goal: To use reference sources to find information.

To find the answers to the questions below, use the Reference Sources of this text-workbook. Write or print your answers in the space at the end of the line.

ANSWERS

1. What is the UPS fee for a
    a. 35-pound commercial parcel to ZIP Code 82733?   **1a.** _____
    b. 17-pound residential parcel to ZIP Code 29193?   **1b.** _____
    c. 26-pound next day air parcel to ZIP Code 93381?   **1c.** _____

2a. Who is the author of *Personality Development for Work*?   **2a.** _____

2b. What is the title of the English book written by Norman Schacter and Alfred T. Clark, Jr.?   **2b.** _____

2c. What is the name of the publisher of the job search book by Martin John Yate?   **2c.** _____

3a. What is the stock number of paper clips?   **3a.** _____

3b. What is the balance on the stock record card for stock number AG88 on September 11?   **3b.** _____

3c. What is the balance of stock number AG88 on September 10? (You did not make an entry. You only look at the balance.)   **3c.** _____

4a. How many degrees is the temperature forecast to *rise* (from low to high) in Juneau on Thursday?   **4a.** _____

4b. In which city is the temperature forecast *lowest* on Wednesday: Charleston, SC; Charlotte, NC; or Columbia, SC?   **4b.** _____

4c. Of the three cities (Houston, Jackson, Omaha), which has the *best* weather forecast on Wednesday?   **4c.** _____

5a. What is the proofreader's mark for *insert period*?   **5a.** _____

5b. What mark would you use to correct *theproof*?   **5b.** _____

5c. What does the mark *DS* mean?   **5c.** _____

6a. What river runs along the Texas–Mexico border?   **6a.** _____

6b. In what state will you find the Great Salt Lake?   **6b.** _____

6c. What is the capital of Massachusetts?   **6c.** _____

EXERCISE 99
Goal: To add words to your vocabulary.

The words in Column 1 are among those words most frequently mispronounced and misspelled. Spend time in study and in drill before you finish the exercise. In your home study, pronounce the words as they are divided in Column 2. Drill on the correct spelling and meanings. You will find these words and meanings on the unit test.

COLUMN 1	COLUMN 2	COLUMN 3
1. allotted	al-lot-ted	divided, measured, rationed, doled out, distributed
2. candidate	can-di-date	office seeker, nominee, applicant, contestant, contender
3. distinct	dis-tinct	different, clear, unconnected, audible, visible
4. explanation	ex-pla-na-tion	reason, answer, meaning, description, interpretation
5. fragrance	fra-grance	perfume, scent, odor, smell, aroma
6. handsome	hand-some	good looking, beautiful, attractive, pleasing, generous
7. individual	in-di-vid-u-al	person, somebody, unique, lone, distinct
8. jubilee	ju-bi-lee	celebration, festival, holiday, fete, frolic
9. mutilate	mu-ti-late	damage, spoil, destroy, demolish, butcher
10. notify	no-ti-fy	make known, inform, announce, tell, publish
11. opponent	op-po-nent	foe, competitor, challenger, enemy, rival
12. prohibit	pro-hib-it	ban, forbid, prevent, obstruct, constrain
13. surplus	sur-plus	extra, leftover, overload, excess, overage
14. unnecessary	un-nec-es-sa-ry	unneeded, unrequired, needless, superfluous, useless
15. wealthiest	wealth-i-est	richest, most affluent, most prosperous, most abundant

Look at the meanings in Column 1. Circle the *correctly spelled* word in Column 2 that matches the meanings in Column 1.

COLUMN 1	COLUMN 2
1. inform, tell	notafy notify notefy notufy
2. leftover, extra	surpulus serplus surplus suplus
3. reason, answer	explainaton explination explernation explanation
4. unneeded, unrequired	unneccesery unnessisary unnecessary unnesessary
5. celebration, festival	jubilee jubalee jubelee jubulee
6. richest, most abundant	wealtheriest wealthiest wealtherest wealtiest
7. foe, competitor	oponent opponnent opponent opponnant
8. odor, perfume	fragrance fragrence fregrance fregrunce
9. different, clear	distink distinct disstink disstinct
10. nominee, applicant	canadate canerdate candidate canudate
11. damage, spoil	mutilate mudilate muttilate mudulate
12. divided, rationed	allottid alloted alotted allotted
13. forbid, prevent	perhibit prohibit prehibit prohibbit
14. person, lone	indivijual indervidual indavidual individual
15. good looking, attractive	handsom handsum handsome hansome

Unit 3D

EXERCISE 100
Goal: To fill in bubble forms.

Businesses often use "bubble" forms to put information into computer memory. Some forms require a special pen or pencil. When the bubbles have been filled in, the form is put into the scanner. The computer receives the information from the scanner.

Fig. 3-4 Sample Bubble Form

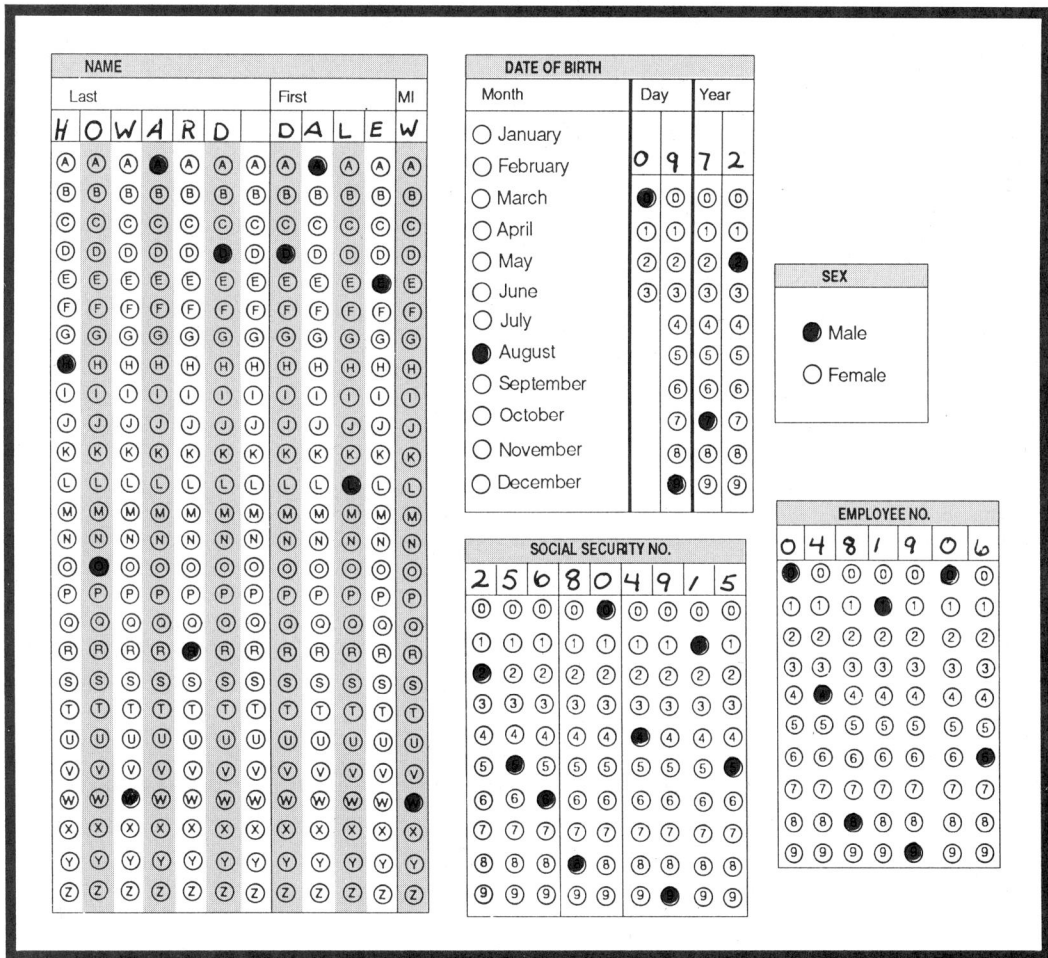

Use the information and forms on pages 258 and 259 to finish this exercise. Use the bubble form above as a guide. Before you bubble the name, date of birth, social security number, and employee number, write the information in the boxes above the bubbles. Print the last name, first name, and middle initial in ALL CAPITAL LETTERS. If a last name has more than seven letters in it, you will print the first seven letters of the name. For example, Shallenberger would be printed and bubbled SHALLEN. For a first name, you will print only four letters. For example, Stephanie would be printed and bubbled STEP.

Stephanie J. Shallenberger
Soc. Sec. No. 288-06-5229
Employee No. 0926093
Female, born September 1, 1959

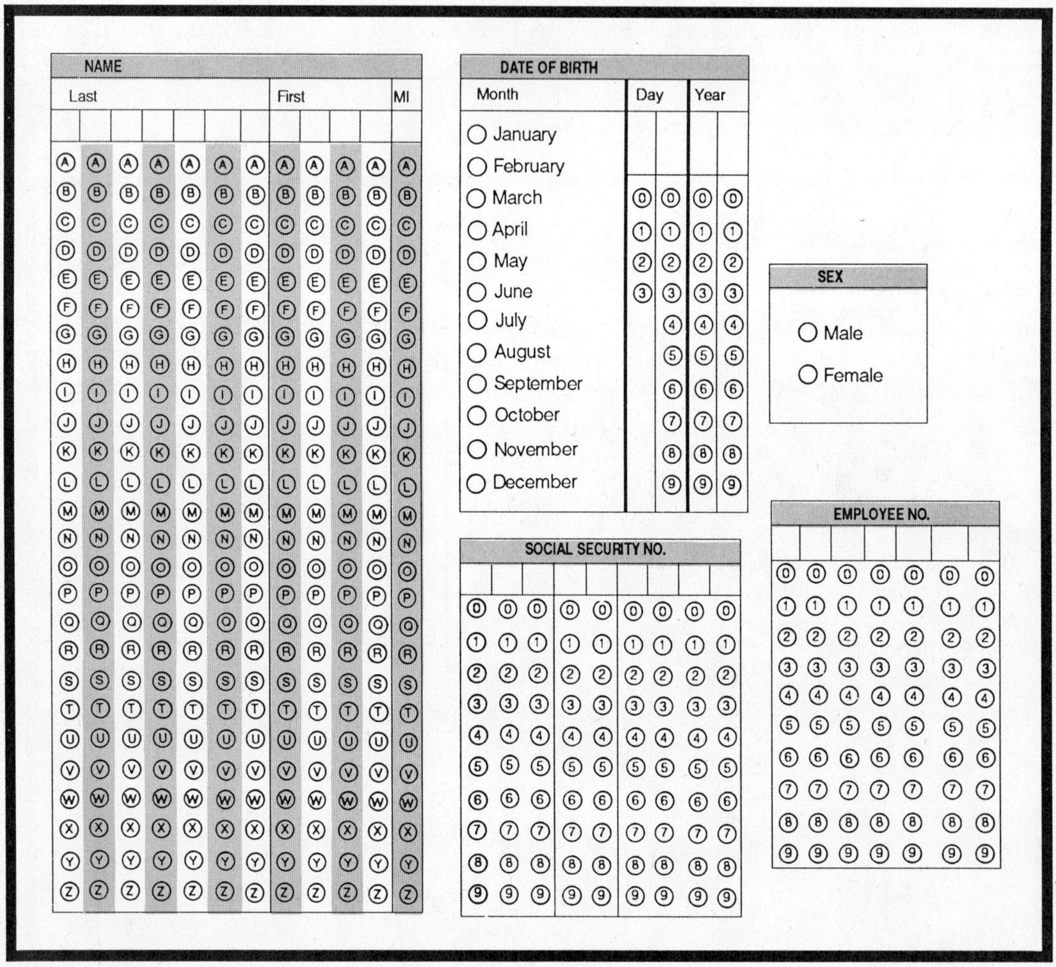

NAME											
Last							First				MI

(grid of bubbles A–Z for each letter position)

DATE OF BIRTH

Month	Day	Year
○ January		
○ February		
○ March	⓪ ⓪	⓪ ⓪
○ April	① ①	① ①
○ May	② ②	② ②
○ June	③ ③	③ ③
○ July	④	④ ④
○ August	⑤	⑤ ⑤
○ September	⑥	⑥ ⑥
○ October	⑦	⑦ ⑦
○ November	⑧	⑧ ⑧
○ December	⑨	⑨ ⑨

SEX

○ Male

○ Female

SOCIAL SECURITY NO.

(grid of bubbles 0–9 for each digit position)

EMPLOYEE NO.

(grid of bubbles 0–9 for each digit position)

Merlin R. Barrineau
Soc. Sec. No. 150-72-9480
Employee No. 0082608
Male, born May 12, 1962

NAME			
Last		First	MI

Letters A through Z in columns for Last name, First name, and MI.

DATE OF BIRTH		
Month	Day	Year

Months: ○ January, ○ February, ○ March, ○ April, ○ May, ○ June, ○ July, ○ August, ○ September, ○ October, ○ November, ○ December

Day and Year columns with digits 0–9.

SEX
○ Male
○ Female

SOCIAL SECURITY NO.

Digits 0–9 in columns.

EMPLOYEE NO.

Digits 0–9 in columns.

Congratulations! You have now finished the exercises for Unit 3. Before you ask your teacher for the unit test, study the vocabulary, spelling, and filing exercises in this unit. You will also need to know the states and capitals. Ask your teacher for instructions for turning in your work.

Exercise 100

REFERENCE SOURCES

delete

SP

CVG

$151.65

02052

[

543-6278

CONTENTS

These airport codes are alphabetized by the code letters. They are not alphabetized by city names. Sometimes airport codes and city names do not start with the same letter. The airport code for the Kansas City, MO airport is MCI. You may have to read the list carefully to find the airport you are looking for.

AIRPORT CODES

Codes	Cities	Codes	Cities
ABQ	Albuquerque, NM	LBB	Lubbock, TX
AMA	Amarillo, TX	LEX	Lexington, KY
ANC	Anchorage, AK	LGA	New York, NY (LaGuardia Airport)
ATL	Atlanta, GA	LNK	Lincoln, NE
AUS	Austin, TX	MCI	Kansas City, MO
BDL	Hartford, CT/Springfield, MA	MCO	Orlando, FL
BHM	Birmingham, AL	MEM	Memphis, TN
BNA	Nashville, TN	MGM	Montgomery, AL
BOS	Boston, MA	MIA	Miami, FL
BTR	Baton Rouge, LA	MOB	Mobile, AL
BUF	Buffalo, NY	MSY	New Orleans, LA
CAE	Columbia, SC	OMA	Omaha, NE
CVG	Cincinnati, OH	ONT	Ontario, Canada
DCA	Washington, DC	ORD	Chicago, IL
DEN	Denver, CO	PDX	Portland, OR
DFW	Dallas/Ft. Worth, TX	PHX	Phoenix, AZ
DTW	Detroit, MI	RDU	Raleigh/Durham, NC
ELP	El Paso, TX	ROC	Rochester, NY
EWR	Newark, NJ	SAN	San Diego, CA
FAI	Fairbanks, AK	SAT	San Antonio, TX
FLL	Ft. Lauderdale, FL	SDF	Louisville, KY
FOE	Topeka, KS	SEA	Seattle/Tacoma, WA
HNL	Honolulu, HI	SFO	San Francisco, CA
IAH	Houston, TX (International)	SHV	Shreveport, LA
ICT	Wichita, KS	SLC	Salt Lake City, UT
IND	Indianapolis, IN	TPA	Tampa/St. Petersburg, FL
JAN	Jackson, MS	TUL	Tulsa, OK
JFK	New York, NY (Kennedy Airport)	TUS	Tucson, AZ
LAS	Las Vegas, NV	TYS	Knoxville, TN
LAX	Los Angeles, CA	YUL	Montreal, QUE

FLIGHT INFORMATION

Flight Number	Cities Served	Air Miles	Flying Times	Meals Served	Aircraft Used
100	ATL-HNL	4502	9:24	B	L10
132	BOS-SFO	2704	5:17	L	DC10
166	TPA-MSY	487	1:23	L	L10
185	JFK-LAX	2475	5:30	D	DC10
190	MCC-BDL	1050	2:24	D	757
242	LGA-DEN	1632	4:01	B	767
258	YUL-MIA	1394	3:09	L	727
281	SEA-DFW	1660	3:31	D	757
290	ORD-LAS	1514	3:32	B	DC8
304	EWR-FLL	1072	2:35	B	DC8
333	MEM-DCA	733	1:48		727
355	CVG-IAH	889	2:05	D	DC9
411	SLC-PDX	630	1:36	B	727
435	SDF-LEX	63	:22		DC9
492	LNK-OMA	55	:25		727
505	IND-DTW	241	:45		DC9
536	ONT-SAN	94	:36		767
555	JAN-BTR	138	:31		737
603	LBB-AMA	108	:26		737
625	SHV-MOB	351	:56		DC9
660	MGM-BHM	90	:25		DC9
687	AUS-SAT	70	:32		727
704	TYS-BNA	152	:38		737
726	ANC-FAI	261	:53		767
778	PHX-TUS	109	:34		727
825	MCI-FOE	55	:27		737
861	ELP-ABQ	224	:53		737
895	ICT-TUL	132	:36		727
901	RDU-CAE	188	:46		737
972	BUF-ROC	55	:26		737

CODES FOR AIRCRAFT USED

DC8	Douglas DC8
DC9	Douglas DC9
DC10	Douglas DC10
L10	Lockheed L-1011
727	Boeing 727
737	Boeing 737
757	Boeing 757
767	Boeing 767

CODES FOR MEALS SERVED

B	Breakfast
L	Lunch
D	Dinner

FLYING TIMES

9:24 = 9 hours, 24 minutes
:45 = 45 minutes

Airlines

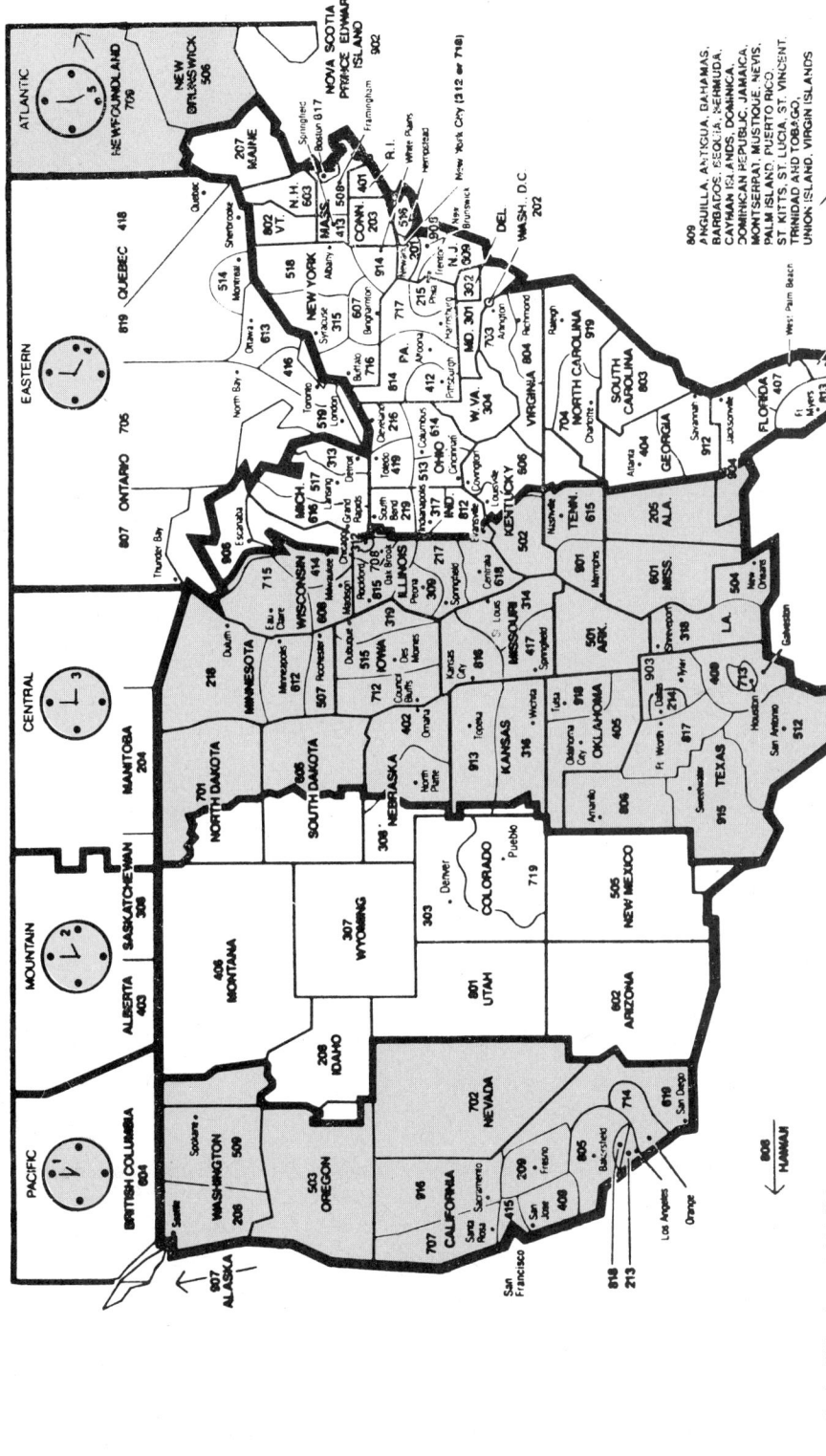

Area codes are shown as numbers within each state. Time zones are shown below the five clocks at the top of the chart. Read across the top of the chart to see the name of the time zone and time: Pacific, 1; mountain, 2; central, 3; eastern, 4; and Atlantic, 5. From these times you can learn that if it is 4 o'clock in the eastern time zone, it is 2 o'clock in the mountain time zone.

708 Area Code Effective 11/11/89
908 Area Code Effective 1/1/90
903 Area Code Effective 11/4/90

BUS/AIRPORT EXPRESS SCHEDULE

Rugby Manor	St. Anne on the River	Union Plaza	Arrive Airport	Rugby Manor	St. Anne on the River	Union Plaza	Arrive Airport
0500A	0505A	0510A	0555A	0200P	0205P	0210P	0255P
0530A	0535A	0540A	0625A	0230P	0235P	0240P	0325P
0600A	0605A	0610A	0655A	0300P	0305P	0310P	0355P
0630A	0635A	0640A	0725A	0330P	0335P	0340P	0425P
0700A	0705A	0710A	0755A	0400P	0405P	0410P	0455P
0730A	0735A	0740A	0825A	0430P	0435P	0440P	0525P
0800A	0805A	0810A	0855A	0500P	0505P	0510P	0555P
0830A	0835A	0840A	0925A	0530P	0535P	0540P	0625P
0900A	0905A	0910A	0955A	0600P	0605P	0610P	0655P
0930A	0935A	0940A	1025A	0630P	0635P	0640P	0725P
1000A	1005A	1010A	1055A	0700P	0705P	0710P	0755P
1030A	1035A	1040A	1125A	0730P	0735P	0740P	0825P
1100A	1105A	1110A	1155A	0800P	0805P	0810P	0855P
1130A	1135A	1140A	1225P	0830P	0835P	0840P	0925P
1200P	1205P	1210P	1255P	0900P	0905P	0910P	0955P
1230P	1235P	1240P	0125P	0930P	0935P	0940P	1025P
0100P	0105P	0110P	0155P	1000P	1005P	1010P	1055P
0130P	0135P	0140P	0225P				

All schedules can change due to delays caused by traffic and/or weather conditions.

Bus/Airport Express Schedule

| LONG-DISTANCE CALLS REGISTER | | | | Month of _July_ | | 19-- |

Date	Time	O/I*	Caller	Person Called	City Called	Number
19-- 7-1	9:15	O	Bette Dilbeck	Gary Idens	Joliet, IL	555-3782
7-1	2:05	O	Leroy Norton	Rosa Vazquez	Des Moines, IA	555-5814
7-5	8:20	O	Colleen Scott	Harley Mason	St. Louis, MO	555-1968
7-6	11:10	I	Danny Lavant	Butch Medina	Anaheim, CA	555-8650
7-8	9:05	O	Calvin Ivey	Nell Free	Hyattsville, MD	555-2431
7-10	1:15	O	Eula Garber	Goro Okano	Camden, NJ	555-7749
7-10	2:40	O	Carlos Ruiz	Annette Dano	Hilo, HI	555-1352
7-12	10:25	O	Lachanda Potts	Toshi Kato	Dayton, OH	555-6910
7-15	2:15	O	Kevin Huang	Clarke Ashley	Marco, FL	555-4521
7-18	11:30	O	Antonio Reese	Ester Salas	Chester, PA	555-9254
7-21	9:00	I	Elease Mayes	Howard Epps	Sumter, SC	555-1680
7-21	1:45	O	Rufus Vestal	Max Logan	Clio, AL	555-9443
7-22	10:15	O	Margo Barna	Lu-yin Wu	Detroit, MI	555-2735
7-22	3:00	O	Willie Turkel	Norma Briggs	Omaha, NE	555-8115
7-25	9:37	O	Zoe Ann Elkins	Grace Speer	Monroe, LA	555-5672
7-25	1:00	O	Li-ming Chang	Nolan Paine	Abilene, TX	555-1560
7-26	10:40	O	Peter Quinn	Rachael Gomez	Ogden, UT	555-6237
7-26	1:05	O	Geneva Ferrell	Chien Li	Dover, DE	555-3928
7-29	9:50	I	Randall Hattaway	Lillie Sue Olden	White Plains, NY	555-7576
7-29	1:12	O	Wylene Jenson	Eugene New	Littleton, CO	555-2184
7-29	3:50	O	Eduardo Lamas	Tim Taylor	Duluth, MN	555-4718
7-30	11:08	O	Gwynne Askew	Rebekah Caffon	Bend, OR	555-1420
7-31	2:45	O	Saul Klein	Juanita Ham	Nashva, NH	555-6359
7-31	3:30	O	Denise Upshaw	Lamar Russ	Dublin, IN	555-3567

* O, Outgoing; I, Incoming Collect

1314	BALANCE BROUGHT FORWARD	2,065	65
Mar 1 19 —			
General Gas Co.			
Monthly service			
DEPOSIT			
BALANCE			
AMOUNT THIS CHECK		85	65

1315	BALANCE BROUGHT FORWARD	1,980	00
Mar 3 19 —			
The Ching Co.			
Invoice 278			
Mar. 2 DEPOSIT		1,350	00
BALANCE		3,330	00
AMOUNT THIS CHECK		527	75

1316	BALANCE BROUGHT FORWARD	2,802	25
Mar 6 19 —			
United Parcel			
Service for			
April			
DEPOSIT			
BALANCE			
AMOUNT THIS CHECK		622	45

1317	BALANCE BROUGHT FORWARD	2,179	80
Mar 8 19 —			
Postmaster			
Meter Service			
Mar 8 DEPOSIT		1,240	00
BALANCE		3,419	80
AMOUNT THIS CHECK		500	00
BALANCE		2,919	80

1318	BALANCE BROUGHT FORWARD	2,919	80
Mar 9 19 —			
City of Kent			
License			
DEPOSIT			
BALANCE			
AMOUNT THIS CHECK		75	00

1319	BALANCE BROUGHT FORWARD	2,844	80
Mar 10 19 —			
Boxwood			
Gardens			
Florist bill			
DEPOSIT			
BALANCE			
AMOUNT THIS CHECK		85	75

1320	BALANCE BROUGHT FORWARD	2,759	05
Mar 18 19 —			
Daily News			
Ads			
Mar 15 DEPOSIT		1,850	00
BALANCE		4609	05
AMOUNT THIS CHECK		350	00

1321	BALANCE BROUGHT FORWARD	4,259	05
Mar 19 19 —			
Your Choice			
Answering Service			
April service			
DEPOSIT			
BALANCE			
AMOUNT THIS CHECK		180	00
BALANCE		4,079	05

1322	BALANCE BROUGHT FORWARD	4,079	05
Mar 22 19 —			
SYS Office			
Supplies			
Invoice 1386			
DEPOSIT			
BALANCE			
AMOUNT THIS CHECK		176	90

1323	BALANCE BROUGHT FORWARD	3,902	15
Mar 25 19 —			
Corner Service			
Auto repairs			
DEPOSIT			
BALANCE			
AMOUNT THIS CHECK		526	10

1324	BALANCE BROUGHT FORWARD	3,376	05
Mar 31 19 —			
Salvation Army			
Contribution			
Mar 27 DEPOSIT		2,209	95
BALANCE		5,586	00
AMOUNT THIS CHECK		500	00

1325	BALANCE BROUGHT FORWARD	5,086	00
Mar 31 19 —			
Kent Power Co.			
Electric bill			
DEPOSIT			
BALANCE			
AMOUNT THIS CHECK		230	00
BALANCE		4,856	00

Checkbook

UPS Ground Service

Commercial Deliveries
Delivery to a place of business†

WEIGHT NOT TO EXCEED	\$ 2	3	4	5	6	7	8
1 lb.	\$ 2.08	\$ 2.22	\$ 2.42	\$ 2.50	\$ 2.58	\$ 2.65	\$ 2.71
2	2.10	2.24	2.67	2.76	2.95	3.05	3.27
3	2.19	2.40	2.84	2.98	3.22	3.39	3.68
4	2.28	2.53	2.96	3.14	3.41	3.62	4.00
5	2.38	2.64	3.03	3.21	3.56	3.79	4.21
6	2.48	2.72	3.08	3.26	3.66	3.96	4.36
7	2.58	2.78	3.13	3.31	3.76	4.13	4.60
8	2.68	2.83	3.18	3.37	3.89	4.38	4.97
9	2.77	2.91	3.23	3.46	4.08	4.70	5.38
10	2.86	2.99	3.28	3.63	4.31	5.03	5.75
11	2.94	3.08	3.36	3.86	4.57	5.38	6.20
12	3.02	3.18	3.47	4.07	4.89	5.73	6.63
13	3.09	3.29	3.64	4.29	5.18	6.11	7.07
14	3.16	3.41	3.82	4.51	5.47	6.46	7.51
15	3.23	3.55	4.00	4.74	5.75	6.83	7.95
16	3.30	3.70	4.18	4.98	6.06	7.19	8.38
17	3.37	3.84	4.36	5.19	6.34	7.55	8.82
18	3.44	3.97	4.53	5.42	6.63	7.92	9.25
19	3.55	4.10	4.71	5.63	6.94	8.28	9.69
20	3.68	4.24	4.89	5.87	7.22	8.63	10.13
21	3.82	4.38	5.07	6.10	7.51	9.01	10.57
22	3.93	4.53	5.24	6.31	7.80	9.36	11.01
23	4.05	4.65	5.42	6.54	8.10	9.72	11.43
24	4.16	4.80	5.59	6.76	8.39	10.09	11.88
25	4.27	4.92	5.76	6.99	8.67	10.46	12.31
26	4.37	5.07	5.95	7.22	8.98	10.80	12.75
27	4.48	5.22	6.13	7.44	9.26	11.18	13.20
28	4.55	5.36	6.30	7.66	9.56	11.54	13.62
29	4.64	5.49	6.48	7.89	9.85	11.90	14.08
30	4.75	5.61	6.67	8.14	10.18	12.30	14.56
31	4.85	5.76	6.89	8.40	10.51	12.69	15.03
32	4.94	5.91	7.08	8.67	10.84	13.10	15.51
33	5.04	6.06	7.29	8.93	11.17	13.49	15.99
34	5.13	6.22	7.48	9.14	11.48	13.88	16.47
35	5.23	6.38	7.64	9.37	11.77	14.29	16.92

Residential Deliveries
Delivery to a home†

WEIGHT NOT TO EXCEED	\$ 2	3	4	5	6	7	8
1 lb.	\$ 2.53	\$ 2.67	\$ 2.87	\$ 2.95	\$ 3.03	\$ 3.10	\$ 3.16
2	2.55	2.69	3.12	3.21	3.40	3.50	3.72
3	2.64	2.85	3.29	3.43	3.67	3.84	4.13
4	2.73	2.98	3.41	3.59	3.86	4.07	4.45
5	2.83	3.09	3.48	3.66	4.01	4.24	4.66
6	2.93	3.17	3.53	3.71	4.11	4.41	4.81
7	3.03	3.23	3.58	3.76	4.21	4.58	5.05
8	3.13	3.28	3.63	3.82	4.34	4.83	5.42
9	3.22	3.36	3.68	3.91	4.53	5.15	5.83
10	3.31	3.44	3.73	4.08	4.76	5.48	6.20
11	3.39	3.53	3.81	4.31	5.02	5.83	6.65
12	3.47	3.63	3.92	4.52	5.34	6.18	7.08
13	3.54	3.74	4.09	4.74	5.63	6.56	7.52
14	3.61	3.86	4.27	4.96	5.92	6.91	7.96
15	3.68	4.00	4.45	5.19	6.20	7.28	8.40
16	3.75	4.15	4.63	5.43	6.51	7.64	8.83
17	3.82	4.29	4.81	5.64	6.79	8.00	9.27
18	3.89	4.42	4.98	5.87	7.08	8.37	9.70
19	4.00	4.55	5.16	6.08	7.39	8.73	10.14
20	4.13	4.69	5.34	6.32	7.67	9.08	10.58
21	4.27	4.83	5.52	6.55	7.96	9.46	11.02
22	4.38	4.98	5.69	6.76	8.25	9.81	11.46
23	4.50	5.10	5.87	6.99	8.55	10.17	11.88
24	4.61	5.25	6.04	7.21	8.84	10.54	12.33
25	4.72	5.37	6.21	7.44	9.12	10.91	12.76
26	4.82	5.52	6.40	7.67	9.43	11.25	13.20
27	4.93	5.67	6.58	7.89	9.71	11.63	13.65
28	5.00	5.81	6.75	8.11	10.01	11.99	14.07
29	5.09	5.94	6.93	8.34	10.30	12.35	14.53
30	5.20	6.06	7.12	8.59	10.63	12.75	15.01
31	5.30	6.21	7.34	8.85	10.96	13.14	15.48
32	5.39	6.36	7.53	9.12	11.29	13.55	15.96
33	5.49	6.51	7.74	9.38	11.62	13.94	16.44
34	5.58	6.67	7.93	9.59	11.93	14.33	16.92
35	5.68	6.83	8.09	9.82	12.22	14.74	17.37

UPS Air Service

UPS 2ND DAY AIR

WEIGHT NOT TO EXCEED	48 STATES 12	*ALASKA & HAWAII 14	PUERTO RICO 15	*ALASKA RURAL 16
LETTER	\$ 5.00	\$ 8.00	\$ 7.50	\$10.00
1 lb.	5.25	8.50	8.00	16.50
2	6.00	9.75	9.00	18.00
3	6.75	10.75	10.25	19.00
4	7.25	12.75	12.00	20.50
5	8.00	13.75	13.00	21.75
6	9.00	15.00	14.25	23.25
7	10.00	16.00	15.50	24.25
8	11.25	17.25	16.75	25.25
9	12.50	18.50	18.00	26.25
10	13.50	19.50	19.50	27.25
11	14.75	20.75	21.25	28.25
12	16.00	22.00	22.50	29.25
13	17.00	23.50	23.75	30.50
14	18.25	24.50	24.75	31.75
15	19.25	26.00	26.00	33.00
16	20.50	27.50	27.25	34.25
17	21.75	29.00	28.50	35.50
18	22.75	30.50	29.75	36.75
19	23.75	32.00	31.00	38.00
20	25.00	33.50	32.25	39.50
21	26.00	34.50	33.75	40.50
22	27.25	36.00	34.75	41.50
23	28.25	37.25	35.75	42.50
24	29.25	38.25	36.50	43.50
25	30.25	39.50	37.50	44.50
26	31.25	40.50	38.50	45.50
27	32.25	41.50	39.50	46.50
28	33.25	42.50	40.50	47.50
29	34.25	43.75	41.50	48.50
30	35.25	45.00	42.50	49.75
31	36.25	46.00	43.25	51.00
32	37.25	47.00	44.25	52.50
33	38.25	48.00	45.25	53.50
34	39.25	49.00	46.00	54.50
35	40.25	50.00	47.00	55.50

UPS NEXT DAY AIR

WEIGHT NOT TO EXCEED	48 STATES 22	*ALASKA & HAWAII 24	PUERTO RICO 25
LETTER	\$10.00	\$11.00	\$11.00
1 lb.	13.50	17.50	18.00
2	14.00	19.00	19.75
3	15.75	20.50	21.50
4	17.50	22.00	23.25
5	19.25	23.50	25.00
6	21.00	25.00	26.50
7	22.75	26.50	28.00
8	24.50	28.00	29.50
9	26.25	29.50	31.00
10	27.50	31.00	32.50
11	28.50	32.50	34.00
12	29.50	34.00	35.50
13	30.50	35.50	37.00
14	31.50	37.00	38.50
15	32.50	38.50	40.00
16	33.75	40.00	41.50
17	34.75	41.50	43.00
18	35.75	43.00	44.50
19	36.75	44.50	46.00
20	37.75	46.00	47.50
21	39.00	47.50	48.75
22	40.00	48.75	50.00
23	40.50	50.00	51.25
24	42.00	51.25	52.50
25	43.00	52.50	53.75
26	44.50	53.75	55.00
27	46.00	55.00	56.25
28	47.50	56.25	57.50
29	48.50	57.50	58.75
30	49.25	58.75	60.00
31	50.25	60.00	61.25
32	51.50	61.25	62.50
33	52.75	62.50	63.75
34	54.00	63.75	65.00
35	55.25	65.00	66.25

UPS NEXT DAY AIR LETTER $10.00
(48 States)

SATURDAY DELIVERY $10.00 FOR NEXT DAY AIR
(See UPS Air Service Guide and Supplement for Details.)

UPS 2ND DAY AIR LETTER $5.00
(48 States)

ANY FRACTION OF A POUND OVER THE WEIGHT SHOWN TAKES THE NEXT HIGHER RATE.

Maximum size per package — 130 inches in length and girth combined with a maximum length of 108 inches per package
Minimum charge for a package measuring over 84 inches in length and girth combined will be equal to the charge for a package weighing 25 pounds

AIR RESTRICTIONS:
The maximum value for an air service package is $25,000 and the maximum carrier liability is $25,000
No Call Tag service provided in UPS Air Service
Hazardous Materials are prohibited in UPS Air Service

NOTES:
†For ground service, a commercial delivery is one made to a place of business. A residential delivery is one made to a home which may include a business operated out of a home
Some Air Shipments may be shipped by Surface Transportation
*See UPS Air Service Guide for Alaska and Hawaii zone designations and time in transit

ADDITIONAL CHARGES:
For each Address Correction — $3.50
For each Call Tag — $1.60 ($1.10 if submitted in electronic transmission format)
For each COD received for collection — $4.00
For each package with a declared value over $100 — 30 cents for each additional $100 or fraction thereof
For each Delivery Confirmation Response — 75 cents
Signature Required — 25 cents additional
Request-Specific Reply Address — 25 cents additional
For each Hazardous Materials ground package — $5.00 (for those packages requiring shipping papers under 49 C F R Section 172 200)
For each Next Day Air Saturday delivery — $10.00 per piece
Weekly service charge — $5.00

WEIGHT AND SIZE LIMITS:
Maximum weight per package — 70 POUNDS

017239 Rev 2 92

Service to 48 Continental United States

To determine zone, take first three digits of ZIP Code to which parcel is addressed and refer to chart below.

ZIP CODE PREFIXES	UPS ZONE	ZIP CODE PREFIXES	UPS ZONE	ZIP CODE PREFIXES	UPS ZONE	ZIP CODE PREFIXES	UPS ZONE
010-041	5	300-312	2	490-492	4	821	7
042-049	6	313-316	3	493-499	5	822-823	6
050-089	5	317-319	2	———		824-825	7
———		320-326	3	500-525	5	826-828	6
100-149	5	327-339	4	526	4	829-834	7
150-163	4	342	4	527-564	5	835-838	8
164-165	5	350-353	2	565-567	6	840-864	7
166	4	354-355	3	570-571	5	865-884	6
167	5	356-362	2	572	6	890-893	7
168	4	363-367	3	573	5	894-897	8
169	5	368	2	574-588	6	898	7
170-174	4	369-372	3	590-592	7	———	
175-198	5	373-374	2	593	6	900-961	8
199	4	375	4	594-598	7	970-986	8
———		376	3	599	8	988-994	8
200-218	4	377-379	2	———			
219	5	380-381	4	600-609	4		
220-241	4	382-385	3	610-612	5		
242-243	3	386-387	4	613-634	4		
244-245	4	388	3	635	5		
246-248	3	389-392	4	636-639	4		
249-268	4	393	3	640-649	5		
270-274	3	394-396	4	650-659	4		
275-279	4	397	3	660-690	5		
280-282	3	———		691-693	6		
283-285	4	400-402	4				
286	3	403-409	3	700-729	4		
287-289	2	410-412	4	730-748	5		
290-292	3	413-418	3	749	4		
293	2	420	4	750-754	5		
294-295	3	421-422	3	755-756	4		
296	2	423-424	4	757-796	5		
297	3	425-427	3	797-799	6		
298	2	430-482	4	———			
299	3	483-489	5	800-820	6		

See separate charts for UPS Next Day Air (where available), 2nd Day Air and Service to Canada. Air service is provided to all points in Hawaii.

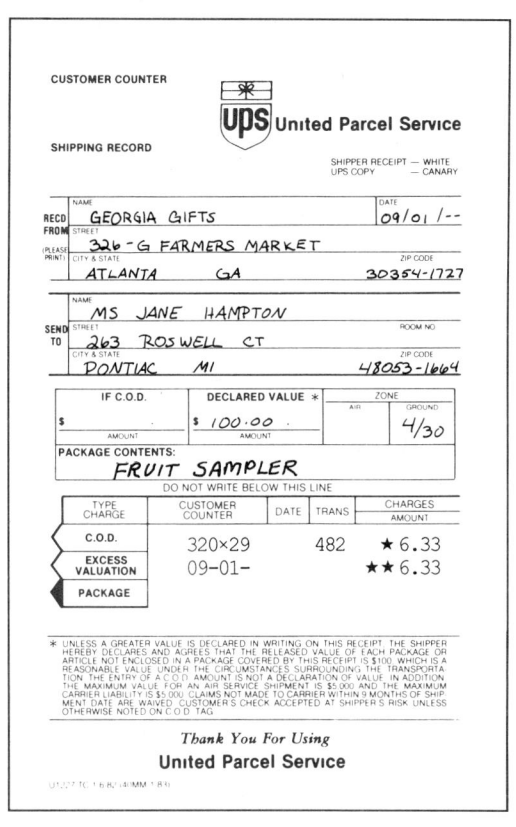

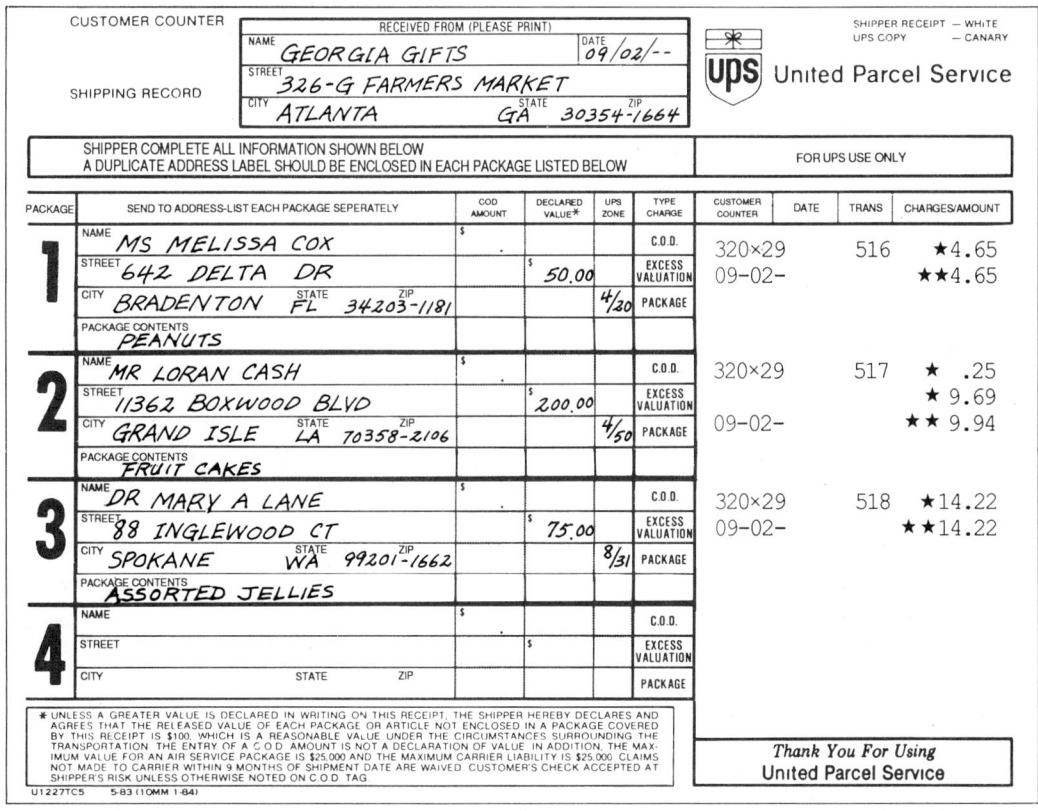

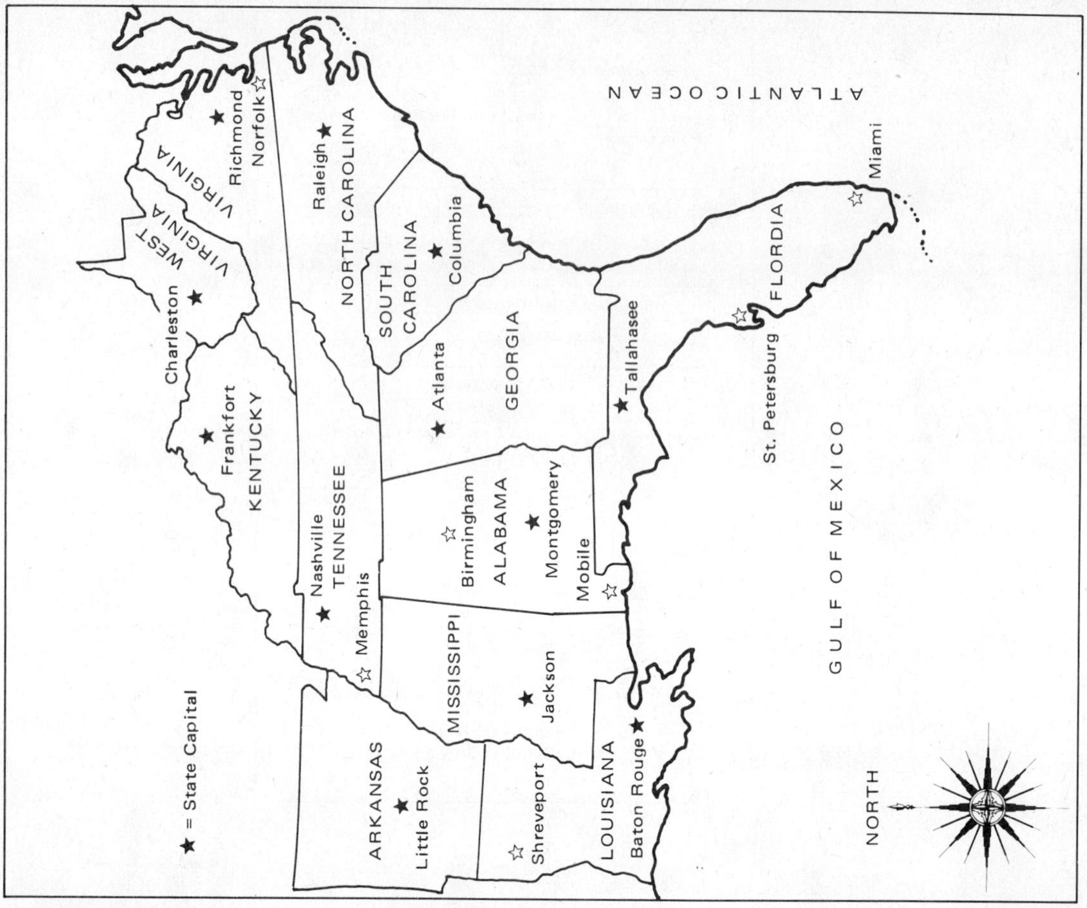
★ = State Capital
WEST VIRGINIA
Charleston
VIRGINIA
Richmond
Norfolk
NORTH CAROLINA
Raleigh
SOUTH CAROLINA
Columbia
KENTUCKY
Frankfort
TENNESSEE
Nashville
Memphis
GEORGIA
Atlanta
ALABAMA
Birmingham
Montgomery
Mobile
MISSISSIPPI
Jackson
ARKANSAS
Little Rock
LOUISIANA
Shreveport
Baton Rouge
FLORIDA
Tallahasee
St. Petersburg
Miami
ATLANTIC OCEAN
GULF OF MEXICO
NORTH

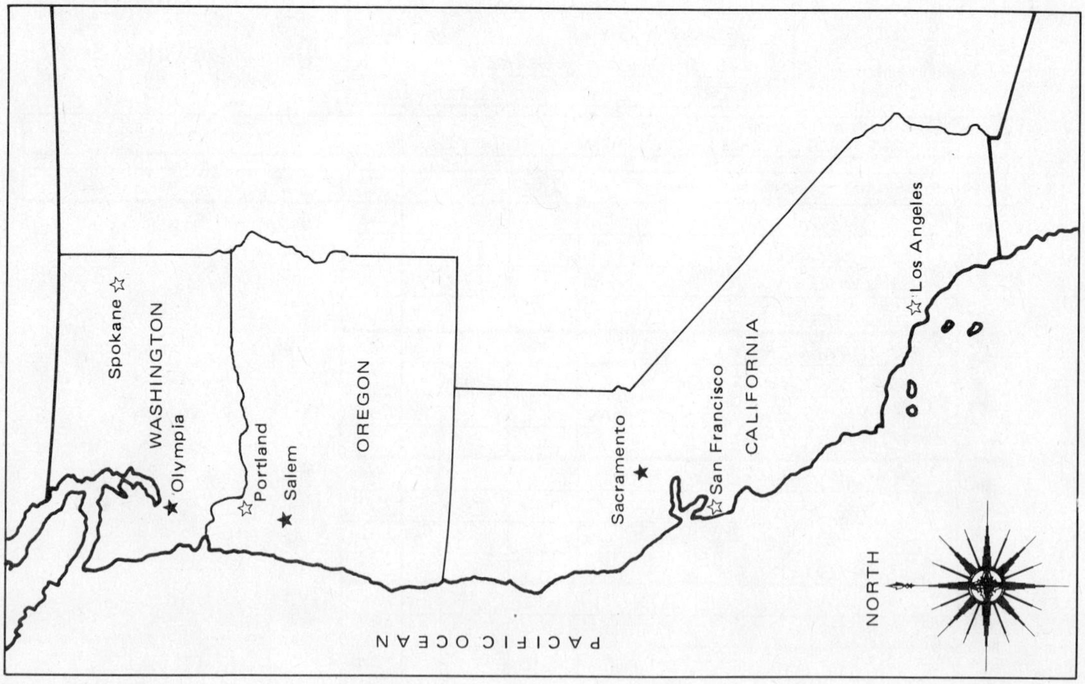
WASHINGTON
Spokane
Olympia
OREGON
Portland
Salem
CALIFORNIA
Sacramento
San Francisco
Los Angeles
PACIFIC OCEAN
NORTH

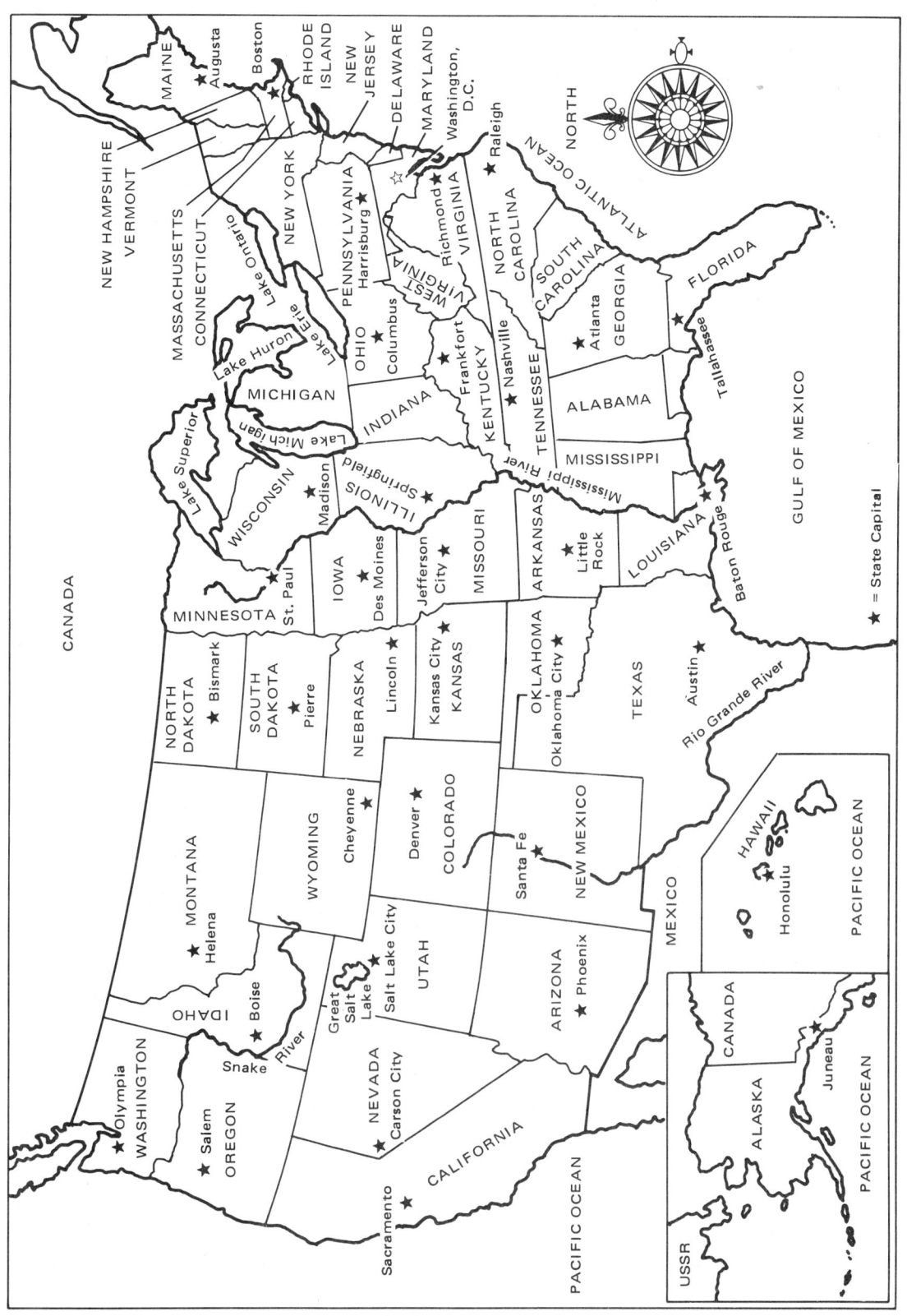

Map—United States

273

Business Section DAILY NEWS

Index

100

Announcements

Bids or Contracts Wanted	192
Personals	193
Business Personals	194
Ticket Mart	195
Articles Lost or Found	197
Pets, Lost, Missing	198
Pets Found	199

Service Guide

See the SERVICE GUIDE for a complete list of classifications

Legal Services	102
Domestic Care and Services	103-107
Medical Services	109
Home and Business Services	11-190

Business Classifieds

See BUSINESS TO BUSINESS in today's Business Section

Business Services	005-004
Equipment, Machinery, Supplies	050-067
Commercial and Industrial Real Estate	075-095

200
Real Estate For Sale

Real Estate Wanted	203
Realty Related Services	206
Condominiums, Townhomes	209
Homes, Inside Northwest	212
Homes, Northwest	215
Homes, Inside North	218
Homes, North	221
Homes, Inside Northeast	224
Homes, Northeast	227
Homes, Inside Southeast	230
Homes, Southeast	233
Homes, South	236
Homes, Inside Southwest	239
Homes, Southwest	242
Restoration Homes	245
Homes With Acreage	248
Mobile Homes, Sites	251
Lots and Subdivision Prop.	254
Mountain Property	257
Lake, River, and Coastal Prop.	260
Farms and Land	263
Other Georgia Real Estate	266
Out of State Real Estate	269
Income Investment Property	272

300
Real Estate For Rent

Wanted to Rent	305
Rental Services	310
Rentals to Share	315
Rooms	320
Rooms and Board	325
Hotels, Motels	330
Furnished Apartments	335
Unfurnished Apartments	340
Furnished Duplexes	345
Unfurnished Duplexes	350
Condominiums, Townhomes	355
Furnished Houses	360
Unfurnished Houses	365
Mobile Homes, Parks	370
Resort Rentals	375

400
Financial

Business Opp'ty Wanted	405
Wanted to Borrow	410
Business Opportunities	415
Investments	420
Money to Lend	425

500
Employment

Jobs Wanted	505
Resume Services	510
Career Services	515
Schools/Instruction	520
Part-Time Help Wanted	525
Help Wanted	530
Manufacturers' Reps	535
Domestic Help Wanted	540

600
Pets and Livestock

Dogs, Needs	602
Cats, Needs	619
Miscellaneous Pets, Needs	630
Horses, Needs	652
Farm Livestock	660

700
Merchandise

Wanted to Buy	703
Miscellaneous For Sale	706
Sales, Flea Markets	709
Household Goods	712
Antiques	715
Collectibles	718
Jewelry, Gems, Metals	721
Musical Merchandise	724
Photo, Needs	727
Radio, Needs	730
TV, Video	733
Computers, Needs	736
Telephones, Needs	739
Lawn & Garden, Supplies	742
Farm Equipment, Supplies	745
Shop Machines, Tools	754
Building Materials	757
Auctions	799

800
Recreational

Aviation, Needs	805
Sailboats, Needs	810
Boats, Needs	815
Hunting, Fishing, Camping	820
Travel Trailers, Campers	825
Motor Homes, RVs	830
Sports Equipment	835
Bicycles, Mopeds	840
Motorcycles, Needs	845

900
Automotive

Cars, Trucks Wanted	905
Auto Parts, Service	910
Heavy Trucks, Buses	915
Pickups, Vans, 4 W/D	920
Antique/Classic Cars	925
Imported Autos	930
Autos	935

Page 4 E　　　　*THE SUN*

SERVICES

201 Advertising Svc.	225 Concrete Service	250 Heating Services	275 Resume Service
202 Air Cond. Service	226 Construction Service	251 Home Rep./Remodel	276 Roofing Service
203 Aircraft Service	227 Consumer Svc. Misc.	252 Interior Design	277 Screens- Rep./Install.
204 Alteration	228 Copy/Duplicating Svc.	253 Janitor/Maid Svc.	278 Secretarial Service
205 Answering Service	229 Daycare/Childcare Svc.	254 Kennel Service	279 Security Service
206 Appliance Service	230 Delivery/Courier Svc.	255 Kitchen Remodeling	280 Septic Tank Service
207 Appraisal Service	231 Dental Service	256 Landscape/Lawncare	281 Sewing Machine Rep.
208 Asphalt Service	232 Detective Service	257 Leasing Service	282 Siding
209 Attorney/Legal Svc.	233 Drapery/Curtain Svc.	258 Locksmiths	283 Sign Service
210 Automotive Service	234 Drywall Service	259 Machine Rep. (Small)	284 Sitting Svcs. Misc.
211 Bathroom Rem./Rep.	235 Electrical Service	260 Mental Health Svc.	285 Solar Energy Svcs.
212 Beauty Services	236 Employment Service	261 Mobile Home Services	286 Tax Service
213 Boats/Marine Svc.	237 Energy Consv. Svc.	262 Motorcycle Service	287 Tile Service/Repair
214 Bonding/Bail Service	238 Entertainment Svc.	263 Moving/Hauling Svc.	288 Tree Service
215 Bookkeeping Service	239 Farm Services	264 Office Svc/Supplies	289 Tutoring
216 Building Contractors	240 Fencing Service	265 Page/Signaling Svc.	290 TV/Stereo Service
217 Building Materials	241 Financial Services	266 Painting	291 Upholstery Service
218 Bus. Machine Rep.	242 Firewood Services	267 Pest Control	292 Vacuum Cleaner Rep.
219 Business Svc. Misc.	243 Fireplace Service	268 Pet Grooming Svc.	293 Wall Design Service
220 Carpentry Service	244 Furniture Rep./Refin.	269 Photography Service	294 Wallpapering/Covering
221 Carpet/Rug Services	245 Glass - Home/Auto	270 Piano Tuning/Repair	295 Wedding Party Svc.
222 Catering Service	246 Grading Service	271 Plumbing Service	296 Window Cleaning
223 Charter Limo Svc.	247 Gunsmiths	272 Pool Svc./Supplies	297 Word Processing Svc.
224 Computer Svc./Rep.	248 Gutter Services	273 Printing Service	298 Wrecker Service
	249 Health Services	274 Rental Service	299 Misc. Services

274　　　　　　　　　　　　　　　　　　　　　　　Newspapers

SINGLE Persons–MONTHLY Payroll Period

And the wages are–		And the number of withholding allowances claimed is–										
At least	But less than	0	1	2	3	4	5	6	7	8	9	10
		The amount of income tax to be withheld shall be–										
$0	$116	$0	$0	$0	$0	$0	$0	$0	$0	$0	$0	$0
116	120	1	0	0	0	0	0	0	0	0	0	0
560	580	60	47	35	23	12	3	0	0	0	0	0
580	600	63	50	38	26	15	5	0	0	0	0	0
600	640	68	55	42	30	18	8	0	0	0	0	0
640	680	74	61	48	36	24	13	3	0	0	0	0
680	720	80	67	54	41	29	18	7	0	0	0	0
720	760	87	73	60	47	35	23	12	2	0	0	0
760	800	93	79	66	53	40	28	17	7	0	0	0
800	840	100	86	72	59	46	34	22	11	2	0	0
840	880	106	92	78	65	52	39	27	16	6	0	0
880	920	113	99	85	71	58	45	33	21	10	1	0
920	960	121	105	91	77	64	51	38	26	15	5	0
960	1,000	128	112	97	84	70	57	44	32	20	10	0
1,000	1,040	135	119	104	90	76	63	50	38	25	14	4

MARRIED Persons--MONTHLY Payroll Period

And the wages are–		And the number of withholding allowances claimed is–										
At least	But less than	0	1	2	3	4	5	6	7	8	9	10
		The amount of income tax to be withheld shall be–										
$0	$212	$0	$0	$0	$0	$0	$0	$0	$0	$0	$0	$0
212	216	1	0	0	0	0	0	0	0	0	0	0
216	220	1	0	0	0	0	0	0	0	0	0	0
880	920	88	76	63	51	40	29	19	9	0	0	0
920	960	93	81	69	57	45	34	24	14	4	0	0
960	1,000	100	87	75	63	50	39	28	18	9	0	0
1,000	1,040	106	92	80	68	56	44	33	23	13	3	0
1,040	1,080	112	99	86	74	62	49	38	28	17	8	0
1,080	1,120	119	105	91	79	67	55	43	32	22	12	3
1,120	1,160	125	111	98	85	73	61	49	37	27	17	7
1,160	1,200	132	118	104	91	78	66	54	42	32	21	12
1,200	1,240	138	124	110	96	84	72	60	48	36	26	16
1,240	1,280	144	131	117	103	90	77	65	53	41	31	20
1,280	1,320	151	137	123	109	95	83	71	59	47	36	25
1,320	1,360	158	143	130	116	102	89	77	64	52	40	30
1,360	1,400	165	150	136	122	108	94	82	70	58	46	35
1,400	1,440	172	157	142	128	115	101	88	76	63	51	40
1,440	1,480	180	164	149	135	121	107	93	81	69	57	45
1,480	1,520	187	171	156	141	127	114	100	87	75	63	50
1,520	1,560	194	178	163	148	134	120	106	92	80	68	56
1,560	1,600	201	186	170	154	140	126	112	99	86	74	62
1,600	1,640	208	193	177	162	147	133	119	105	91	79	67
1,640	1,680	216	200	184	169	153	139	125	111	98	85	73

SINGLE Persons–WEEKLY Payroll Period

And the wages are–		And the number of withholding allowances claimed is–										
At least	But less than	0	1	2	3	4	5	6	7	8.	9	10
		The amount of income tax to be withheld shall be–										
$0	$30	$0	$0	$0	$0	$0	$0	$0	$0	$0	$0	$0
30	32	1	0	0	0	0	0	0	0	0	0	0
32	34	1	0	0	0	0	0	0	0	0	0	0
34	36	1	0	0	0	0	0	0	0	0	0	0
120	125	13	10	7	4	2	0	0	0	0	0	0
125	130	13	10	8	5	2	0	0	0	0	0	0
130	135	14	11	8	5	3	1	0	0	0	0	0
135	140	15	12	9	6	4	1	0	0	0	0	0
140	145	16	13	10	7	4	2	0	0	0	0	0
145	150	16	13	10	8	5	2	0	0	0	0	0
150	160	18	14	11	9	6	3	1	0	0	0	0
160	170	19	16	13	10	7	4	2	0	0	0	0
170	180	21	18	14	11	9	6	3	1	0	0	0
180	190	22	19	16	13	10	7	4	2	0	0	0
190	200	24	21	18	14	11	9	6	3	1	0	0
200	210	26	22	19	16	13	10	7	4	2	0	0
210	220	27	24	21	18	14	11	9	6	3	1	0
220	230	29	26	22	19	16	13	10	7	4	2	0
230	240	31	27	24	21	18	14	11	9	6	3	1

MARRIED Persons–WEEKLY Payroll Period

And the wages are–		And the number of withholding allowances claimed is–										
At least	But less than	0	1	2	3	4	5	6	7	8	9	10
		The amount of income tax to be withheld shall be–										
$0	$52	$0	$0	$0	$0	$0	$0	$0	$0	$0	$0	$0
52	54	1	0	0	0	0	0	0	0	0	0	0
54	56	1	0	0	0	0	0	0	0	0	0	0
150	160	13	10	8	5	3	1	0	0	0	0	0
160	170	14	11	9	6	4	2	0	0	0	0	0
170	180	16	13	10	8	5	3	1	0	0	0	0
180	190	17	14	11	9	6	4	2	0	0	0	0
190	200	18	16	13	10	8	5	3	1	0	0	0
200	210	20	17	14	11	9	6	4	2	0	0	0
210	220	21	18	16	13	10	8	5	3	1	0	0
220	230	23	20	17	14	11	9	6	4	2	0	0
230	240	24	21	18	16	13	10	8	5	3	1	0
240	250	26	23	20	17	14	11	9	6	4	2	0
250	260	28	24	21	18	16	13	10	8	5	3	1
260	270	29	26	23	20	17	14	11	9	6	4	2
270	280	31	28	24	21	18	16	13	10	8	5	3
280	290	32	29	26	23	20	17	14	11	9	6	4
290	300	34	31	28	24	21	18	16	13	10	8	5
300	310	36	32	29	26	23	20	17	14	11	9	6
310	320	38	34	31	28	24	21	18	16	13	10	8
320	330	39	36	32	29	26	23	20	17	14	11	9
330	340	41	38	34	31	28	24	21	18	16	13	10

DOMESTIC POSTAL RATES AND FEES
Effective February 3, 1991

FIRST-CLASS

SINGLE-PIECE LETTER RATES:

1st ounce			$0.29
Each additional ounce			0.23

For pieces not exceeding (oz.)	The rate Is	For pieces not exceeding (oz.)	The rate Is
1	$0.29	7	$1.67
2	0.52	8	1.90
3	0.75	9	2.13
4	0.98	10	2.36
5	1.21	11	2.59
6	1.44		

FOR PIECES OVER 11 OUNCES, SEE PRIORITY MAIL RATES

Presort rates	Consult Postmaster
Business reply mail	Consult Postmaster

CARD RATES:

Single postal cards sold by the post office	$0.19 each
Double postal cards sold by the post office	0.38 ($0.19 each half)
Single post cards	0.19 each
Double post cards (reply-half of double post card does not have to bear postage when originally mailed)	$0.38 ($0.19 each half)

Note: To qualify for card rates, a card may not be larger than 4¼ by 6 inches, nor smaller than 3½ by 5 inches. The thickness must be uniform and not less than 0.007 of an inch

SECOND-CLASS

(Regular and preferred second-class rates are available only to newspapers and periodicals that have been authorized second-class mail privileges.)

Copies mailed by the public are charged at the applicable Express Mail, Priority Mail, or single piece First-, third-, or fourth-class rate.

THIRD-CLASS

REGULAR AND SPECIAL BULK RATES AVAILABLE ONLY TO AUTHORIZED MAILERS—CONSULT POSTMASTER FOR DETAILS

Circulars, books, catalogs, and other printed matter; merchandise, seeds, cuttings, bulbs, roots, scions, and plants, weighing less than 16 ounces.

Single-piece rates
for piece not exceeding

1 oz.	$0.29	8 ozs.	$1.33
2 ozs.	0.52	10 ozs.	1.44
3 ozs.	0.75	12 ozs.	1.56
4 ozs.	0.98	14 ozs.	1.67
6 ozs.	1.21	Over 14 but less than 16 ozs.	1.79

MONEY ORDERS

For safe transmission of money

$0.01 to 700.00	$0.75

PRIORITY MAIL We Deliver.

Weight, up to but not exceeding— pound(s)	Local 1, 2, and 3	ZONES 4	5	6	7	8
1	2.90	2.90	2.90	2.90	2.90	2.90
2	2.90	2.90	2.90	2.90	2.90	2.90
3	4.10	4.10	4.10	4.10	4.10	4.10
4	4.65	4.65	4.65	4.65	4.65	4.65
5	5.45	5.45	5.45	5.45	5.45	5.45
6	5.55	5.75	6.10	6.85	7.65	8.60
7	5.70	6.10	6.70	7.55	8.50	9.65
8	5.90	6.50	7.30	8.30	9.40	10.70
9	6.10	7.00	7.95	9.05	10.25	11.75
10	6.35	7.55	8.55	9.80	11.15	12.80
11	6.75	8.05	9.20	10.55	12.05	13.80
12	7.15	8.55	9.80	11.30	12.90	14.85
13	7.50	9.10	10.40	12.05	13.80	15.90
14	7.90	9.60	11.05	12.80	14.65	16.95
15	8.30	10.10	11.65	13.55	15.55	18.00
16	8.70	10.65	12.30	14.30	16.45	19.05
17	9.10	11.15	12.90	15.05	17.30	20.10
18	9.50	11.65	13.55	15.80	18.20	21.10
19	9.90	12.20	14.15	16.50	19.05	22.15
20	10.30	12.70	14.75	17.25	19.95	23.20
21	10.70	13.25	15.40	18.00	20.85	24.25
22	11.10	13.75	16.00	18.75	21.70	25.30
23	11.50	14.25	16.65	19.50	22.60	26.35
24	11.90	14.80	17.25	20.25	23.45	27.40
25	12.30	15.30	17.90	21.00	24.35	28.45
26	12.70	15.80	18.50	21.75	25.25	29.45
27	13.10	16.35	19.10	22.50	26.10	30.50
28	13.50	16.85	19.75	23.25	27.00	31.55
29	13.90	17.35	20.35	24.00	27.85	32.60
30	14.30	17.90	21.00	24.75	28.75	33.65
31	14.70	18.40	21.60	25.50	29.65	34.70
32	15.10	18.95	22.20	26.20	30.50	35.75
33	15.50	19.45	22.85	26.95	31.40	36.75
34	15.90	19.95	23.45	27.70	32.25	37.80
35	16.30	20.50	24.10	28.45	33.15	38.85
36	16.70	21.00	24.70	29.20	34.05	39.90
37	17.10	21.50	25.35	29.95	34.90	40.95
38	17.45	22.05	25.95	30.70	35.80	42.00
39	17.85	22.55	26.55	31.45	36.65	43.05
40	18.25	23.05	27.20	32.20	37.55	44.05
41	18.65	23.60	27.80	32.95	38.45	45.10
42	19.05	24.10	28.45	33.70	39.30	46.15
43	19.45	24.60	29.05	34.45	40.20	47.20
44	19.85	25.15	29.65	35.15	41.05	48.25
45	20.25	25.65	30.30	35.90	41.95	49.30
46	20.65	26.20	30.90	36.65	42.85	50.35
47	21.05	26.70	31.55	37.40	43.70	51.35
48	21.45	27.20	32.15	38.15	44.60	52.40
49	21.85	27.75	32.80	38.90	45.45	53.45
50	22.25	28.25	33.40	39.65	46.35	54.50
51	22.65	28.75	34.00	40.40	47.25	55.55
52	23.05	29.30	34.65	41.15	48.10	56.60
53	23.45	29.80	35.25	41.90	49.00	57.65
54	23.85	30.30	35.90	42.65	49.85	58.65
55	24.25	30.85	36.50	43.40	50.75	59.70
56	24.65	31.35	37.15	44.15	51.65	60.75
57	25.05	31.90	37.75	44.85	52.50	61.80
58	25.45	32.40	38.35	45.60	53.40	62.85
59	25.85	32.90	39.00	46.35	54.25	63.90
60	26.25	33.45	39.60	47.10	55.15	64.95
61	26.65	33.95	40.25	47.85	56.05	65.95
62	27.05	34.45	40.85	48.60	56.90	67.00
63	27.40	35.00	41.45	49.35	57.80	68.05
64	27.80	35.50	42.10	50.10	58.65	69.10
65	28.20	36.00	42.70	50.85	59.55	70.15
66	28.60	36.55	43.35	51.60	60.45	71.20
67	29.00	37.05	43.95	52.35	61.30	72.25
68	29.40	37.55	44.60	53.10	62.20	73.25
69	29.80	38.10	45.20	53.80	63.05	74.30
70	30.20	38.60	45.80	54.55	63.95	75.35

Source: United States Postal Service, 2/3/91.

SPECIAL SERVICES—DOMESTIC MAIL ONLY

INSURANCE
for Coverage Against Loss or Damage

Fees (in addition to postage)

Liability	Fee
$ 0.01 to $ 50.00	$0.75
50.01 to 100.00	1.60
100.01 to 200.00	2.40
200.01 to 300.00	3.50
300.01 to 400.00	4.60
400.01 to 500.00	5.40
500.01 to 600.00	6.20

REGISTRY
For Maximum Protection and Security

Value	Fees in addition to postage	
	For articles covered by Postal Insurance	For articles not covered by Postal Insurance
$0.01 to 100.00	$4.50	$4.40
$100.01 to 500.00	4.85	4.70
500.01 to 1,000.00	5.25	5.05
For higher values, consult Postmaster		

SPECIAL DELIVERY
(In addition to required postage)

Class of Mail	Not more than 2 pounds	Weight	
		More than 2 pounds but not more than 10 pounds	More than 10 pounds
First-Class	$7.65	$7.95	$8.55
All other classes	8.05	8.65	9.30

SPECIAL HANDLING
Third- and fourth-class only (In addition to required postage)

10 pounds and less	$1.80
More than 10 pounds	2.50

COD

THE MAXIMUM VALUE FOR C.O.D. SERVICE IS $600.00
Consult Postmaster for fees and conditions of mailing

ADDITIONAL SERVICES

CERTIFIED MAIL—Fee (in addition to postage)	$1.00
CERTIFICATE OF MAILING—Fee (in addition to postage) (For Bulk mailings and Firm mailing books, see Postmaster)	$0.50
RESTRICTED DELIVERY (For Insured*, Certified, and Registered Mail)	$2.50

RETURN RECEIPT (with Insured*, Certified, and Registered Mail)

REQUESTED AT TIME OF MAILING:

Showing to whom (signature) and date delivered	$1.00
Showing to whom (signature), date, and address were delivered	1.35

REQUESTED AFTER MAILING:

Showing to whom and date delivered	$6.00

*NOT AVAILABLE FOR MAIL INSURED FOR $50 OR LESS

RETURN RECEIPT FOR MERCHANDISE

Showing to whom (signature) and date of delivery	$1.10
Showing to whom (signature), date, and address where delivered	1.50

Source: United States Postal Service, 2/3/91.

SIZE STANDARDS FOR DOMESTIC MAIL

MINIMUM SIZE

Pieces that do not meet the following requirements are prohibited from the mails
a All pieces must be at least .007 inch thick, and
b All pieces (except keys and identification devices) that are ¼ inch or less in thickness must be
  (1) Rectangular in shape.
  (2) At least 3½ inches high, and
  (3) At least 5 inches long.
  Note: Pieces greater than ¼ inch thick can be mailed even if they measure less than 3½ by 5 inches.

NONSTANDARD MAIL

First-Class Mail, except Presort First-Class and carrier route First-Class, weighing one ounce or less, and all single-piece rate third-class mail weighing one ounce or less is nonstandard (and subject to a $0.10 surcharge in addition to the applicable postage and fees) if
1 Any of the following dimensions are exceeded:
  Length—11½ inches.
  Height—6⅛ inches.
  Thickness—¼ inch, or
2 The length divided by the height is not between 1.3 and 2.5, inclusive.

The nonstandard surcharge for Presort First-Class and carrier route First-Class is $0.05.

FOURTH-CLASS

Weight, up to but not exceeding— (pounds)	ZONES							
	Local	1 & 2	3	4	5	6	7	8
2	2.12	2.19	2.32	2.46	2.74	2.85	2.85	2.85
3	2.19	2.29	2.49	2.70	3.12	3.54	4.00	4.05
4	2.25	2.39	2.65	2.94	3.50	4.06	4.35	4.60
5	2.31	2.49	2.81	3.17	3.88	4.58	5.20	5.40
6	2.38	2.59	2.98	3.41	4.26	5.10	6.33	8.55
7	2.44	2.68	3.14	3.65	4.64	5.62	7.06	9.60
8	2.50	2.78	3.31	3.89	5.02	6.14	7.78	10.65
9	2.57	2.88	3.47	4.12	5.40	6.67	8.51	11.70
10	2.63	2.98	3.63	4.36	5.78	7.19	9.24	12.75
11	2.69	3.08	3.80	4.60	6.16	7.71	9.97	13.75
12	2.76	3.18	3.96	4.83	6.54	8.23	10.69	14.80
13	2.80	3.25	4.08	4.99	6.79	8.57	11.17	15.85
14	2.85	3.32	4.19	5.16	7.04	8.92	11.65	16.90
15	2.89	3.38	4.28	5.27	7.23	9.17	11.99	17.95
16	2.93	3.43	4.36	5.39	7.40	9.40	12.31	19.00
17	2.97	3.48	4.44	5.49	7.56	9.62	12.61	19.91
18	3.01	3.53	4.51	5.60	7.72	9.83	12.90	20.38
19	3.05	3.58	4.59	5.69	7.87	10.03	13.17	20.83
20	3.08	3.63	4.65	5.79	8.01	10.22	13.43	21.26
21	3.12	3.68	4.72	5.88	8.15	10.40	13.68	21.66
22	3.15	3.72	4.79	5.97	8.28	10.57	13.91	22.05
23	3.18	3.77	4.85	6.05	8.40	10.74	14.14	22.43
24	3.22	3.81	4.91	6.13	8.52	10.90	14.36	22.78
25	3.25	3.85	4.97	6.21	8.64	11.05	14.57	23.13
26	3.28	3.89	5.03	6.29	8.76	11.20	14.77	23.46
27	3.32	3.93	5.09	6.36	8.87	11.35	14.97	23.78
28	3.35	3.97	5.14	6.44	8.97	11.49	15.16	24.09
29	3.38	4.01	5.20	6.51	9.08	11.63	15.34	24.39
30	3.41	4.05	5.25	6.58	9.18	11.76	15.52	24.68
31	3.44	4.09	5.30	6.65	9.28	11.89	15.69	24.96
32	3.47	4.13	5.36	6.71	9.37	12.01	15.86	25.23
33	3.50	4.17	5.41	6.78	9.47	12.14	16.02	25.50
34	3.53	4.20	5.46	6.84	9.56	12.26	16.18	25.75
35	3.56	4.24	5.51	6.91	9.65	12.37	16.34	26.01
36	3.59	4.28	5.55	6.97	9.74	12.49	16.49	26.25
37	3.62	4.31	5.60	7.03	9.82	12.60	16.64	26.49
38	3.65	4.35	5.65	7.09	9.91	12.71	16.79	26.72
39	3.68	4.38	5.69	7.15	9.99	12.81	16.93	26.95
40	3.71	4.42	5.74	7.20	10.07	12.92	17.07	27.17
41	3.74	4.45	5.78	7.26	10.15	13.02	17.20	27.39

CLASSIC AUTO PARTS
5963 Beverly Drive
Hollywood, CA 90028
(213) 555-9864

Part No.	Price (each)	Part No.	Price (each)	Part No.	Price (each)
00053473	$151.65	00411611	$ 56.65	32363878	$ 67.70
00053474	86.70	00411612	66.65	32638370	44.50
00053475	15.50	00556328	123.00	36338637	55.40
00053476	23.35	00556329	132.00	38863783	45.00
00053477	36.90	00556330	135.50	43516653	8.75
00145570	5.55	00556331	155.30	43536655	7.85
00145571	4.35	00556332	135.50	43558658	8.85
00145572	7.00	00683382	87.50	48356685	7.85
00145573	3.35	00683383	88.80	51173714	66.00
00145574	5.20	00683384	78.80	51177341	65.50
00204833	117.75	00683385	77.75	57117437	57.50
00204834	106.60	00683386	87.50	57717337	77.50
00204835	115.00	11745905	45.50	57773374	220.00
00204836	139.75	11749505	55.75	64036893	115.75
00204837	108.80	11838233	45.50	64366389	88.70
00399455	65.00	11883283	75.75	64554369	11.75
00399456	43.40	11935575	57.75	64649693	9.90
00399457	95.50	11985357	175.00	77173947	135.65
00399458	37.50	25787385	175.50	77474197	15.90
00399459	25.75	25873758	170.75	77477947	37.75
00411608	55.55	25961608	177.75	77744749	88.30
00411609	65.35	25996808	178.85	91179771	103.50
00411610	60.65	32268357	87.75	91797974	44.40

BUSINESS FORMS (packs of 100)

Code	Price	Code	Price	Code	Price
AA35	$12.24	JA25	$32.67	SE23	$ 5.88
AB53	22.43	JA52	36.35	SE32	5.08
AD35	11.45	JM53	38.00	SF38	5.58
AD53	21.50	JN55	38.25	SF88	8.58
BA85	8.87	KA16	4.55	TC95	13.35
BB38	7.70	KA66	5.45	TC98	13.85
BD81	6.95	KR02	3.88	TG17	18.35
BD88	9.65	KR20	8.33	TG77	18.55
CC40	32.88	LC19	6.39	US04	41.50
CD34	43.38	LC94	3.69	US40	44.50
CE80	23.46	LQ38	8.15	UZ23	41.05
CF08	23.58	LQ83	8.75	UZ28	44.00
DD16	18.48	MM34	14.45	VI53	17.75
DE76	11.25	MM48	15.55	VI58	17.70
DG92	17.52	MN44	14.45	VT63	17.77
DO29	17.85	MN48	15.45	VT68	17.57
EA38	5.55	NM18	8.53	WA17	2.95
EE83	7.75	NM81	8.35	WA77	2.59
EF88	9.09	NN18	3.38	WC59	2.90
EP88	5.39	NN81	5.83	WC99	2.99
FA02	8.06	OA35	8.05	WO99	2.09
FE20	8.86	OA55	8.80	XE25	23.05
FF22	6.88	OY85	8.08	XE28	22.35
FP32	8.88	OY88	8.80	XF38	23.30
GC44	27.50	PJ30	12.25	XF88	22.35
GC74	20.00	PJ38	12.55	XP38	23.35
GG77	25.35	PO80	12.35	YB11	23.85
GQ27	27.70	PO88	12.45	YB17	28.35
HB22	41.50	QV72	9.00	YP11	32.85
HB82	44.65	QV77	9.90	YP27	38.35
HD33	40.90	QW41	9.45	YR11	35.58
HD83	43.38	QW44	9.54	ZC47	6.88
IA91	7.30	RB09	22.74	ZC74	8.85
II32	7.53	RB90	27.47	ZO61	8.55
II91	7.33	RP89	24.75	ZO66	5.85
IT99	7.55	RP98	25.75	ZQ61	5.05

BYTE SOFTWARE WAREHOUSE

4982 Garden Plaza
Woodstown, NJ 08098

DISKS AND CARTRIDGES

5.25″ Floppy Disks (10 per box)

	Price
Double sided, double density	$12.10
Double sided, high density	21.70
Double sided, double density, 286 format	13.10
Double sided, high density, 286 format	22.80

3.5″ Micro Floppy Disks (10 per box)

Double sided, double density	$18.90
Double sided, high density, 286 format	36.00
Double sided, double density, 512 format	19.90

Color Diskettes (10 per box)

5.25	Double sided, double density	$12.70
	Double sided, high density	22.80
3.5	Double sided, double density	19.90
	Double sided, high density	36.00

Data Cartridges

High density, high capacity, 150 megabyte	$49.99
High density, high capacity, PC/T systems	34.85
High density, mini ¼″-Advanced PC systems	27.20

Symbol	Instruction	Example	Result
∧	insert copy	Te proof the	The proof of the
⊂	close up	The pr oof	The proof
#	add space	Theproof	The proof
∪	transpose	The porof (the of)	The proof of the
lc or /	lowercase	The PRoof	The proof
℘	delete	The proof of of thee	The proof of the
/	replace	The proof in the	The proof of the
⊙	insert period	the proof⊙ However,	the proof. However,
___	underline or italicize	The proof	The proof
≡	capitalize	the best proof	The BEST proof
sp	spell out	sp (5) (WP) centers	five word processing centers
¶	new paragraph	proof.¶ However, the	proof. However, the
No ¶	no paragraph (run together)	proof. No ¶ However, the	proof. However, the
.... or stet.	leave as is; ignore the correction	The stet. proof of the	The proof of the
∧∧∧ ? ↑	insert punctuation	the proof however,	the proof; however,
∧̄	insert hyphen	The age old proof	The age-old proof
∨	insert apostrophe	The proofs effect	The proof's effect
∨ ∨	insert quotation marks	The proof of the	The "proof" of the
⊐	move right	The proof	The proof
⊏	move left	The proof	The proof
⟳	move copy as indicated	The (matter) proof of the is	The proof of the matter is
SS	single-space	600 Broad Street SS Mt. Pleasant, PA	600 Broad Street Mt. Pleasant, PA
DS	double-space	DS Dear Mr. Sofranko	Dear Mr. Sofranko
QS	quadruple-space	QS THE PROOF The proof of the	THE PROOF The proof of the

PERSONAL/PROFESSIONAL DEVELOPMENT

Balderidge, Leticia. *Complete Guide to the New Manners for the 90's.* New York: Rawson Associates, 1990.

Brothers, Joyce. *The Successful Woman.* New York: Simon and Schuster, 1988.

Ford, Charlotte. *Charlotte Ford's Book of Modern Manners.* New York: C. N. Patten, 1988.

Wallace, Harold R., and Ann Masters. *Personality Development for Work.* Cincinnati: South-Western Publishing Co., 1989.

GRAMMAR, STYLE, PUNCTUATION, CAPITALIZATION, AND ABBREVIATIONS

Azar, Betty Schrampfer. *Understanding and Using English Grammar.* Englewood Cliffs: Prentice-Hall Regents, 1989.

Booker, Dianna Daniels. *Good Grief, Good Grammar.* New York: Facts on File Publications, 1988.

Bryant, Nerissa Bell. *Language in Daily Living.* Austin: Steck-Vaughn, 1985.

Kleinman, Howard H. *Everyday Consumer English.* Lincolnwood: National Textbook Co., 1985.

Mosenfelder, Donn, Caleb Crowell, and Jennifer Sylvor. *Vocabulary for Competency, Book 1.* New York: Educational Design, Inc., 1986.

Schacter, Norman. *Words, Words, Words.* 2nd Ed. Cincinnati: South-Western Publishing Co., 1986.

Schacter, Norman, and Alfred T. Clark, Jr. *English the Easy Way.* 5th Ed. Cincinnati: South-Western Publishing Co., 1985.

Shertzen, Margaret D. *The Elements of Grammar.* New York: Collier Books, 1986.

Wolf, Morris P., and Shirley Kuiper. *Effective Communication for Today.* 9th Ed. Cincinnati: South-Western Publishing Co., 1991.

JOB SEARCH SOURCES

Kent, George E. *How to Get Hired Today!* Lincolnwood: VGM Career Horizons, 1991.

Kushner, John A. *How to Find and Apply for a Job.* Cincinnati: South-Western Publishing Co., 1989.

Schuman, Nancy, and William Lewis. *Back to Work: How to Re-enter the Working World.* Hauppauge: Barron's, 1985.

Wallace, Janet. *Looks That Work.* New York: Viking, 1986.

Yate, Martin John. *Resumes That Knock 'em Dead.* Boston: Bob Adams, 1988.

4½%	SALES TAX CHART				

SALES			SALES		
From	To	Tax	From	To	Tax
.15 —	.33	.01	6.78 —	6.99	.31
.34 —	.55	.02	7.00 —	7.22	.32
.56 —	.77	.03	7.23 —	7.44	.33
.78 —	.99	.04	7.45 —	7.66	.34
1.00 —	1.22	.05	7.67 —	7.88	.35
1.23 —	1.44	.06	7.89 —	8.11	.36
1.45 —	1.66	.07	8.12 —	8.33	.37
1.67 —	1.88	.08	8.34 —	8.55	.38
1.89 —	2.11	.09	8.56 —	8.77	.39
2.12 —	2.33	.10	8.78 —	8.99	.40
2.34 —	2.55	.11	9.00 —	9.22	.41
2.56 —	2.77	.12	9.23 —	9.44	.42
2.78 —	2.99	.13	9.45 —	9.66	.43
3.00 —	3.22	.14	9.67 —	9.88	.44
3.23 —	3.44	.15	9.89 —	10.11	.45
3.45 —	3.66	.16	10.12 —	10.33	.46
3.67 —	3.88	.17	10.34 —	10.55	.47
3.89 —	4.11	.18	10.56 —	10.77	.48
4.12 —	4.33	.19	10.78 —	10.99	.49
4.34 —	4.55	.20	11.00 —	11.22	.50
4.56 —	4.77	.21	11.23 —	11.44	.51
4.78 —	4.99	.22	11.45 —	11.66	.52
5.00 —	5.22	.23	11.67 —	11.88	.53
5.23 —	5.44	.24	11.89 —	12.11	.54
5.45 —	5.66	.25	12.12 —	12.33	.55
5.67 —	5.88	.26	12.34 —	12.55	.56
5.89 —	6.11	.27	12.56 —	12.77	.57
6.12 —	6.33	.28	12.78 —	12.99	.58
6.34 —	6.55	.29	13.00 —	13.22	.59
6.56 —	6.77	.30	13.23 —	13.44	.60

SALES			SALES		
From	To	Tax	From	To	Tax
44.70 —	44.89	2.24	50.30 —	50.49	2.52
44.90 —	45.09	2.25	50.50 —	50.69	2.53
45.10 —	45.29	2.26	50.70 —	50.89	2.54
45.30 —	45.49	2.27	50.90 —	51.09	2.55
45.50 —	45.69	2.28	51.10 —	51.29	2.56
45.70 —	45.89	2.29	51.30 —	51.49	2.57
45.90 —	46.09	2.30	51.50 —	51.69	2.58
46.10 —	46.29	2.31	51.70 —	51.89	2.59
46.30 —	46.49	2.32	51.90 —	52.09	2.60
46.50 —	46.69	2.33	52.10 —	52.29	2.61
46.70 —	46.89	2.34	52.30 —	52.49	2.62
46.90 —	47.09	2.35	52.50 —	52.69	2.63
47.10 —	47.29	2.36	52.70 —	52.89	2.64
47.30 —	47.49	2.37	52.90 —	53.09	2.65
47.50 —	47.69	2.38	53.10 —	53.29	2.66
47.70 —	47.89	2.39	53.30 —	53.49	2.67
47.90 —	48.09	2.40	53.50 —	53.69	2.68
48.10 —	48.29	2.41	53.70 —	53.89	2.69
48.30 —	48.49	2.42	53.90 —	54.09	2.70
48.50 —	48.69	2.43	54.10 —	54.29	2.71
48.70 —	48.89	2.44	54.30 —	54.49	2.72
48.90 —	49.09	2.45	54.50 —	54.69	2.73
49.10 —	49.29	2.46	54.70 —	54.89	2.74
49.30 —	49.49	2.47	54.90 —	55.09	2.75
49.50 —	49.69	2.48	55.10 —	55.29	2.76
49.70 —	49.89	2.49	55.30 —	55.49	2.77
49.90 —	50.09	2.50	55.50 —	55.69	2.78
50.10 —	50.29	2.51	55.70 —	55.89	2.79

6%	SALES TAX CHART				
SALES			**SALES**		
From	To	Tax	From	To	Tax
0.01 — 0.10		0.00	4.92 — 5.08		.30
.11 — .24		.01	5.09 — 5.24		.31
.25 — .41		.02	5.25 — 5.41		.32
.42 — .58		.03	5.42 — 5.58		.33
.59 — .74		.04	5.59 — 5.74		.34
.75 — .91		.05	5.75 — 5.91		.35
.92 — 1.08		.06	5.92 — 6.08		.36
1.09 — 1.24		.07	6.09 — 6.24		.37
1.25 — 1.41		.08	6.25 — 6.41		.38
1.42 — 1.58		.09	6.42 — 6.58		.39
1.59 — 1.74		.10	6.59 — 6.74		.40
1.75 — 1.91		.11	6.75 — 6.91		.41
1.92 — 2.08		.12	6.92 — 7.08		.42
2.09 — 2.24		.13	7.09 — 7.24		.43
2.25 — 2.41		.14	7.25 — 7.41		.44
2.42 — 2.58		.15	7.42 — 7.58		.45
2.59 — 2.75		.16	7.59 — 7.74		.46
2.75 — 2.91		.17	7.75 — 7.91		.47
2.92 — 3.08		.18	7.92 — 8.08		.48
3.09 — 3.24		.19	8.09 — 8.24		.49
3.25 — 3.41		.20	8.25 — 8.41		.50
3.42 — 3.58		.21	8.42 — 8.58		.51
3.59 — 3.74		.22	8.59 — 8.74		.52
3.75 — 3.91		.23	8.75 — 8.91		.53
3.92 — 4.08		.24	8.92 — 9.08		.54
4.09 — 4.24		.25	9.09 — 9.24		.55
4.25 — 4.41		.26	9.25 — 9.41		.56
4.42 — 4.58		.27	9.42 — 9.58		.57
4.59 — 4.74		.28	9.59 — 9.74		.58
4.75 — 4.91		.29	9.75 — 9.91		.59

STOCK RECORD CARD

ITEM *Staples*   Maximum **250**

STOCK No. **ST 96**   Minimum **100**

UNIT **BOX**

Date	Quantity Received	Quantity Issued	Balance

STOCK RECORD CARD

ITEM *Paper Clips*   Maximum **150**

STOCK No. **CP 24**   Minimum **25**

UNIT **Box**

Date	Quantity Received	Quantity Issued	Balance

STOCK RECORD CARD

ITEM *Index Cards* Maximum **100**

STOCK No. **IC 34**   Minimum **25**

UNIT **PKG**

Date	Quantity Received	Quantity Issued	Balance

STOCK RECORD CARD

ITEM *Envelopes*   Maximum **200**

STOCK No. **AG 88**   Minimum **50**

UNIT **EACH**

Date	Quantity Received	Quantity Issued	Balance
19-- Sept 1			200
8		70	130
11		80	50
15	150		200
18		60	140
22		50	90
23		40	50
25	150		200
30		60	140

ACCOUNTING DEPARTMENT
INVENTORY

Month Ended _June, 19_

Product Number	Item	Unit Size	Closing Inventory	Unit Price	Inventory Value
AG88	Window envelopes, #1	500	12	10.75	129.00
AG89	Window envelopes, #2	500	12 *	14.85	178.20
AG93	Regular envelopes	500	15	10.10	151.50
CP24	Paper clips	box	35	1.79	62.65
GL70	Rubber cement	qt.	8	5.19	41.52
GL75	Rubber cement	4 oz.	11	1.45	15.95
GL88	Glue sticks	each	6	.65	3.90
IC34	Index cards, 3x5	pkg.	18	.99	17.82
IC36	Index cards, 4x6	pkg.	16	1.16	18.56
IC38	Index cards, 5x7	pkg.	15	1.89	28.35
IC75	Card file box	each	2	3.79	7.58
LA18	Info processing labels	pkg.	12	3.99	47.88
LA47	File folder labels	pkg.	12	3.75	45.00
PA42	Phone message pads	doz.	8	1.98	15.84
PA55	Legal pads	doz.	8	12.25	98.00
PA73	Steno notebook	each	10	.98	9.80
PA94	Calculator rolls	each	25	.45	11.25
PE29	Pencils	doz.	10	.89	8.90
RB23	Rubber bands	lb.	18	3.50	63.00
RU07	Ruler	each	4	1.55	6.20
SP73	Stamp pad	each	8	1.95	15.60
SP75	Stamp pad ink	each	8	1.75	14.00
ST96	Staples	box		.95	11.40
WP37	Typewriter ribbon	each		12.50	150.00
WP45	Printwheel	each		7.50	135.00
				TOTAL	1,286.90

Stock Record

Business Section

~~~

NATIONAL WIRE WORKS
11734 Telford Rd..................................555-2045
National Youth Foundation
3298 Congress Blvd.............................555-1930
Nation's Gardeners
958 Old Yale Rd.................................555-0395
Nations Cheryl M atty
437 Candler Blvd...............................555-9356
Nationwide Business Forms
117 Rainbow Dr..................................555-2284
NATIONWIDE FLORAL SERVICE
11545 Circle 85 Pkwy..........................555-3000
Nationwide Haulers
1037 Gordon St.................................555-6530
Native Thos J CPA
945 Tara Cir....................................555-4480
NATKIN PERSONNEL
775 Dogwood Hwy.............................555-1986
Natural Health Foods, Inc.
2348 Phoenix Byway............................555-0038
Natural You Hair Styles
654-E Exchange Pl..............................555-3380
Naturally Nutritious Co
655 Business Park Dr...........................555-8734

Navy Recruiting Station--
3529 Lake Plaza...............................555-3422
847 Cobb Pkwy................................555-9394
Naylon G Philip DDS
633 Hembree Cir...............................555-0238
Naylor Kim B DVM
3487 Armour Hwy..............................555-9939
NBS Car Rentals
937 Northcliff Ter..............................555-0203
NECCO SEWING CENTER
554 Ford Road Ext.............................555-7721
238 Lake Hearn Dr............................555-4480
955 Light Cir...................................555-3238
Needle Geo G rl est............................555-5388
Needle Point Village...........................555-2211
Needlepoint Junction...........................555-0045
Neel Thelma J MD PC
11947 N Landing Run..........................555-9993
Neil M Thos Rev................................555-6645
NELSON-JOHNSON, INC invstmnts
Municipal Bldg................................555-2020
News-Daily
3458 Old Dayton Hwy..........................555-4440
Classified Want Ads...........................555-4444

~~~

Government Section

United S

Continued From Last Page   Continued From Last Column

U.S. Government--
LABOR DEPT OF --
Minimum Wage/Overtime........................555-3490
Employment & Training Programs................555-7070
Federal Workers' Compensation.................555-2894
Job Safety & Health............................555-5023
Labor Statistics................................555-4419
Pensions......................................555-0354
Public Affairs.................................555-4952
Women's Activities............................555-6620
Bureau of Apprenticeship & Trainiing
11543 Pierce Ave--
Area Office...................................555-7745
Regional Office...............................555-2993
State Office...................................555-4147
Bureau of Labor Statistics--
Administrative................................555-4290
Regional Commissioner........................555-8821
Statistical Information.........................555-8823

U.S. Government--
POSTAL SERVICE--
ZIP Code Information..........................555-1010
Rates and Information.........................555-2325
Employee & Labor Relations....................555-2041
Finance.......................................555-3210
Mail Processing...............................555-4002
Customer Services.............................555-1110
Postmaster....................................555-9219
Retail Sales and Service.......................555-5521
Personnel.....................................555-4349
Express Mail Service...........................555-0202
Passport Information..........................555-3337
Public Affairs.................................555-9110
Postique/Stamp Collecting Center...............555-8883
Philately/Stamp Collecting.....................555-0366
Claims and Inquiry............................555-1988
Airport Mail Facility...........................555-6661
Special Delivery...............................555-4433

FROM/TO	ATLANTA, GA	CHICAGO, IL	DALLAS, TX	LOS ANGELES, CA	NEW YORK, NY	WASHINGTON, DC
			NUMBER OF MILES			
Atlanta, GA	---	674	795	2182	841	608
Birmingham, AL	150	642	645	2032	969	736
Charleston, SC	289	877	1072	2459	733	500
Dallas, TX	795	917	---	1387	1552	1319
Jacksonville, FL	306	980	990	2377	959	726
Knoxville, TN	193	527	837	2202	715	482
Lexington, KY	362	352	861	2180	703	514
Miami, FL	655	1329	1300	2687	1308	1075
New Orleans, LA	479	912	496	1883	1311	1078
Orlando, FL	435	1109	1078	2465	1098	865
Raleigh, NC	372	784	1166	2545	489	256
St. Louis, MO	541	289	630	1845	948	793

USPS ABBREVIATIONS

The abbreviations listed here are recommended by the U.S. Postal Service (USPS). By using the city and state abbreviations, it is possible to enter the city, state, and ZIP Code on the last line of an address with a maximum of 28 positions: 13 positions for the city, 1 space between the city and state, 2 positions for the state, 2 spaces between the state and ZIP Code, and 10 positions for the ZIP+4 Code.

U.S. State, District, Possession, or Territory	Two-Letter Abbreviation	U.S. State, District, Possession, or Territory	Two-Letter Abbreviation
Alabama	AL	North Carolina	NC
Alaska	AK	North Dakota	ND
Arizona	AZ	Ohio	OH
Arkansas	AR	Oklahoma	OK
California	CA	Oregon	OR
Canal Zone	CZ	Pennsylvania	PA
Colorado	CO	Puerto Rico	PR
Connecticut	CT	Rhode Island	RI
Delaware	DE	South Carolina	SC
District of Columbia	DC	South Dakota	SD
Florida	FL	Tennessee	TN
Georgia	GA	Texas	TX
Guam	GU	Utah	UT
Hawaii	HI	Vermont	VT
Idaho	ID	Virgin Islands	VI
Illinois	IL	Virginia	VA
Indiana	IN	Washington	WA
Iowa	IA	West Virginia	WV
Kansas	KS	Wisconsin	WI
Kentucky	KY	Wyoming	WY

U.S. State, District, Possession, or Territory	Two-Letter Abbreviation	Canadian Province, Possession, or Territory	Two-Letter Abbreviation
Louisiana	LA	Alberta	AB
Maine	ME	British Columbia	BC
Maryland	MD	Labrador	LB
Massachusetts	MA	Manitoba	MB
Michigan	MI	New Brunswick	NB
Minnesota	MN	Newfoundland	NF
Mississippi	MS	Northwest Territories	NT
Missouri	MO	Nova Scotia	NS
Montana	MT		
Nebraska	NE		
Nevada	NV	Ontario	ON
New Hampshire	NH	Prince Edward Island	PE
New Jersey	NJ	Quebec	PQ
New Mexico	NM	Saskatchewan	SK
New York	NY	Yukon Territory	YT

ABBREVIATIONS FOR STREET DESIGNATORS
(STREET SUFFIXES)

Word	Abbreviation	Word	Abbreviation	Word	Abbreviation	Word	Abbreviation
Alley	ALY	Drive	DR	Lake	LK	Rapids	RPDS
Annex	ANX	Estates	EST	Lakes	LKS	Rest	RST
Arcade	ARC	Expressway	EXPY	Landing	LNDG	Ridge	RDG
Avenue	AVE	Extension	EXT	Lane	LN	River	RIV
Bayou	BYU	Fall	FL	Light	LGT	Road	RD
Beach	BCH	Falls	FLS	Loaf	LF	Row	ROW
Bend	BND	Ferry	FRY	Locks	LCKS	Run	RUN
Bluff	BLF	Field	FLD	Lodge	LDG	Shoal	SHL
Bottom	BTM	Fields	FLDS	Loop	LOOP	Shoals	SHLS
Boulevard	BLVD	Flats	FLT	Mall	MALL	Shore	SHR
Branch	BR	Ford	FRD	Manor	MNR	Shores	SHRS
Bridge	BRG	Forest	FRST	Meadows	MDWS	Spring	SPG
Brook	BRK	Forge	FRG	Mill	ML	Springs	SPGS
Building	BLDG	Fork	FRK	Mills	MLS	Spur	SPUR
Bureau	BUR	Forks	FRKS	Mission	MSN	Square	SQ
Burg	BG	Fort	FT	Mount	MT	Station	STA
Bypass	BYP	Freeway	FWY	Mountain	MTN	Stream	STRM
Camp	CP	Gardens	GDNS	National	NATL	Street	ST
Canyon	CYN	Gateway	GRWY	Neck	NCK	Summit	SMT
Cape	CPE	Glen	GLN	Orchard	ORCH	Terrace	TER
Causeway	CSWY	Green	GRN	Oval	OVAL	Trace	TRCE
Center	CTR	Grove	GRV	Park	PARK	Track	TRAK
Circle	CIR	Harbor	HBR	Parkway	PKY	Trail	TRL
Cliffs	CLFS	Haven	HVN	Pass	PASS	Trailer	TRLR
Club	CLB	Heights	HTS	Path	PATH	Tunnel	TUNL
Corner	COR	Highway	HWY	Pike	PIKE	Turnpike	TPKE
Corners	CORS	Hill	HL	Pines	PNES	Union	UN
Course	CRSE	Hills	HLS	Place	PL	Valley	VLY
Court	CT	Hollow	HOLW	Plain	PLN	Viaduct	VIA
Courts	CTS	Inlet	INLT	Plains	PLNS	View	VW
Cove	CV	Island	IS	Plaza	PLZ	Village	VLG
Creek	CRK	Islands	ISS	Point	PT	Ville	VL
Crescent	CRES	Isle	ISLE	Port	PRT	Vista	VIS
Crossing	XING	Junction	JCT	Prairie	PR	Walk	WALK
Dale	DL	Key	KY	Radial	RADL	Way	WAY
Dam	DM	Knolls	KNLS	Ranch	RNCH	Wells	WLS
Divide	DV						

THE NATION

City	Tuesday Low	High	Wednesday F'cast	Low	High	Thursday F'cast	Low	High
Albuquerque......	33	53	PtCldy	35	56	PtCldy	35	65
Anchorage.........	24	35	Cloudy	25	35	Cloudy	24	38
Asheville............	21	62	Sunny	31	65	Cloudy	41	55
Atlanta..............	33	63	PtCldy	31	65	Rain	52	60
Atlantic City......	23	46	Sunny	30	54	Sunny	29	47
Austin..............	53	67	Cloudy	54	66	Sunny	45	67
Billings	31	58	Sunny	33	60	Windy	28	48
Birmingham......	33	68	Cloudy	42	65	Shwrs	57	62
Bismarck	25	56	PtCldy	27	54	PtCldy	32	55
Boise.................	26	60	Sunny	27	59	PtCldy	24	53
Boston	18	42	PtCldy	31	55	Sunny	26	42
Brownsville........	56	78	Cloudy	66	81	PtCldy	57	76
Buffalo	21	44	PtCldy	28	39	PtCldy	18	35
Charleston, SC..	40	54	Sunny	37	66	Cloudy	49	67
Charlotte, NC ...	25	60	Sunny	34	65	Cloudy	43	58
Cheyenne	33	52	Sunny	28	53	Sunny	29	51
Chicago	37	63	PtCldy	30	45	Fair	28	48
Cincinnati.........	30	67	PtCldy	32	54	PtCldy	34	57
Cleveland	22	59	PtCldy	34	46	Sunny	26	48
Columbia, SC....	22	65	Sunny	29	46	Rain	46	63
Dallas...............	52	67	Strms	42	64	PtCldy	42	60
Dayton..............	29	65	PtCldy	35	52	Sunny	27	54
Denver..............	35	53	Sunny	31	58	Sunny	27	62
Des Moines	43	63	PtCldy	33	56	Cloudy	34	53
Detroit..............	26	57	Sunny	28	46	Sunny	21	42
El Paso	41	62	PtCldy	36	65	Fair	36	72
Fairbanks...........	05	36	PtCldy	03	34	PtCldy	05	37
Fargo	28	49	PtCldy	24	49	PtCldy	29	50
Flagstaff	25	37	Sunny	22	52	PtCldy	23	54
Hartford............	13	48	PtCldy	26	50	Sunny	21	43
Helena..............	24	57	Sunny	25	53	Windy	25	44
Honolulu...........	69	81	Sunny	69	81	Sunny	69	81
Houston	56	65	TStrms	59	68	PtCldy	47	68
Indianapolis	32	66	Sunny	35	56	Cloudy	34	53
Jacksonville	32	65	Sunny	36	72	PtCldy	50	74
Jackson.............	37	73	TStrms	50	72	PtCldy	50	74
Juneau..............	34	41	SnoShw	32	41	PtCldy	33	41
Kansas City	40	70	Cloudy	43	59	Cloudy	37	54

THE NATION

City	Tuesday Low	Tuesday High	Wednesday F'cast	Wednesday Low	Wednesday High	Thursday F'cast	Thursday Low	Thursday High
Las Vegas..........	43	73	Sunny	46	74	PtCldy	48	71
Little Rock	46	72	Rain	50	59	Cloudy	49	59
Los Angeles	46	69	Sunny	48	70	Fair	49	70
Louisville	34	69	PtCldy	42	62	Cloudy	50	58
Lubbock	39	52	Rain	36	54	Fair	35	64
Memphis	45	71	Cloudy	49	64	Rain	49	58
Miami Beach......	57	69	PtCldy	67	76	PtCldy	69	80
Milwaukee	29	60	Sunny	33	46	Sunny	25	47
Minneapolis.......	31	55	Fair	29	44	Sunny	29	50
Nashville...........	30	70	PtCldy	39	68	Rain	49	60
New Orleans.....	42	71	TStrms	56	73	Cloudy	58	73
New York..........	22	47	PtCldy	35	55	Sunny	32	45
Norfolk..............	31	54	PtCldy	35	64	Cloudy	39	48
Oklahoma City..	45	66	Rain	48	54	PtCldy	41	60
Omaha..............	40	63	Sunny	31	62	Sunny	32	64
Orlando............	41	71	Sunny	46	77	PtCldy	57	80
Philadelphia	19	48	Sunny	30	55	Sunny	28	47
Phoenix	50	59	Sunny	47	77	Sunny	52	80
Pittsburgh..........	18	57	PtCldy	37	48	Sunny	25	45
Portland, ME	14	41	PtCldy	27	47	Sunny	20	40
Portland, OR	38	57	Shwrs	40	52	PtCldy	35	56
Raleigh-Drhm ...	21	57	Sunny	31	65	Cloudy	42	56
Reno.................	30	62	Windy	28	62	PtCldy	30	56
Sacramento	44	64	Fair	44	65	PtCldy	42	68
Salt Lake City ...	41	58	Fair	32	60	Shwrs	36	50
San Antonio......	53	67	Cloudy	54	69	Sunny	44	67
San Diego..........	54	66	Sunny	52	66	Fair	55	65
San Francisco....	50	65	PtCldy	48	60	PtCldy	46	61
Seattle...............	42	51	Shwrs	37	50	Rain	39	49
St. Louis...........	48	71	Shwrs	38	58	Shwrs	39	55
St. Pete/Tampa .	37	75	Sunny	46	75	PtCldy	61	78
Shreveport	40	75	TStrms	50	68	Cloudy	45	62
Spokane............	31	55	PtCldy	33	52	PtCldy	27	45
Topeka.............	39	70	PtCldy	40	60	PtCldy	36	54
Tucson	44	55	Sunny	39	71	Sunny	46	77
Tulsa	47	70	Rain	50	56	PtCldy	43	61
Washington.......	24	54	PtCldy	39	65	PtCldy	36	50

DELAWARE

(Abbreviation: DE)

Post office and county	ZIP Code
Bear, New Castle,	19701
Bethany Beach, Sussex,	19930
Bethel, Sussex,	19931
Bridgeville, Sussex, C	19933
Brookside, B (See Newark)	
Camden-Wyoming, Kent, C	19934
Cheswold, Kent,	19936
Clarksville, Sussex,	19937
Claymont, New Castle, C	19703
Clayton, Kent,	19938
Dagsboro, Sussex,	19939
Delaware City, New Castle,	19706
Delmar, Sussex, C	19940
Dewey Beach, CPO Rehoboth Beach	19971
Dover, Kent, C	19901
Dover A F B B x G	
Dover A F B E	19902
Main Office Boxes X (Sussex Co.)	19903
Marydel P	19964
Dover A F B, B x G Dover	19901
Dover A F B, E Dover	19902
Edgemoor, B x G (See Wilmington)	
Ellendale, Sussex,	19941
Farmington, Kent,	19942
Federal, S x G (See Newark)	
Felton, Kent,	19943
Fenwick Island, CPO Selbyville	19944
Frankford, Sussex,	19945
Frederica, Kent,	19946
Georgetown, Sussex, G C	19947
Greenville, B x Wilmington	19807
Greenwood, Sussex,	19950
Harbeson, Sussex,	19951
Harrington, Kent, G C	19952
Hartly, Kent,	19953
Hockessin, New Castle,	19707
Houston, Kent,	19954
Kenton, Kent,	19955
Kirkwood, New Castle,	19708
Laurel, Sussex, G C	19956
Lewes, Sussex, G C	19958
Lincoln, Sussex,	19960
Little Creek, Kent,	19961
Magnolia, Kent,	19962
Main Office Boxes, X Dover	19903
Manor, B x New Castle	19720
Marshallton, B x Wilmington	19808
Marydel, P Dover	19964
Middletown, New Castle, C	19709
Midway, CPO Rehoboth Beach	19971
Milford, Sussex, C	19963
Millsboro, Sussex,	19966
Millville, Sussex,	19967
Milton, Sussex, C	19968
Montchanin, New Castle,	19710
Nassau, Sussex,	19969
NEWARK, New Castle, † G C (SEE PAGE 406)	
Brookside B	
Federal S x G	
Polly Drummond B	
New Castle, New Castle, G C	19720
Manor B x	
Newport, B x Wilmington	19804
Ocean View, Sussex,	19970
Odessa, New Castle,	19730
Polly Drummond, B Newark	19711
Port Penn, New Castle,	19731
Rehoboth Beach, Sussex, G C	19971
Dewey Beach CPO	
Midway CPO	
Rockland, New Castle,	19732
Rodney Square, S x (See Wilmington)	
Saint Georges, New Castle,	19733
Seaford, Sussex, G C	19973
Selbyville, Sussex, G	19975
Fenwick Island CPO	19944
Smyrna, Kent, C	19977
Stanton, B x Wilmington	19804
Talleyville, B x (See Wilmington)	
Townsend, New Castle,	19734
Union Street, S x (See Wilmington)	
Viola, Kent,	19979
WILMINGTON, New Castle, † G C (SEE PAGE 407)	
Edgemoor B x G	
Greenville B x	19807
Marshallton B x	19808
Newport B x	19804
Rodney Square S x	
Stanton B x	19804
Talleyville B x	
Union Street S x	
Winterthur CPO	19735
Winterthur, CPO Wilmington	19735
Woodside, Kent,	19980
Yorklyn, New Castle,	19736

NEWARK DE

POST OFFICE BOXES MAIN OFFICE, STATIONS AND BRANCHES

Box Nos.	ZIP
1-4999 Federal Sta	19715
7000-9999 Main Office	19714
15000-15177 Polly Drummond Br	19711

RURAL ROUTES

1	19702
2	19711

POSTMASTER AND GENERAL DELIVERY

General Delivery	19715
Postmaster	19711

APARTMENTS, HOTELS, MOTELS

Admiral Club	19711
Allandale	19713
Aston Court, 400 Wollaston Ave	19711
Brookside Plaza	19713
Cavalier Country Club	19702
Cedarwood, 758 Christiana Rd	19713
Chestnut Crossing	19713
Churchmans Village, 4949 Ogletown-Stanton Rd	19713
College Town, 163 Elkton Rd	19711
Colonial Garden, 334 E Main St	19711
Country Squire, 900 Capitol Trail	19711
Drummond Hill	19711
English Village	19711
Fairfield	19711
Foxcroft, 120 Wilbur St	19711
Garden Quarter	19711
Greenfield Manor	19702
Harbor Club	19713
Holiday Inn, 1203 Christiana Rd	19713
Howard Johnsons, 1119 S College Ave	19713
Iron Hill	19702
Iron Hill Inn, 1120 S College Ave	19713
Kimberton	19713
La Villa Belmont	19713
Little Sisters Of The Poor, 185 Salem Church Rd	19713
Main Towers, 330 E Main St	19711
Mcintosh Inn, 100 Mcintosh Plz	19713
Millcroft Retirement Home, 255 Possum Park Rd	19711
Oak Tree	19713
Paper Mill	19711
Park Place	19711
Possum Park, 630 Capitol Trl	19711
Regency Square	19711
Royale, 54 Cheswold Blvd	19713
Salem Village	19713
Sandalwood	19713
Sheraton Inn, 300 Chapman Rd	19702
Shoneys, 900 Churchmans Rd	19713
Southgate	19713
Spring Run	19713
Strawberry Run	19702
The Bluffs	19711
Towne Court	19711
Travel Lodge, 268 E Main St	19711
University Garden, 281 Beverly Rd	19711
University Village	19702
Victoria Mews	19711
Village Ii	19713
Village Of Kent	19702
Village Of Windover	19702
Wellington Arms	19713
West Knoll, 260 Elkton Rd	19711

BUILDINGS

Chapel Main, 70 S Chapel St	19711
Chapel North, 62 N Chapel St	19711
Continental, 300 Continental Dr	19713
Drummond Plaza, 1401 Capital Trl	19711
Kelway Plaza, 314 E Main St	19711
Newark Medical, 325-327 E Main St	19711
Robscott, 153 Chestnut Hill Rd	19713
White Clay Center, 1401 Ogletown Rd	19711

GOVERNMENT OFFICES

City Of Newark, 220 Elkton Rd	19711
Delaware Dept Of Labor, 37 Marrows Rd	19713
Delaware Turnpike Adm, 1200 Whitaker Rd	19702
Floyd Hudson Service Ctr, 501 Ogletown Rd	19711
New Castle County Ascs Ofc, 4 Peoples Plz	19702
New Castle County Engineering, 2701 Capital Trl	19711
U S Dept Of Labor, 261 Chapman Rd	19702

HOSPITALS

Medical Ctr Of De, Christiana, Po Box 6001	19718

UNIVERSITIES AND COLLEGES

Delaware Tech Comm College, 400 Stanton Christiana Rd	19713
Univ Of De Students, Agriculture Dept Bk Store, Library	19717
Univ Of Delaware, Administrative	19716

NAMED STREETS

Aaa Blvd	19713
Abbey Hall	19711
Academy St	19711
Adams Dr	19711
Addison Cir & Dr	19702
Adrian Ct	19713
Albe Dr	19702
Albert St	19702
Aldershot Dr	19713
Aleph Dr	19702
Alexandria Dr	19711
Alice Ct	19702
Allan Dr	19711
Allandale Dr	19713
Allcorn Ct	19711
Allison Ln	19711
Alton Ct & Rd	19711
Alton Wood Dr	19711
Alvin Dr	19702
Alwyn Rd	19713
Amherst Dr	19711
Amstel Ave	19711
Anderson Ln	19711
Anderson Rd	19713
Andrea Rd	19702
Andries Rd	19711
Anglin Rd	19713
Anita Dr	19713
Annabelle St	19711
Ansonia Ct	19711
Anthony Cir	19702
Apache Ct	19702
Apple Rd	19711
Arbour Dr	19713
Archer Cir & Way	19702
Ardmore Dr	19713
Argyle Rd	19713
Arkfield Ct	19713
Arlene Ct	19702
Arlington St	19711
Aronimink Dr	19711
Art Ln	19713
Ash Ave	19711
Ashkirk Pl	19702
Ashley Rd	19711
Aster Ave	19711
Astro Shopping Ctr	19711
Atram Hall	19711
Aubrey Ln	19711
Augusta Dr	19713
Autumn Horseshoe Bnd	19702
Aylesboro St	19713
Azalea Rd	19711
Bach Dr	19702
Bala Rd	19713
Balanger Rd	19711
Ballad Dr	19702
Banyan Rd	19713
Barberry Ct	19702
Barclay Hall	19711
Bark Dr	19713
Barksdale Plz	19711
Barksdale Rd	
1-1999	19711
Barksdale Prof Ctr	19711
Barnaby St	19702
Barnard St	19711
Bartley Dr	19702
Bartow Cir	19713
Bass Ct	19713
Bassett Pl	19711
Bayard St	19702
Baylor Dr	19711
Belfield Rd	19713
Bellevue Rd	19713
Bemis Rd	19711
Render Dr	19711
Benny St	19711
Bent Ln	19711
Berwick Dr	19702
Berwyn Hall	19711
Beverly Rd	19711
Birch Ln	19702
Birchbrook Dr	19702
Birchwood Dr	19713
Bisbee Ct & Rd	19711
Biscayne Blvd	19713
Blackstone Rd	19713
Blair Ct	19711
Blatty Pl	19702
Blue Hen Dr	19713
Blue Hen Rdg	19711
Blue Jay Dr	19713
Bluefield Rd	19713
Bobby Dr	19713
Bonnie Ln	19713
Bowfin Dr	19702
Boxwood Ave	19711
Boyds Valley Dr	19711
Bradford Ln	19711
Bradley Dr	19702
Branch Rd	19711
Brandywine Ct	19702
Breezewood Turn	19713
Brennen Ct & Dr	19713
Brentwood Ln	19711
Brewster Dr	19711
Briar Ln	19711
Bridlebrook Ln	19711
Bridleshire Ct & Rd	19711
Bristol Rd	19711
Broadfield Rd	19713
Brook Dr	19713
Brookbend Dr	19713
Brookedge Ct	19702
Brookhill Dr	19702
Brookmeade Rd	19711
Brookmont Dr	19702
Brookside Blvd	19713
Brownleaf Rd, N & S	19713
Browns Ln	19702
Bryant Ct	19713
Bunker Hill Ct	19702
Burbank St	19702
Burleigh Ct	19702
Burningbush Dr	19711
Burns Way	19702
Byron Ct	19702
Cadagan St	19702
Cain Rue	19711
Caladium Ln	19711
Caldwell Pl	19711
Calgary Rd	19711
Calyso Ct	19711
Cambridge Dr	19711
Cameron Ln	19713
Campfield Rd	19713
Candate Ct	19711
Cann Rd	19702
Canoe Ct	19702
Canoe Club Rd	19702
Canter Cir	19711
Canzonet Dr	19702
Capano Dr	19702
Capital Pl & Trl	19711
Carlin Ln	19713
Carlisle Rd	19713
Carlo Rd	19702
Carnaby Hall	19711
Carnegie Ct	19713
Carole Rd	19713
Carriage Ln	19711
Cartier Ct	19711
Casho Mill Rd	19711
Cassandra Rd	19702
Castle Mall	19713
Catalina Dr	19711
Cauline Ct	19711
Cedar Ct	19702
Cedarwood Ln	19702
Center St	19711
Cervantes Ct	19702
Chadd Rd	19711
Chambers St	19711
Chambers Rock Rd	19711
Chancellor Dr	19713
Chapel St, N	19711
Chapel St, S	
1-315	19711
316-999	19713
1000-OUT	19702
Chapel Hill Dr	19711
Chapel Hill Dr, W	19711
Chapman Rd	
1-99	19713
100-OUT	19702
Chatham Ln	19713
Chaucer Dr	19713
Chelmsford Cir	19713
Cheltenham Rd	19711
Cherokee Dr, E & W	19713
Chesbee Dr	19711
Chesmar Plz	19713
Chestnut Ave	19711
Chestnut Xing	19713
Chestnut Hill Plz	19713
Chestnut Hill Rd, E & W	19713
Cheswold Blvd	19713
Cheyenne Ct	19702
Chippendale Cir	19713
Choate St	19711
Christiana Mall	19702
Christiana Rd	19713
Christiana Medical Ctr	19702
Christiana Towers Dr, E & W	19711
Christiana Vlg Prof Ctr	19702
Chrysler Ave	19711
Church Rd	19702
Church Rd, N & W	19711
Church St	19711
Churchmans Rd	
1-799	19702
800-1499	19713
Clairmont Dr, E & W	19702
Clarion Ct	19713
Clemson Ct	19711
Cleveland Ave, E & W	19711
Clipper Ct	19702
Clover Ln	19713
Cloverlea Rd	19711
Cobble Creek Curve	19702
Cohansey Cir	19702
Cold Spring Run Run	19711
Colfax Rd	19713
Colgate Ln	19711
College Ave, N	19711
College Ave, S	
1-499	19711
500-1199	19713
1200-OUT	19702
College Sq	19711
Comet Ln	19711
Concord Bridge Pl	19702

Conne
Contin
Contin
Cook
Copper
Coral
Corbit
Cordele
Cordrey
Corner
Cornw
Cornw
Coron
Count
Countr
Count
Court
Covent
Cover
Cox
Creek
Creek
Cros
Croyd
Crysta
Curlew
Curry
Curtis
Cynthia
Cypre
Daise
Dale
Dallam
Dallas
Dan S
Danna
Darby
Darien
Darwin
Darwin
David
Davies
Dawes
Dawso
Decke
Deer R
Deer R
Deerfie
Defoe
Dekal
Del Gr
Delapl
Delawa
Delawa
Delawa
Delpa
Delre
Demp
Dennis
Denny
Deville
Devon
Dewal
Dicke
Dillw
Dixie
10
Dixon
Doe L
Doe R
Dogw
Dolphi
Donald
Donak
Donna
Dorche
Dougf
Dove
Dove
Drexe
Drex
Duff
Duma
Dunba
Dunsm
Durha
Dursc
Eagle
Earling
Eastbu
Eastfie
Eastw
Eberly
Eden
Edgeb
Edgem

OFFICE FILES/DATABASES

CONTENTS

```
             JUST JEANS, INCORPORATED
           SCHEDULE OF ACCOUNTS RECEIVABLE
                  NOVEMBER 30, 19--


     ALL STAR CLOTHING STORES        1,200.00
     BETTY LACY'S STYLE CENTER         850.00
     DALE'S DEPT STORES                675.00
     GEORGE MOSS CLOTHING OUTLET     2,525.00 B
     J & J SPECIALTY SHOPPES         1,750.00
     MCRAE CLOTHING DEPOT              655.00 C
     'SPECIALLY FOR YOU STORES       2,500.00
     TEEN TOWN CLOTHIERS               950.00 A

                        TOTAL        11,105.00




   CODES:   A=60 days      B=90 days        C=COLLECT. AGCY
```

KA___ KEY AIR FLIGHT SCHEDULE

From LITTLE ROCK, AR					From MEMPHIS, TN				
Reservations 555-4440					Reservations 555-2311				
Air Cargo 555-4488					Air Cargo 555-2335				
Lv	Ar	Flight Number	Stops or Via	Meals	Lv	Ar	Flight Number	Stops or Via	Meals
To MEMPHIS, TN				130 miles	To LITTLE ROCK, AR				130 miles
630a	702a	236	0		735a	807a	507	0	
1215p	1247p	298	0		110p	139p	583	0	
305p	337p	218	0		505p	537p	551	0	
700p	732p	154	0		845p	917p	717	0	

```
                    Receiving Report

                      05/20/--


Purchase Order No.

Vendor          ELLIS PAPER PRODUCTS

Vendor Invoice No.       73904

Item                   Quantity  Quantity
No.  Description  Unit  Ordered   Received   Remarks

LD65 ENVELOPES     BOX     150       145        5D
MW29 MAILING TAPE  ROLL     15        10        5B




   CODES:  B=Backordered    D=Damaged    O=Over
           X=Discontinued   S=Short
```

Screen 1

```
              SPEAKERS AND JUDGES

ALY CHAMBRA  ALY'S DEPT STORE
3892 W VICTORY DR
LEBANON MO    65536-3047
555-4584

BURDETT BILLIE ANNE  MAYOR'S AIDE
717 FELDWOOD PL
AURORA MO    65605-5320
555-9200 EXT 28

CARLTON JACOB  RETIRED REAL EST BROKER
1974 LAKESHORE TR
MONETT MO  65708-3371
555-2348
```

Screen 2

```
ORRICK RAY  LAWYER
1225 TOM LEWIS BLDG
JOPLIN MO  64801-4582
555-6119

PAUL LINDA  OWNER  WP SERVICES INC
11957 COLLINS BLVD  SUITE G-34
SPRINGFIELD MO  65804-9135
555-3387

WALKER HILDA  TRNG DIR  METRO TEMP SVS
483 GRANDE VISTA PKWY
BOLIVAR MO  65613-0357
555-9295
```

```
                         PRICE QUOTATION


                                    STOCK NO:  FF86
     ITEM:    File Folders              UNIT:  500 per carton


     ────────────────────────────────────────────────────────────────
     Date    Firm and Address        Price     Terms      Contact
     ────────────────────────────────────────────────────────────────
     July 1  Adams Company
             814 Rice Avenue
             Bronx, NY 10467-1283     55.75     60 days    Leroy Durst

          1  Chang Company
             140 Key Street
             Carlstadt, NJ 07072-1082 52.80     45 days    Ming-li

          1  Riggs Company
             292 Melville Road
             White Plains, NY 10607-2218 55.25  30 days    Helen Ashe
```

```
                         PRICE QUOTATION

                                    STOCK NO:  JM29
     ITEM:    Jiffy Mailers             UNIT:  500 per carton


     ────────────────────────────────────────────────────────────────
     Date    Firm and Address        Price     Terms      Contact
     ────────────────────────────────────────────────────────────────
     July 1  Adams Company
             814 Rice Avenue
             Bronx, NY 10467-1283     99.75     60 days    Leroy Durst

          1  Bigelow Company
             1058 Anchor Place
             Newark, NJ 07102-1557    98.50     60 days    Joe Orr

          1  Harding Company
             726 Wall Boulevard
             Yonkers, NY 10704-6021   101.50    90 days    Margo Lea
```

POSTAL ANSWER LINE

—it's the nearest thing to having your own personal post office.

Information at your fingertips.

Now you don't have to stand in information lines at the post office. Or make unnecessary trips. (Much as we like to see you, we know you're busy.)

That's because POSTAL ANSWER LINE—the post office's new automated telephone service—puts information at your fingertips.

It couldn't be easier.

How to use POSTAL ANSWER LINE

1. Look up the message number for the information you want.
2. In the Atlanta area, call 555-7689 on your touch-tone telephone.
3. The recorded instructions will tell you when to push the buttons that correspond with the desired message number.
4. Wait a few moments for your message to begin.
5. For information on another service or to have the message repeated, wait for the tone, then press the appropriate message number.

	Message No.
First-Class Mail—Up to but over twelve (12) ounces	101
First-Class Mail—Over 12 ounces, up to but not over 32 ounces (2 pounds)	155
First-Class Mail—Over 32 ounces, up to 60 ounces (5 pounds)	355
First-Class Mail—Over 60 ounces (5 pounds) call your local post office for costs	
Parcel Post—Packages weighing up to but not over fifteen pounds	301
Parcel Post—Packages weighing over fifteen pounds—Call your local post office	

Sending Valuables/Proof of Mailing or Delivery

When you send valuables or need proof of mailing or delivery.

How to send valuables through the mail	Message No.
Registered mail	135
Insurance	337
How to file a claim for items lost or damaged in the mail	113
How to obtain proof of mailing or delivery	
Certificate of mailing	111
Certified mail	121
Return receipt service (proof of delivery)	334

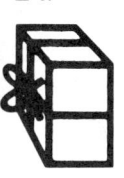

Moving or Vacationing/Mail Holding/Mail Forwarding

Whenever you travel, we'll mind your mail. And when you move, we'll move your mail right along with you.

Moving or going on vacation? Here's what to do.	Message No.
Relocating permanently: File a change of address at least one month before you move.	137
When you'll be away six months or less: File a temporary change of address.	312
While you're on vacation: Notify the post office to hold your mail.	340

International Mail/Sending Packages

We can make international mailing as easy as mailing to the nearest town.

This page has message numbers for the dos and don'ts of mailing packages.

	Message No.
International mail	
Rates for First-Class surface mail	319
Airmail rates and information	134
Express Mail International Service	318
Parcel Post rates and information	317
Customs	308
Special services available	142
International Reply Coupons	307
How to send packages	
Which mailing option should I select?	310
Special services available for packages	143
How to prepare packages for mailing	139
Sending parcels to the military	109

Resolving Problems/Mail Order/Fraud/Security

This page has message numbers for reporting problems or complaints, for protecting yourself from mail fraud and for mail security.

Resolving mail difficulties	Message No.
How to report a service problem, compliment or complaint	335
Removing your name from mailing lists	140
Tracing or recalling mail	117
Unsolicited merchandise	306
Illegal mail items	106
Dogs can delay your mail	148
Sexually oriented ads	338
Mail Order	
Mail order tips	348
Mail order problems	311
Mail order and mail fraud publications	105

Christiansen Insurance Agency

IMPORTANT MESSAGE

TO: _Ron Abbott_

Mʳˢ _Sylvia Jensen_

of _Minn. Ins. Commission_

FROM: _C. Canning_

DATE: _10-2- —_

TIME: _2:35 P.M._

✓ TELEPHONED	CAME TO SEE YOU
✓ PLEASE PHONE	WOULD LIKE TO SEE YOU
WILL CALL AGAIN	WILL STOP BY LATER
RETURNED YOUR CALL	OTHER

MESSAGE/COMMENTS _Regarding Insurance Meeting on Oct. 18_

APPOINTMENTS—TUESDAY, OCTOBER 2, 19-

TIME	NAME/TITLE	COMPANY
9:00	Dennis Erickson, Owner	Lithonia Finance Co.
9:30	Gina Terveen, Systems Analyst	J&T Computer Corp.
10:00	Tom Lear, Auto Mechanic	Self-employed
10:30	Dottie Henlin, Piano Tuner	Self-employed
11:00	Sheila Seville, Attorney	Seville, Ling, Frye
11:30	Preston Dawson, CPA	Dawson & Associates
1:00	Rowanne Liles, Representative	Metro Exterminators
1:30	Billie Gershon, News Reporter	Van Nuys Journal
2:00	Keith McCue, President	Western Reliance
2:30	Margie Boyle, Author	Self-employed
3:00	Earl Greenberg, Professor	Clay College
3:30	Brett Souters, Sales Manager	Shamrock Industries

FAX TRANSMISSION COVER SHEET

Today's Date: _Oct. 1, 19--_

Person to Receive FAX Message: _Ms. Yoko Umeki_

Person Sending FAX Message: _Mr. James Lowery_

FAX Telephone Number: _(740) 555-4590_ (or) Auto Dial No._____

(NOTE: If FAX message is being sent overseas, a country code, usually three digits, is necessary.)

This page and _____ page(s) transmitted.

_10-1-— 10:40 A.M._

Date and Time Message Transmitted

NATIONAL INSURANCE ASSOCIATION
2976 Madison Boulevard
Coshocton, OH 43812-1004

October 1, 19—

Ms. Yoko Umeki, CLU
Christiansen Insurance Agency
11974 Perimeter Industrial Blvd.
High Point, NC 27261-2389

Dear Ms. Umeki:

Thank you for accepting the assignment as the keynote speaker at the 3 p.m. session on Thursday, June 25, at the National Insurance Association Convention in Denver.

Please forward a glossy black and white photograph and a brief biographical sketch to my office no later than January 15. You will receive further correspondence from Convention Program Chairperson Catherine Jackson.

Give my best regards to your chapter members in High Point.

Sincerely,

NATIONAL INSURANCE ASSOCIATION

James Lowery
Executive Director

vcw

IMPORTANT MESSAGE

TO: _Yoko Umeki_   FROM: _C. Canning_

Ms _Marcy Eisenberg_   DATE: _10-1-—_

of _Consumer League_   TIME: _11:15 A.M._

TELEPHONED	✓ CAME TO SEE YOU
✓ PLEASE PHONE	WOULD LIKE TO SEE YOU
WILL CALL AGAIN	WILL STOP BY LATER
RETURNED YOUR CALL	OTHER

MESSAGE/COMMENTS _____

_____

_____

SOUTHWESTERN OFFICE AUTOMATION CONFERENCE REGISTRATION

Name	Company	Address	Phone
Early, Edward	Sands Software	373 Walnut Lane Cincinnati, OH 45227-2882	(513) 555-4001
Fuentes, Carla	Century Electronics	23814 Valley Blvd. Beaumont, TX 77706-0478	(409) 555-1092
Hilty, Owen	The Creamery	12 Penn Avenue Pittsburgh, PA 15202-3302	(412) 555-8813
Ingram, Deloris	Mahalia Word Processing Service	8316 Mahalia Road Houma, LA 70360-2257	(318) 555-8294
Naylon, J. Steven	Self-Employed Author	984 Victory Circle Lake Charles, LA 70605-2843	(318) 555-7117
Proctor, Tony	Budget Software Distributors	1100 Terrell Mill Tpke. Columbus, MS 39701-6251	(601) 555-8309

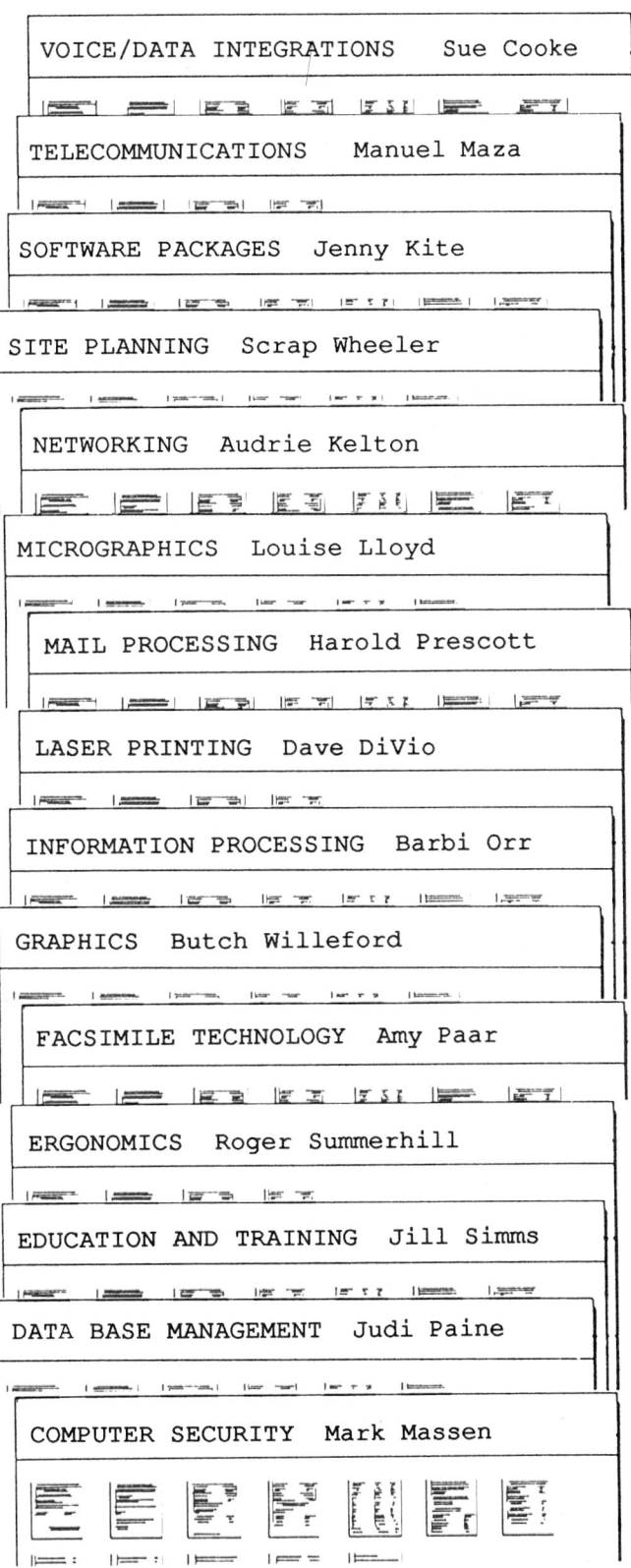

VOICE/DATA INTEGRATIONS   Sue Cooke

TELECOMMUNICATIONS   Manuel Maza

SOFTWARE PACKAGES   Jenny Kite

SITE PLANNING   Scrap Wheeler

NETWORKING   Audrie Kelton

MICROGRAPHICS   Louise Lloyd

MAIL PROCESSING   Harold Prescott

LASER PRINTING   Dave DiVio

INFORMATION PROCESSING   Barbi Orr

GRAPHICS   Butch Willeford

FACSIMILE TECHNOLOGY   Amy Paar

ERGONOMICS   Roger Summerhill

EDUCATION AND TRAINING   Jill Simms

DATA BASE MANAGEMENT   Judi Paine

COMPUTER SECURITY   Mark Massen

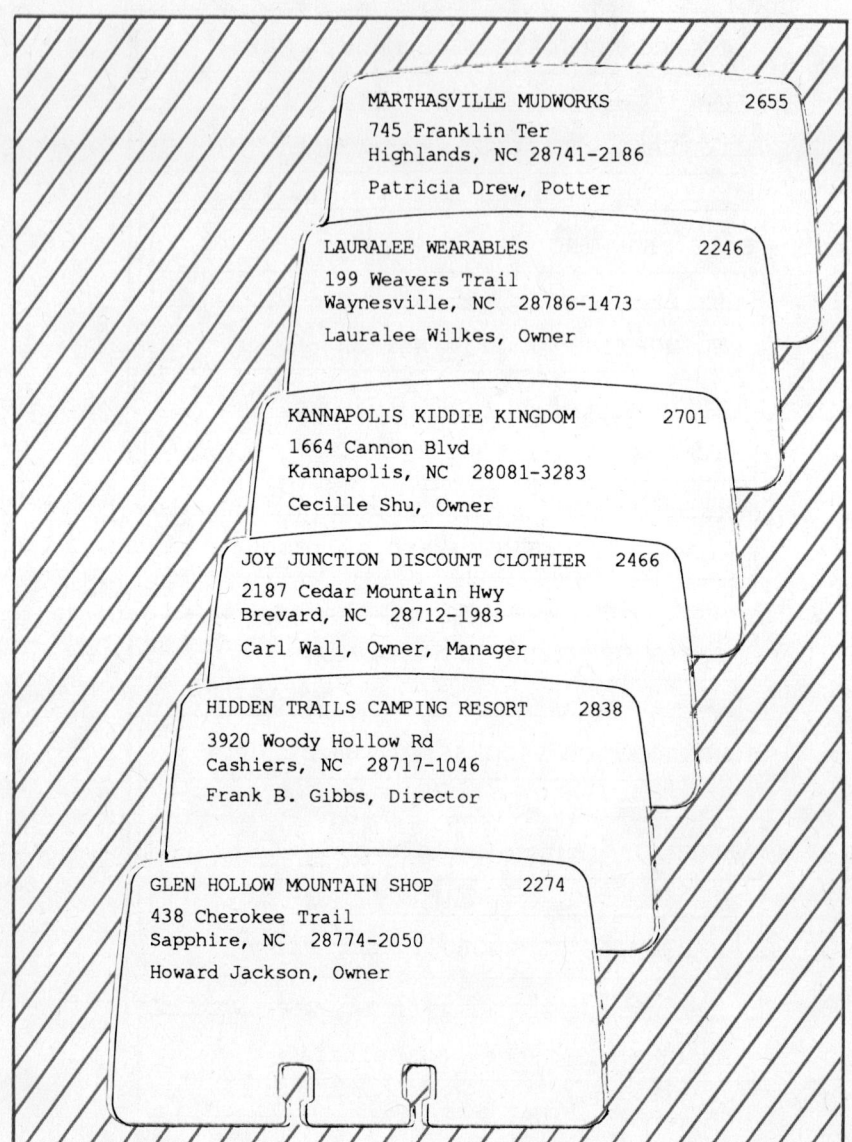

MARTHASVILLE MUDWORKS   2655

745 Franklin Ter
Highlands, NC 28741-2186

Patricia Drew, Potter

LAURALEE WEARABLES   2246

199 Weavers Trail
Waynesville, NC 28786-1473

Lauralee Wilkes, Owner

KANNAPOLIS KIDDIE KINGDOM   2701

1664 Cannon Blvd
Kannapolis, NC 28081-3283

Cecille Shu, Owner

JOY JUNCTION DISCOUNT CLOTHIER   2466

2187 Cedar Mountain Hwy
Brevard, NC 28712-1983

Carl Wall, Owner, Manager

HIDDEN TRAILS CAMPING RESORT   2838

3920 Woody Hollow Rd
Cashiers, NC 28717-1046

Frank B. Gibbs, Director

GLEN HOLLOW MOUNTAIN SHOP   2274

438 Cherokee Trail
Sapphire, NC 28774-2050

Howard Jackson, Owner

MED-FUND VOLUNTEER ENROLLMENT FORM

PLEASE PRINT

MR MS MRS	LAST NAME	FIRST NAME	MI
MS	FORSYTH	JESSICA	H

COMPANY: VIP AIRLINES

STREET ADDRESS: MUNICIPAL AIRPORT   SUITE APT / NO

CITY	STATE	ZIP
LOUISVILLE	KY	40216-5114

AREA CODE	BUSINESS PHONE	EXTENSION	AREA CODE	HOME PHONE
502	555-1125	40	502	555-8392

MED-FUND VOLUNTEER ENROLLMENT FORM

PLEASE PRINT

MR MS MRS	LAST NAME	FIRST NAME	MI
MR	HOLLOWAY	WINSTON	S

COMPANY: CHAMBER OF COMMERCE

STREET ADDRESS: P O BOX 78   SUITE APT / NO

CITY	STATE	ZIP
BARDSTOWN	KY	40004-0078

AREA CODE	BUSINESS PHONE	EXTENSION	AREA CODE	HOME PHONE
502	555-1102		502	555-0395

MED-FUND VOLUNTEER ENROLLMENT FORM

PLEASE PRINT

MR MS MRS	LAST NAME	FIRST NAME	MI
MRS	MARROW	EDITH	J

COMPANY: CITY OF SHEPHERDSVILLE

STREET ADDRESS: 1210 CENTRAL AVE   SUITE APT / NO

CITY	STATE	ZIP
SHEPHERDSVILLE	KY	40165-2635

AREA CODE	BUSINESS PHONE	EXTENSION	AREA CODE	HOME PHONE
502	555-6306	2	502	555-9604

MED-FUND VOLUNTEER ENROLLMENT FORM

PLEASE PRINT

MR MS MRS	LAST NAME	FIRST NAME	MI
MR	OGLESBY	LOUIS	R

COMPANY: ACME ELECTRIC AUTHORITY

STREET ADDRESS: 4520 LOUISVILLE HWY   SUITE APT / NO.

CITY	STATE	ZIP
JEFFERSONTOWN	KY	40299-1482

AREA CODE	BUSINESS PHONE	EXTENSION	AREA CODE	HOME PHONE
502	555-8294	28	502	555-7206

This Lease Witnesseth:

THAT Norris J. Dundas and Cecily W. Dundas, husband and wife, HEREBY LEASE TO Michael G. Farmer

the premises situate in the City *of* Alexandria *in the County of* Thayer *and State of* Nebraska *described as follows:*

Building to be used as an office located at 730 North Street Alexandria, Nebraska

with the appurtenances thereto, for the term of five (5) years *commencing* June 1, 19 -- *at a rental of* Nine hundred (900)----------

dollars per month *. payable* monthly.

SAID LESSEE AGREES *to pay said rent, unless said premises shall be destroyed or rendered untenantable by fire or other unavoidable accident; to not commit or suffer waste; to not use said premises for any unlawful purpose; to not assign this lease, or underlet said premises, or any part thereof, or permit the sale of* his *interest herein by legal process, without the written consent of said lessor* S; *to not use said premises or any part thereof in violation of any law relating to intoxicating liquors; and at the expiration of this lease, to surrender said premises in as good condition as they now are, or may be put by said lessor* S, *reasonable wear and unavoidable casualties, condemnation or appropriation excepted. Upon nonpayment of any of said rent for* thirty *days, after it shall become due, and without demand made therefor; or if said lessee or any assignee of this lease shall make an assignment for the benefit of his creditors; or if proceedings in bankruptcy shall be instituted by or against lessee or any assignee; or if a receiver or trustee be appointed for the property of the lessee or any assignee; or if this lease by operation of law pass to any person or persons; or if said lessee or any assignee shall fail to keep any of the other covenants of this lease, it shall be lawful for said lessor* s, their *heirs or assigns, into said premises to reenter, and the same to have again, repossess and enjoy, as in* their *first and former estate; and thereupon this lease and everything herein contained on the said lessor* s '*behalf to be done and performed, shall cease, determine, and be utterly void.*

SAID LESSORS AGREE *(said lessee having performed* his *obligations under this lease) that said lessee shall quietly hold and occupy said premises during said term without any hindrance or molestation by said lessor* s, their *heir* s *or any person lawfully claiming under* them.

Signed this first *day of* May *A. D. 19 --*

IN THE PRESENCE OF:

Lilian Beemer

Gerald Vickery

Michael G. Farmer

Norris J. Dundas

Cecily W. Dundas

MED-FUND VOLUNTEER ENROLLMENT FORM

PLEASE PRINT

MR MS MRS	LAST NAME	FIRST NAME	MI
MS	FORSYTH	JESSICA	H

COMPANY
VIP AIRLINES

STREET ADDRESS	SUITE APT / NO
MUNICIPAL AIRPORT	

CITY	STATE	ZIP
LOUISVILLE	KY	40216-5114

AREA CODE	BUSINESS PHONE	EXTENSION	AREA CODE	HOME PHONE
502	555-1125	40	502	555-8392

MED-FUND VOLUNTEER ENROLLMENT FORM

PLEASE PRINT

MR MS MRS	LAST NAME	FIRST NAME	MI
MR	HOLLOWAY	WINSTON	S

COMPANY
CHAMBER OF COMMERCE

STREET ADDRESS	SUITE APT / NO
P O BOX 718	

CITY	STATE	ZIP
BARDSTOWN	KY	40004-0078

AREA CODE	BUSINESS PHONE	EXTENSION	AREA CODE	HOME PHONE
502	555-1102		502	555-0395

MED-FUND VOLUNTEER ENROLLMENT FORM

PLEASE PRINT

MR MS MRS	LAST NAME	FIRST NAME	MI
MRS	MARISOW	EDITH	J

COMPANY
CITY OF SHEPHERDSVILLE

STREET ADDRESS	SUITE APT / NO
1210 CENTRAL AVE	

CITY	STATE	ZIP
SHEPHERDSVILLE	KY	40165-2635

AREA CODE	BUSINESS PHONE	EXTENSION	AREA CODE	HOME PHONE
502	555-6306	2	502	555-9604

MED-FUND VOLUNTEER ENROLLMENT FORM

PLEASE PRINT

MR MS MRS	LAST NAME	FIRST NAME	MI
MR	OGLESBY	LOUIS	R

COMPANY
ACME ELECTRIC AUTHORITY

STREET ADDRESS	SUITE APT. / NO.
4520 LOUISVILLE HWY	

CITY	STATE	ZIP
JEFFERSONTOWN	KY	40299-1482

AREA CODE	BUSINESS PHONE	EXTENSION	AREA CODE	HOME PHONE
502	555-8294	28	502	555-7706

𝔗𝔥𝔦𝔰 𝔏𝔢𝔞𝔰𝔢 𝔚𝔦𝔱𝔫𝔢𝔰𝔰𝔢𝔱𝔥:

THAT Norris J. Dundas and Cecily W. Dundas, husband and wife,
HEREBY LEASE TO Michael G. Farmer

the premises situate in the City *of* Alexandria *in the County of* Thayer *and State of* Nebraska *described as follows:*

Building to be used as an office located at 730 North Street Alexandria, Nebraska

with the appurtenances thereto, for the term of five (5) years *commencing* June 1, *19 __ at a rental of* Nine hundred (900)----------

dollars per month *. payable* monthly.

SAID LESSEE AGREES *to pay said rent, unless said premises shall be destroyed or rendered untenantable by fire or other unavoidable accident; to not commit or suffer waste; to not use said premises for any unlawful purpose; to not assign this lease, or underlet said premises, or any part thereof, or permit the sale of* his *interest herein by legal process, without the written consent of said lessor* s; *to not use said premises or any part thereof in violation of any law relating to intoxicating liquors; and at the expiration of this lease, to surrender said premises in as good condition as they now are, or may be put by said lessor* s, *reasonable wear and unavoidable casualties, condemnation or appropriation excepted. Upon nonpayment of any of said rent for* thirty *days, after it shall become due, and without demand made therefor; or if said lessee or any assignee of this lease shall make an assignment for the benefit of his creditors; or if proceedings in bankruptcy shall be instituted by or against lessee or any assignee; or if a receiver or trustee be appointed for the property of the lessee or any assignee; or if this lease by operation of law pass to any person or persons; or if said lessee or any assignee shall fail to keep any of the other covenants of this lease, it shall be lawful for said lessor* s, their *heirs or assigns, into said premises to reenter, and the same to have again, repossess and enjoy, as in* their *first and former estate; and thereupon this lease and everything herein contained on the said lessor* s '*behalf to be done and performed, shall cease, determine, and be utterly void.*

SAID LESSORS AGREE *(said lessee having performed* his *obligations under this lease) that said lessee shall quietly hold and occupy said premises during said term without any hindrance or molestation by said lessor* s, their *heirs or any person lawfully claiming under* them.

Signed this first *day of* May *A. D. 19 __*

IN THE PRESENCE OF:

Lillian Beemer *Norris J. Dundas*
Gerald Vickery *Cecily W. Dundas*
Michael G. Farmer

Cut here and give the certificate to your employer. Keep the top portion for your records.

Form **W-4**
Department of the Treasury
Internal Revenue Service

Employee's Withholding Allowance Certificate

▶ For Privacy Act and Paperwork Reduction Act Notice, see reverse.

OMB No. 1545-0010

1992

1 Type or print your first name and middle initial IVAN T.	Last name WELLS	2 Your social security number 358-04-0966

Home address (number and street or rural route) 1705 WESTWOOD AVE	3 ☐ Single ☒ Married ☐ Married, but withhold at higher Single rate.
City or town, state, and ZIP code HEBRON NE 68370-5027	Note: If married, but legally separated, or spouse is a nonresident alien, check the Single box.

4 If your last name differs from that on your social security card, check here and call 1-800-772-1213 for more information ▶ ☐

5	Total number of allowances you are claiming (from line G above or from the Worksheets on back if they apply)	5	4
6	Additional amount, if any, you want deducted from each paycheck	6	$

7 I claim exemption from withholding and I certify that I meet **ALL** of the following conditions for exemption:
   • Last year I had a right to a refund of **ALL** Federal income tax withheld because I had **NO** tax liability; **AND**
   • This year I expect a refund of **ALL** Federal income tax withheld because I expect to have **NO** tax liability; **AND**
   • This year if my income exceeds $600 and includes nonwage income, another person cannot claim me as a dependent.
   If you meet all of the above conditions, enter the year effective and "EXEMPT" here . . ▶ | 7 | 19

8 Are you a full-time student? (**Note:** *Full-time students are not automatically exempt.*) . . . . | 8 ☐ Yes ☐ No

Under penalties of perjury, I certify that I am entitled to the number of withholding allowances claimed on this certificate or entitled to claim exempt status.

Employee's signature ▶ *Ivan T. Wells*   Date ▶ 9-28-   , 19

9 Employer's name and address (Employer: Complete 9 and 11 only if sending to the IRS)	10 Office code (optional)	11 Employer identification number

Cat. No. 10220Q

Cut here and give the certificate to your employer. Keep the top portion for your records.

Form **W-4**
Department of the Treasury
Internal Revenue Service

Employee's Withholding Allowance Certificate

▶ For Privacy Act and Paperwork Reduction Act Notice, see reverse.

OMB No. 1545-0010

1992

1 Type or print your first name and middle initial CHERYL M. NIX	Last name	2 Your social security number 380-61-8297

Home address (number and street or rural route) 682 LINCOLN TER	3 ☒ Single ☐ Married ☐ Married, but withhold at higher Single rate.
City or town, state, and ZIP code FAIRBURY NE 68352-7214	Note: If married, but legally separated, or spouse is a nonresident alien, check the Single box.

4 If your last name differs from that on your social security card, check here and call 1-800-772-1213 for more information ▶ ☐

5	Total number of allowances you are claiming (from line G above or from the Worksheets on back if they apply)	5	1
6	Additional amount, if any, you want deducted from each paycheck	6	$

7 I claim exemption from withholding and I certify that I meet **ALL** of the following conditions for exemption:
   • Last year I had a right to a refund of **ALL** Federal income tax withheld because I had **NO** tax liability; **AND**
   • This year I expect a refund of **ALL** Federal income tax withheld because I expect to have **NO** tax liability; **AND**
   • This year if my income exceeds $600 and includes nonwage income, another person cannot claim me as a dependent.
   If you meet all of the above conditions, enter the year effective and "EXEMPT" here . . ▶ | 7 | 19

8 Are you a full-time student? (**Note:** *Full-time students are not automatically exempt.*) . . . . | 8 ☐ Yes ☐ No

Under penalties of perjury, I certify that I am entitled to the number of withholding allowances claimed on this certificate or entitled to claim exempt status.

Employee's signature ▶ *Cheryl M. Nix*   Date ▶ 9-28-   , 19

9 Employer's name and address (Employer: Complete 9 and 11 only if sending to the IRS)	10 Office code (optional)	11 Employer identification number

Cat. No. 10220Q

Heintzelman Communication Systems

DATE	FROM	TO	FLIGHT NUMBER	MILES
4-1	DFW	MCI	872	460
4-2	MCI	DFW	859	460
4-8	DFW	SFO	651	1,465
4-14	SFO	MSY	744	1,911
4-18	MSY	DFW	793	447
4-20	DFW	MEM	506	431
4-24	MEM	CVG	320	403
4-28	CVG	BNA	211	230
4-30	BNA	DFW	645	631
5-12	DFW	ATL	104	731
5-15	ATL	SAT	437	874
5-17	SAT	DFW	958	247

FLIGHT LOG OF LAMBROS, A
LAST NAME, INITIAL

LEGAL
DEPARTMENT

DATE	FROM	TO	FLIGHT NUMBER	MILES
5-24	DFW	SDF	920	732
5-25	SDF	LGA	398	657
5-31	LGA	DFW	145	1,386
6-6	DFW	AMA	884	313
6-6	AMA	LBB	461	108
6-7	LBB	DFW	532	282
6-10	DFW	BHM	278	597
6-12	BHM	JAN	767	211
6-15	JAN	DFW	619	408
6-26	DFW	BDL	196	1,470
6-28	BDL	BOS	285	91
6-30	BOS	DFW	933	1,561

```
                    TRAVEL SUMMARY
              A. Lambros--Legal Department

      Month      Miles      Month      Miles

      Jan        4,983      Ar         6,438
      Feb        7,349      May        4,627
      Mar        5,246      Jun        5,041

      Totals     17,578                16,106
```

EMPLOYEE	JULY				AUGUST					SEPTEMBER			
	Week Beginning				Week Beginning					Week Beginning			
	4	11	18	25	1	8	15	22	29	5	12	19	26
Clementi, Candyce	X				X								
Ergle, Ken							X				X		
Hardison, Rebecca				X								X	
Issacs, Naomi		X								X			
Johanson, Kyle					X	X							
Lambros, Alex	X									X			
Nozaki, Sumiyo							X	X					
Pasquale, Suzann			X					X					
Quintas, Vincent		X								X			
Su, San-li				X									X

Travel America Magazine

MEETING: National Travel Association

TIME: Wednesday, January 11, 19—, 7 p.m.

PLACE: Jefferson Plaza Hotel (Founder's Room)
12837 Mansfield Fwy

SPEAKER: Mr. Jayson Crooksfield, President
National Travel Association

TOPIC: "Improving Your Travel Promotion Programs"

DINNER: $30 (Make checks payable to NTA)

Please return your reservation card to reach the treasurer by January 5. You must cancel reservations by noon of the day of the meeting or you will be billed for the dinner.

TELEPHONE: 555-2048 (Alice McQuaid)

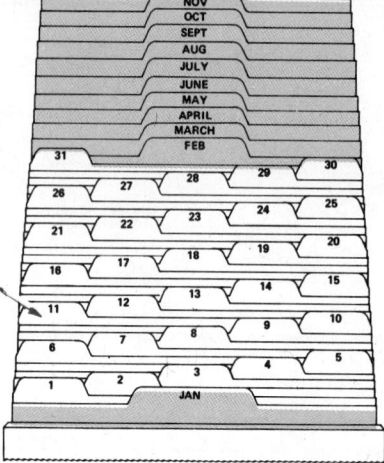

HUMAN RESOURCES DIRECTORY

NAME	DEPARTMENT	EXTENSION
ALLMAN DOUG T	PUB RELATIONS	2380
AVALDO SHELIA	SALES	2854
BADEN CINDY	LEGAL	1875
COHEN ISADORE	ADMN	1105
CY CHARLEEN	ILLUSTRATIONS	2450
DANIEL DAVID	PROD CNTRL	8038
DAVIES GERRI	RESEARCH	4309
EPPS DANA	EDITORIAL	3420
FARGO TED	PRODUCTION	7230
HILTON RON	COST ACCG	2284
JAY JANIS	LEGAL	1877
KOMPTON KARL	SECURITY	1003
LA SALLE LEAH	PRINTING	1106
LETEER AMY	PROD CNTRL	8039
LOY AMBROS	SHIPPING	2455
LYNN CHAS	ADMN	1116